Contentious Politics

CONTENTIOUS POLITICS

SECOND EDITION

FULLY REVISED AND UPDATED

Charles Tilly & Sidney Tarrow

OXFORD
UNIVERSITY PRESS

OXFORD
UNIVERSITY PRESS

Oxford University Press is a department of the University of Oxford.
It furthers the University's objective of excellence in research, scholarship,
and education by publishing worldwide. Oxford is a registered trade mark
of Oxford University Press in the UK and in certain other countries

Published in the United States of America by
Oxford University Press
198 Madison Avenue, New York, NY 10016,
United States of America

Library of Congress Cataloging-in-Publication Data
Tilly, Charles.
  Contentious politics / Charles Tilly and Sidney Tarrow. — Second revised edition.
    p.   cm.
  Includes bibliographical references and index.
  ISBN 978-0-19-025505-3 (paperback)
1. Social movements. 2. Social conflict. 3. Political sociology. I. Tarrow, Sidney G.
II. Title.
  HM881.T54 2015
  303.48'4—dc23
                        2015005732

9 8 7 6 5 4 3

Printed in Canada on acid-free paper

To Doug,
[Not so] Silent Partner

CONTENTS

LIST OF TABLES, FIGURES AND BOXES

List of Tables

List of Figures

List of Boxes

PREFACE TO THE SECOND EDITION

As the twentieth century ended and the new one was about to begin, the redoubtable David S. Meyer and I brought out a book that we hoped would reflect what the last few decades of research had taught us about contentious politics: that social movements had become ever more common since the 1960s; that this commonality was producing a growing familiarity with protest activity among ordinary people and their rulers; and that this general acceptance was leading—if it had not already led—to the routinization of contention—the rise of a *Social Movement Society* (1998).

Of these three claims, the first was correct; the second was partly right and partly questionable; and the third was clearly wrong. Although routine forms of protest like the public march and the demonstration continued to animate popular politics and to engage broader and broader sectors of the public, from the turn of the new century more intensive protests appeared in the United States, and more disruptive and more violent forms of contention began to explode across the globe. Not only that: governments—including the American government—were clearly not becoming better accustomed to dealing with protest and were developing more refined and aggressive forms of policing and surveillance.

Consider the following examples:

- In November 1999, thousands of demonstrators converged on the city of Seattle to protest against the meeting of the World Trade Organization, which they were certain would increase the growing inequality between the world's rich and poor.
- In September 2001 a group of Islamist militants took over four airplanes over United States airspace and flew them into the World Trade Center and the Pentagon, killing over 3,000 people.
- In Genoa, Italy, a few months later, police murdered a young man demonstrating against the G-8 conference that was meeting in that city.

- In 2002, in response to 9/11, the United States invaded Afghanistan, triggering ongoing civil strife both there and in neighboring Pakistan.
- A year later, a threatened American invasion of Iraq led to the largest peace demonstration in world history, with an estimated 16 million people attempting to stop the rush to war. As is well known, they failed, and the world is still reeling from the aftereffects of that invasion.
- In 2004 it emerged that Americans, under the unblinking eyes of higher officials, were routinely torturing Al Qaeda and other detainees in the prison of Abu Ghraib in Iraq and, as it eventually came out, in "dark sites" around the world.
- Also in 2004, a massive demonstration against a stolen election triggered a revolution in Ukraine, a former Soviet Republic that had gained its independence in the aftermath of the collapse of the Soviet empire.
- As we wrote, news began to break that the United States had developed an encompassing network of surveillance that was capable of sweeping up phone calls and Internet traffic from across the globe. This revelation was confirmed by Edward Snowden—a whistleblowing NSA contractor—in 2013.

Meyer and Tarrow's book described the social movements they observed in the 1990s reasonably well. But like many other texts that grew out of the American tradition of contentious politics, *The Social Movement Society* specified the boundaries of contention too narrowly. That book analyzed a narrow spectrum of mainly-secular movements in the mostly-democratic countries of the global North during a period when the last major cycle of contention—that of the 1960s and 1970s—had declined and a new one had not yet begun.

The first edition of this book set out to examine a much broader range of forms of contention. In it, Charles Tilly and I attacked three analytical problems:

> *First*, we believed that while social movements are a vigorous and important sector of contentious politics, they are not alone. Alongside and interacting with movements are riots, strike waves, rebellions, revolutions, civil wars, nationalist episodes, and ethnic strife—the kinds of episodes that we are increasingly faced with in the new century.
>
> *Second*, we thought that if we wish to understand such phenomena, we will need a vocabulary for analysis that is narrower than the enunciation of general laws but broad enough to facilitate comparison among different forms of contention.

Third, forms of contention do not stand still: sometimes pacific forms of protest escalate into violence and revolutions; at other times violent forms of contention are normalized and give way to routine politics. We reasoned that studies that focus only on social movements are unlikely to capture those dynamics.

Contentious Politics argued that the best strategy in facing these three analytical problems was not to proceed movement by movement or episode by episode, but to identify the common mechanisms and processes—in different combinations, to be sure—that operate across the range of contentious politics and bring about change. This edition follows the same analytical strategy, but with some significant changes.

Since 2007, when we published *Contentious Politics*, the world has become even more contentious. Consider the following:

- In the United States in 2010 a conservative populist movement—the Tea Party—erupted against the policies and the person of the country's first African American President, upsetting the internal equilibrium between moderates and conservatives in the Republican party and shifting the center of gravity of that party to the right.
- This was followed by the creation of a left-populist movement, Occupy Wall Street, which spread to street occupations in an estimated 180 cities around the United States and even abroad.
- At roughly the same time, beginning in Spain, what came to be called *indignados* movements diffused across Europe in protest against the draconian austerity policies that had been enforced on member-states of the European Union by the European Central Bank.
- In 2011, a wave of protest exploded against authoritarian governments in North Africa and the Middle East, leading to a military coup on Egypt, to civil wars in Syria and Yemen, and to a near-total breakdown of order in Libya. But as of this writing, desite the great hopes ignited by the so-called "Arab Spring," a constitutional regime survives only in little Tunisia, where the movement began.
- A decade after the "Green Revolution" in Ukraine, which we wrote about in 2006, a new revolution ejected the country's President; but this one led to a Russian takeover of the Crimea and to a separatist rebellion in the country's east that continues as this preface is written.
- In mid-2014, students and democracy campaigners converged in a campaign for free elections in the city of Hong Kong, since 1997 under Communist Chinese rule.

- Later that year, police violence in Ferguson, Missouri, and Islamist terrorism in Paris, France, unleashed waves of peaceful demonstrations on the part of citizens outraged, in the first case, at what they saw as racial profiling and, in the second, in favor of free speech.

While making no attempt to "cover" all the major episodes of contention across the globe, this new edition draws on many of them to reinforce the message of the book. These range from the insurrections against Middle Eastern dictatorships to the civil strife and reactions that followed; from the "Occupy Wall Street" movement in the United States to the "Occupy Central" movement in Hong Kong; from digital contention and the struggle for same-sex marriage in the United States to armed conflicts on the border of the former Soviet Union.

After *Contentious Politics* was published in 2007, both authors continued to extend the approach they employed in new research and writing. Before he left us in 2008, Tilly published two key studies: *Regimes and Repertoires*, published in 2006, and *Contentious Performances*, which appeared two years later, shortly before he passed away. Sidney Tarrow has also been busy, publishing *Strangers at the Gates* in 2012, *The Language of Contention* in 2013, and *War, States, and Contention* in 2015, in honor of his late friend and collaborator. This edition draws on the recent work of both auhors, expanding the horizons of the book beyond what we covered in the first edition.

This new edition will also draw upon the exploding number of specialized studies by other scholars in the broadening field of contentious politics by other scholars over the last decade in an effort to make them available to a student audience. It draws in particular on the work by Eitan Alimi, Javier Auyero, Donatella della Porta, Diana Fu, Michael Heaney and Fabio Rojas, and Neil Ketchley, none of whom has the slightest responsibility for the use I have made of their research. I am especially grateful to these colleagues for reading the parts of the manuscript that draw on their work and making sure I understood the nuances in the contentious episodes they describe. I also wish to thank Chan Suh, Yisook Lim, and Sarah and Susan Tarrow for their help in producing this edition of the book. Chris Tilly was an important source of moral support as I tried to catch up to the creativity and expertise of his father.

The book follows roughly the structure of the first edition, with theoretical propositions leavened by examples of empirical work and case studies in every chapter. Like the first edition, it does not stop with exposition: it regards the analysis of contentious politics not as an arcane art or an unattainable science but as a craft accessible to hard work and intelligent inquiry by students, as well as more senior researchers. There is also a new chapter that focusses on the global protests and transnational violence that have become an important feature of the first fifteen years of the twenty-first century. There is a new conclusion, which draws on three recent phenomena: the campaign for same-sex marriage, the movements that followed the financial crisis of 2008, and the use of social media for mobilization.

Sidney Tarrow
Ithaca, New York
February, 2015
Contentious Politics

Contentious Politics

PART ONE

Introduction

Circa 1830: A slave auction in America (photo by Rischgitz/Getty Images).

CHAPTER 1
Making Claims

When a young English divinity student named Thomas Clarkson won a Latin Prize with an essay on slavery at Cambridge in 1785, neither he nor his listeners imagined the effect it would have on slavery in the British Empire. But as he sat down at the side of the road on his way to London to take up a career as a Protestant minister, Clarkson reflected that if the horrors he had uncovered about slavery were true, "it was time some person should see these calamities to their end" (Hochschild 2005: 89).

Clarkson turned out to be that person. Together with a small band of antislavery advocates, he became the world's first modern social movement organizer. He wrote thousands of letters, organized petition drives, and helped to launch the world's first successful transnational movement. That movement eventually ended the vicious violence of the slave trade and led to the abolition of slavery around the Atlantic. It allowed English reformers to claim moral superiority over the newly independent but slaveholding United States. The antislavery movement went through many phases, suffered reversals during the repressive years of the Napoleonic wars, and required a savage civil war to end slavery in the United States. But it joined religious evangelicalism, the political emancipation of Catholics, and parliamentary reform to create the pattern of modern social movements in eighteenth- and nineteenth-century England.

The movement that Clarkson and his friends started looks decorous and even conservative to us today. But they made their claims much as social movements still do. They stimulated the formation of committees, took out newspaper ads, encouraged the deposing of petitions, gathered evidence, and laid it before the House of Commons. Although the word *boycott* itself would not enter the language for another century, they organized what was in effect a boycott of slave-produced sugar. Britain's antislavery activists also shocked the nation's conscience by displaying instruments of torture the slave owners used. In the process, they forged alliances with parliamentary and literary opponents of slavery such as William Wilberforce and Samuel Taylor Coleridge. They even sent Clarkson to help antislavery forces in France during the brief period when French republicans were interpreting the Rights of Man to include people of color (Drescher 1991).

It took almost twenty years for Britain's antislavery campaign to bring the Atlantic slave trade to an end and another three decades for slavery to end in Britain's colonies. But less than a year after Clarkson and the committee began their campaign, "Britons were challenging slavery in London debating societies, in provincial pubs, and across dinner tables throughout the country" (Hochschild 2005: 213). In the newly independent United States, opponents of the slave trade would eventually persuade Congress to make the trade illegal, and it took a civil war to end slavery in the South. Clarkson, his allies, his enemies, and public authorities on both sides of the Atlantic were building a social movement.

We could tell many different stories about antislavery. We could treat it as a moral tale showing what determination can accomplish in the face of difficult odds. We could think about it as an application of enlightened values, as an expression of religious zeal, or as English capitalists' attempt to promote free labor and free trade. We could see it as an early example of a transnational social movement, a phenomenon that has become important in this age of globalization (see chapter 9). Different observers of European and American antislavery campaigns have told all these tales, and more. Here we treat it as a dramatic example of *contentious politics*, of people struggling with each other over which political program will prevail. For another dramatic episode of contentious politics, fast-forward 228 years to the Ukrainian capital of Kiev.

THE UKRAINIAN FALL

In November 2013, a protest movement erupted against President Viktor Yanukovych's decision to cancel a long-planned agreement between his economically-strapped country and the European Union (EU). Yanukovych had been persuaded—his enemies would say "bought"—by Russian President Vladimir Putin to draw back from Europe by the inducement of a $15 billion loan if his country joined a Russian-led trade group. Eurupean leaders responded that if Yanukovych accepted the

Russian offer, all bets were off for a Ukrainian link to the EU. Western Ukrainians—including most of the residents of the country's capital, Kiev—were outraged by Yanukovych's move. Protesters in Kiev soon occupied the "Maidan"—the city's central square—evoking the country's "Orange Revolution" of 2002 (Beissinger 2011). They called first for Ukraine's association with Europe, then for an end to corruption, and increasingly for the President to resign.

Those protests were largely peaceful, and they soon "turned violent"— that is to say, the regime's riot police turned on them, killing eighty-four protesters and arresting hundreds more. Outrage at the regime's overreaction spread around the country and across Europe, and the Maidan occupation fell into a pattern of barricade building, police charges, occupation of government buildings, speeches by opposition politicians, and government warnings of fascist infiltration. What had begun as a largely peaceful protest movement rapidly militarized, with groups of young "hundreds" donning helmets and gas masks and carrying improvised shields against the increasingly ineffective, but no less brutal, police.

As the confrontations escalated, international actors mobilized on one side or another. In the West, French, German and Polish envoys tried to forge a compromise that would save Yanukovych's face but give the protesters the link to the EU they wanted; in the East, Russian President Putin offered Ukraine a down payment on his promised loan and urged him to continue to stand fast against the protesters. The Russians then grudgingly agreed to the Europeans' compromise proposal, but suddenly, as quickly as he had cancelled the original EU association deal, Yanukovych disappeared, only to reappear in the Russian Federation, claiming to have been overthrown by a coup d'état. (It later turned out that he had been abandoned by both army units and the special police forces on which he depended for his survival).

While the Maidan occupiers cheered jubilantly, opposition politicians set up an unelected provisional government, and accused Yanukovych of mass killing, threatening to take him to the International Criminal Court. In Washington, President Obama and Secretary of State Kerry cheered the advent of the provisional government, while in Brussels, EU Foreign commissioner Catherine Ashton spoke cautiously of a major injection of cash to bolster the country's economy. But talk of internal democracy and external bailout was soon eclipsed by what happened in the Crimean peninsula of Ukraine between February 28 and March 2. (See map, figure 1.1.)

On those days, "little green men" in uniform began to appear at key points in the Crimea, an area that had been part of Russia since the time of Catherine the Great but was handed to Ukraine by Communist Party

Figure 1.1:
Ukraine, Crimea, and the Kerch Connection to Russia (photo by Lonely Plantet/Getty Images)

chief Nikita Khrushchev in 1954, when the region was still part of the of Soviet Union. The peninsula was heavily peopled by Russian speakers and was the home of the Russian Black Sea fleet. Slowly, at first, and then increasingly insistently, Russian armed forces surrounded Ukrainian military facilities in the region, took over its Parliament, and the Kerch ferry crossing between the Crimea and Russia. Their identity became clear when Sergey Aksyonov, the newly-appointed Prime Minister of the Crimea, called for Russian intervention to protect the region's citizens against armed attacks. Russian armored vehicles soon rolled across the border as the Russian Duma declared it the country's duty to protect Russian-speaking civilians from attacks it claimed were coming from "fascists, nationalists, and anti-Semites" directed from Kiev. A full-scale military intervention, allied with internal pro-Russian demonstrations, was underway. And, in a plebiscite on March 16, a large majority of Crimean voters supported Crimea's attachment to Russia.

In the wake of these events, western observers saw the Russian takeover as the start of the worst foreign policy crisis since the Cold War. In Brussels, the EU and NATO fulminated that the attack violated Russia's commitment to respect Ukraine's territorial integrity. In Washington, President Obama launched a devastating series of economic sanctions, while in Moscow the Kremlin propaganda machine revved up patriotic fervor to support the annexation. But more was still to come: For no sooner was the Crimean peninsula detached from Ukraine than war broke out between pro-Russian militants in the East of the counry, aided by Russian troops, against the near-helpless agents of the Ukrainian state. Soldiers without insignias took over government buildings in twelve southeastern cities of Ukraine. They were helped by the inability of the new Ukrainian government to mount an effective response to their pressures and by the presence of 40,000 Russian troops, backed by a propaganda campaign beamed in from Moscow. A wave of domestic contention against a weak and corrupt state had brought the collapse of a government, an internal countermovement, and a partial military takeover by a neighboring state joined to a nationalist rebellion.

CONTENTIOUS POLITICS

What do the campaign against the slave trade in eighteenth-century England and the partial breakup and civil war in Ukraine in 2014 have in common? Although we can identify many differences, these were both episodes of what we call *contentious politics* In both, actors made claims on authorities, used public performances to do so, drew on inherited forms of collective action (our term for this is *repertoires*) and invented new ones, forged alliances with influential members of their respective polities, took advantage of existing political regime opportunities and made new ones, and used a combination of institutional and extrainstitutional routines to advance their claims.

Contentious politics involves interactions in which actors make claims bearing on other actors' interests, leading to coordinated efforts on behalf of shared interests or programs, in which governments are involved as targets, initiators of claims, or third parties. Contentious politics thus brings together three familiar features of social life: contention, collective action, and politics.

Contention involves making claims that bear on someone else's interests. In everyday life, contention ranges from small matters such as which television show we should watch tonight to bigger questions such as whether your sister Sue should marry the man she is dating. But it also takes place in football matches, rival advertising campaigns, and struggles between cantankerous patients and irritable doctors.

In the simplest version of contention, one party makes claims on another. The parties are often persons, but one or the other can also be a group or even an institution; you can make a claim on your school or file a claim on the government for unemployment benefits. In the elementary version, we can think of one party as a subject (the maker of a claim) and the other as an object (the receiver of a claim). Claims always involve at least one subject's reaching visibly toward at least one object. You (subject) may ask a friend (object) to pay back the money he borrowed from you yesterday. But claims range from timid requests to strident demands to direct attacks, just so long as they would, if realized, somehow affect the object's well-being, the object's interests. Often three or more parties are involved, as when you demand that your friend pay you back the money he was about to hand over to another creditor. Contention always brings together subjects, objects, and claims.

Collective action means coordinating efforts on behalf of shared interests or programs. Football teams engage in collective action, but so do churches, voluntary associations, and neighbors who clear weeds from a vacant lot. When you go to school or to work for a big company, you enter an organization that is carrying on collective action. But most of the collective action involved occurs with no significant contention and no government involvement. The bulk of collective action takes place outside contentious politics.

Most contention also occurs outside politics. We enter the realm of *politics* when we interact with agents of governments, either dealing with them directly or engaging in activities bearing on governmental rights, regulations, and interests. Politics likewise ranges from fairly routine matters such as applying for a driver's license to momentous questions such as whether the country should go to war. But most of politics involves little or no contention. Most of the time, people register for benefits, answer census takers, cash government checks, or show their passports to immigration officers without making significant claims on other people.

The presence or absence of governments in contention makes a difference for three big reasons. First, people who control governments gain advantages over people who don't. Even where the government is weak, controlling it gives you the means of collecting taxes, distributing resources, and regulating other people's behavior. As a result, political contention puts at risk, however slightly, the advantages of those who currently enjoy governmental power.

Second, governments always make rules governing contention: who can make what collective claims, by what means, with what outcomes. Even weak governments have some influence over the prevailing forms of claim making, and they resist anyone else's building up competitive centers of power within their territories.

Third, governments control substantial coercive means: armies, police forces, courts, prisons, and the like. The availability of governmental coercion gives an edge to political contention that rarely exists outside the political arena. In political contention, large-scale violence always remains a possibility, however faint. Contention connected to governments does resemble contention in families, sports, churches, and businesses in some regards. We will sometimes call attention to those parallels. But we single out government-connected contention because it has these distinctive properties.

Let us immediately rule out a few possible misunderstandings. Restriction of contentious politics to claim making that somehow involves governments by no means implies that governments must figure as the makers or receivers of contentious claims. On the contrary, as the book proceeds, we will encounter a wide range of contention in which nongovernmental actors are pitted against each other and make claims on religious, economic, ethnic, or other nongovernmental holders of power. Remember the story with which this chapter began? In both England and America, antislavery activists directed their claims first against slaveholders and only then against governments, which were drawn into the action because they either supported or opposed slavery and only they could resolve the legal and physical conflicts that slavery fostered.

As you move through the book, you will read sustained discussions of many such conflicts: American campus activism against South Africa's apartheid in the 1980s; changes in the repertoire of contention in the United States since the 1960s and in Argentina before and after the dictatorship of the 1970s and 1980s; the rebellion of the Zapatista movement in Chiapas, Mexico, in the 1990s; nationalist and democratization protests in the breakup of the former Soviet Union; transformations of American women's lives by participation in feminist organizations; lethal conflicts in Northern Ireland and Sudan, and the revolution in Nicaragua; the transnational "Global Justice" movement and transnational Islamism; the struggle for marriage equality in the United States and the tumultuous Arab Spring that are ongoing as this book goes to press. All of these conflicts eventually drew governments—local or national—into the action, as did our initial story of the struggle against slavery in England. But they began by pitting nongovernmental actors against each other.

Let us be clear. We do not deny that processes much like those occurring in contentious politics also occur in nonpolitical settings. That is actually the point of distinguishing collective action and contention from politics. We also do not deny that some forms of contention—such as religious movements—aim primarily at internal change within individuals. But even these frequently come into contact with governments—for example, when evangelical Christians attempt to incorporate religious values into the public school curriculum. Finally, sometimes a corporation that runs a company town, an international military force such as NATO, or an international institution such as the United Nations and the World Trade Organization behaves much like a government. Those cases come close enough to our definition of contentious politics for this book to include them. Still, we focus our attention on the convergence of collective action, contention, and politics because the area of their overlap has distinctive—and potentially dangerous—properties.

Figure 1.2 shows how contention, collective action, and politics converge in contentious politics. Many scholars would draw different boundaries—for example, by treating collective action as the fundamental process. In that view, such episodes as antislavery in Britain and the conflicts in Ukraine in 2013–2014 qualify simply as special instances of collective action. Others define politics as consisting of struggles for power however and wherever they occur. They thus take in all of contentious politics, add to it struggles outside the range of government, but treat routine political transactions as something else. In this line of thought, many analysts distinguish between real politics—our contentious politics plus similar struggles outside political arenas—and public administration.

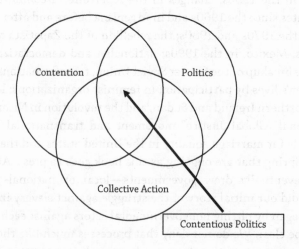

Figure 1.2:
Components of Contentious Politics

Many students of the subject use the term *social movement* to cover most or all of the overlap between contention and collective action, whether it happens in politics or some other arena. The same analysts often extend the term *social movement* to what we will call *social movement bases*: the social background, organizational resources, and cultural frameworks of contention and collective action. Our book provides plenty of evidence about social movements. But we recommend resisting expansion of the term to embrace most or all of contentious politics, its social bases, and its cultural contexts. Such an expansion has several drawbacks. First, it hampers comparison across different types of contention by collecting them under the same label. Second, if different forms of contention all count as social movements, that expansion makes it difficult to examine transitions among them.

Third, it obscures a fundamental fact: that social movements are a *historical*—and not a universal—category. As our story of British antislavery shows, the social movement as we know it took shape about two centuries ago, and it only became widely available as a means of popular claim making during the twentieth century (Tilly and Wood 2009). It emerged through episodes such as antislavery, found its feet in the early nineteenth century through labor and other struggles, and eventually became a staple of popular politics across the world's less authoritarian regimes during the twentieth century. American civil rights activism formed a social movement; so did the movement for same-sex marriage, which ends this book.

What qualifies as a *social movement*? We define a movement as a sustained campaign of claim making, using repeated performances that advertise the claim, based on organizations, networks, traditions, and solidarities that sustain these activities. But most forms of contentious politics are not social movements. Social movements combine (1) sustained *campaigns* of claim making; (2) an array of public performances including marches, rallies, demonstrations, creation of specialized associations, public meetings, public statements, petitions, letter writing, and lobbying; (3) repeated public displays of worthiness, unity, numbers, and commitment by such means as wearing colors, marching in disciplined ranks, sporting badges that advertise the cause, displaying signs, chanting slogans, and picketing public buildings. They draw on (4) the organizations, networks, traditions, and solidarities that sustain these activities—*social movement bases*. As familiar as it has become to citizens of Western countries, this combination of campaigns, performances, and displays only took shape a few hundred years ago, and it is still rare or nonexistent through much of the contemporary world. The recent explosion of digital activism we will see in chapter 10 may even be making social movements obsolete.

The second part of this book compares social movements to other forms of contention. Chapter 7 shows how movement forms of action figured in Poland's Solidarity movement and the American women's movement. These movements' combinations of public displays of worthiness, unity, numbers, and commitment produced significantly less violent confrontation than the three forms of lethal conflict reviewed in chapter 8: ethnic-religious strife, civil wars, and revolutions. Social movement politics and lethal conflicts often co-occur and intersect in the same places, as chapter 4 will show.

CONTENTIOUS INTERACTION

Our two landmark episodes—British antislavery and the Ukrainian-Russian conflicts from 2013 on reveal intersections among contention, politics, and collective action. Though buffeted by the varying winds of reaction and reform, antislavery was a true social movement. Over a period of more than thirty years, its participants sustained a powerful campaign of contentious politics both within and against Britain's political institutions. The Ukrainian conflict ranged from a short-term movement coalition comprising masses in the streets and opposition leaders, to an armed struggle between militants and their state opponents with the backing of a foreign power. It led to the full-scale conflict between Russia and Ukraine, with the backing of its western supporters, that continues as this book goes to press.

When contention, politics, and collective action get together, something distinctive happens: power, shared interests, and government policy come into play. Claims become collective, which means they depend on some sort of coordination among the people making the claims. They also become political, at least by assuming the presence of governments as monitors, guarantors, or regulators of collective claim making and often more directly as subjects or objects of claims. In those circumstances, we will speak about groups that sometimes make claims as *political actors*. We will call the collective names that they give themselves or that other people give them—those workers, we citizens, us women, and so on—their *political identities*.

People often make collective claims on governments, and governments make claims on whole categories of people. Governments also involve themselves in how people outside government make claims on each other.

Sometimes they facilitate contention by opening opportunities for challengers but sometimes they suppress it: Lawmakers make laws banning some kinds of assemblies, police arrest unruly demonstrators, judges try people for seditious claims, and officials intervene when their clients or constituents are fighting collectively. The intersection of contention, politics, and collective action contains events ranging from local ethnic competition to great revolutions.

This book looks hard and systematically at that intersection. It lays out a simple set of tools for describing and explaining contentious politics in all its varieties. The tools consist of concepts and of causal connections among the phenomena singled out by those concepts. We make a rough distinction between *description* and *explanation*. *Description* consists of specifying what special properties and variations in contention deserve serious attention. *Explanation* entails showing what produces those special properties and variations.

The distinction between description and explanation remains rough; sometimes one special property or brand of variation helps to explain another. When we compare Ukraine's quasi-revolution with other mobilizations against authoritarian regimes, we actually move toward explanation by identifying relevant differences among the regimes and their oppositions. Chapter 2 takes up explanatory concepts more directly, and chapters 3 and 4 combine description and explanation by placing different forms of contention in different forms of regimes and examining the role of contention in regime transitions. But this chapter concentrates on concepts describing the interesting features of contention that deserve explanation.

What concepts? This chapter's concepts show how political actors make claims in the names of their political identities, identify various sorts of collective political performances, describe how contentious performances cluster into repertoires of contention, analyze how repertoires change, and apply those ideas to the United States since World War II. The rest of the book returns repeatedly to the United States. But it also draws on cases from Europe, Latin America, the Middle East, and Asia. As the book moves on, much of our descriptive work will involve connecting these concepts with each other.

How? The book shows how repertoires of contention differ between democratic and undemocratic *regimes*. The book explains what difference it makes whether contention takes place within existing *institutions*, outside them, or against them. It considers how *political opportunity structures* affect which political identities people bring into contention. It describes how social movements combine institutional and extrainstitutional forms of action. It shows that actors build on a broad set of *social bases* but that these bases are not sufficient to explain *contentious interaction*, which depends on the triggering of a finite set of *mechanisms and processes*. The book reveals that a similar group of mechanisms and processes—for example, brokerage, certification, mobilization, demobilization, and scale shift—recur in different combinations with substantially different outcomes in revolutions, social movements, ethnic conflict, nationalism, civil war, and other distinct forms of contentious politics. Later chapters will treat all of these elements in detail.

This book presents an *interactive approach* to contentious politics. As Doug McAdam (1999) writes, "a viable model of the individual must take full account of the fundamentally *social/relational* nature of human existence" (xiii). Some students of contention give primary attention to its social bases—for example, to social networks, organizations, cultural predispositions, and the political and ideological traditions that nourish contention. While we give ample space to these bases of contention, we are primarily concerned with the mechanisms and processes that involve challengers with their targets, public authorities, and third parties like the media and the public in sequences of interaction. For example, when we turn to social movements in chapter 7, we focus on the mechanisms and processes that transform the bases of contention into social movement campaigns.

Putting these elements together will help us to resolve a fundamental paradox of contentious politics: its recurring combination of *variations and regularities*. Contentious politics features enormous variation in its issues, actors, interactions, claims, sequences, and outcomes from time to time and place to place. But it also displays great regularities in the ways that contention unfolds. We will see how similar mechanisms and processes produce distinctive political trajectories and outcomes depending on their combinations and on the social bases and political contexts in which they operate. We can begin to capture some of the recurrent, historically embedded character of contentious politics by means of two related theatrical metaphors and a military one: performances, repertoires, and campaigns.

- *Contentious performances* are relatively familiar and standardized ways in which one set of political actors makes collective claims on some other set of political actors. Among other performances, participants in Ukraine's protest movement against President Yanukovych used mass demonstrations as visible, effective performances.
- *Contentious repertoires* are arrays of performances that are currently known and available within some set of political actors. England's

antislavery activists helped to invent the demonstration as a political performance, but they also drew on petitions, lobbying, press releases, public meetings, and a number of other performances. Ukraine's Maidan protesters assembled in a public place, but they also built a tent city, defended it with shields against police repression, and attacked government buildings until the President and his entourage fled the country.

- *Contentious campaigns* are combinations of performances that "focus on a particular policy and usually disassemble when that policy is implemented or overturned" (Almeida 2014: 6). Observers sometimes refer to such campaigns as "movements," but in many cases they involve arrays of actors, including movements, interest groups, political parties, the media, interested onlookers, and state agents, as we will see in chapter 5.

CLAIM MAKING AS PERFORMANCE

Once we look closely at collective making of claims, we see that particular instances improvise on shared scripts. Presentation of a petition, taking a hostage, or mounting a demonstration constitutes a performance that links at least two actors, a claimant, and an object of claims. Innovation occurs incessantly on the small scale, but effective claims depend on a recognizable relation to their setting, on relations between the parties, and on previous uses of the claim-making form.

Performances evolve over time. Consider how Clarkson and his colleagues used petitions to inundate Parliament with antislavery demands. One of the most traditional forms of making claims, petitions originally came from individual petitioners seeking benefits for themselves. They bowed before their lords to request personal exemption from military service or lowering of their excise tax. The British antislavery group turned the petition into an instrument for *mass* claim making, accumulating thousands of signatures on petitions to demand redress for others. This was the origin of the on-line petition of today.

Now think of the massing of protesters in the streets of Kiev in 2013. In the 1830s, British Chartists adopted the mass demonstration, then a new form, as they demanded political rights for working people (Thompson 1984). In the mid–nineteenth century, during what we remember as the 1848 revolution, such demonstrations traversed Europe on the part of workers, nationalists, middle-class reformers, and revolutionary socialists. That led to a known change in the repertoire of contention: By 2013,

Ukrainians knew exactly how to organize demonstrations that would challenge the rules, reinforce their own solidarity, and gain international support.

All forms of contention rest on performances, but performances range from direct assaults on others to theatricals staged for nearby or distant audiences (Taylor and Van Dyke 2004: 271; Tarrow 2011). In the eighteenth century, people mainly engaged in performances that were specific to their particular claims, such as seizing grain, invading landlords' fields, barricading their streets, and pulling down wrongdoers' houses (Tilly 2005). Think of the Boston colonists who attacked the home of an official charged with collecting the hated stamp tax in 1765, or of those who dumped tea into Boston Harbor in 1775. Both groups were engaging in *particular* performances.

But by the twentieth century, many contentious performances had spread around the world and become what we call *modular*: performances that could be adopted and adapted across a wide range of conflicts and sites of contention by a broad range of actors. Think again of the protest demonstration. It grew out of—and at first resembled—the religious procession to a place of worship. It turned contentious as demonstrators moved from a place of assembly to a site from which they could confront the targets of their claims. Later, it became the central form of action, mounted routinely to demonstrate a claim before the public. With the diffusion of mass media, that public expanded from neighbors who witnessed a demonstration passing beneath their windows to a wider range of citizens who could watch it on their television sets. By the twentieth century, it had become the major conventional form of contention used by claim makers across the world. By the early twenty-first century, as we will see, marchers protesting for free speech in Paris knew how to organize a demonstration and what they did not know, they quickly learned from social media.

More recently, reaching people through the Internet has become a favored means of mobilization (see chapter 10). For example, "hactivism," the practice of infiltrating the computer of a transnational firm or a government to disrupt its routines, is becoming more and more common (Samuels 2004). So far the Internet's major role in contentious politics has been either (1) to assemble people in demonstrations at one site or (2) to coordinate demonstrations in many sites across a broad range of territory; and it may also be emerging (3) as a form of "connective action" itself (Bennett and Segerberg 2013). A good example of the Internet's first sort of use was the 1999 Seattle demonstration against the World Trade Organization. A major example of the second was the coordination of demonstrations across the globe against the American invasion of Iraq in 2003. An example of the third was the "Occupy" movement of 2011–2012, which existed "online" as much as "offline." None of these has done away with the classical set of contentious politics performances but they have progressively increased the ability of organizers to expand their reach. The petition, the demonstration, and the Internet-based call to action have become *modular performances*, generic forms that can be adapted to a variety of local and social circumstances.

The advantage of such modular performances is their dual generality and specificity. Seen generically, they have features that adapt to a wide variety of circumstances and have meaning to a wide variety of potential participants and audiences. American students demonstrate on college campuses, French farmers demonstrate outside the prefecture, Israeli settlers demonstrate beside the Wailing Wall, and Hong Kong democracy protesters demonstrate in Hong Kong's business district—all are using some variant of the same modular performance.

But seen in particular circumstances, demonstrations offer a variety of facets that can be attached to local knowledge. Skillful organizers adapt the generic form to local circumstances, embedding a modular form such as the demonstration in the languages, symbols, and practices that make them compelling in those circumstances. This is but one specific version of the duality of similarities and differences that will show up throughout our book.

Of course, not all contentious performances are as orderly, theatrical, and peaceful as the demonstration. Take the confrontational forms of contentious politics that exploded in Western Europe and the United States during the 1960s. The Cold War between the Soviet Union and the United States had dominated the early 1950s, restricting protest in general and confrontational protest in particular. But the African American awakenings of the mid-1950s and the 1960s, the student and antiwar movements of the late 1960s, the women's and gay rights movements of the 1970s, the peace and environmental movements of the 1980s, the collapse of communism at the end of that decade, and the Arab Spring revolutions of 2010–2012 expanded all kinds of protest and particularly of confrontational and violent forms of contention.

Now think of how young protesters after the death of Michael Brown in Ferguson, Missouri burned and overturned cars when a grand jury absolved a police officer of using unnecessary force (see chapter 2). They were using a performance that had become a standard part of the American urban repertoire that emerged in the riots of the mid-1960s against police violence. These two generations of protesters were not connected to each other but the performance of burning cars during social unrest became a standard part of the American repertoire.

Finally, think of the occupation of public space organized by the "Occupy" movement in the United States and the "Indignation" protesters in Europe in response to the Great Recession of 2008–2013; they picked up on a performance that goes back to the nineteenth century and reached its peak in the sit-in protests of the civil rights and anti-Vietnam war era of the 1960s. The same performance with more profound implications was used by the occupants of Tahrir Square in Cairo in 2011, when they launched a revolutionary message that spread across the Middle East and North Africa.

Dieter Rucht has provided us with a running portrait tracing how different forms of contentious politics converged in one archetypical European country, Germany, over this period. Rucht and his colleagues examined contention from major newspapers for the years 1950–1988 for West Germany and for both halves of Germany over the following decade (2005). His findings show a dramatic increase in the numbers of protests in the 1960s and smaller, but still substantial, increases over the next three decades. Protests rose from a low of just over 1,100 in the 1950s to over 4,000 in the 1990s. Not only that: The mix of conventional, confrontational, and violent activities changed dramatically between the beginning of the West German Republic and the end of the century.

Although no linear trend appeared in the proportion of "demonstrative" protests (about 50 percent at the beginning and at the end of the

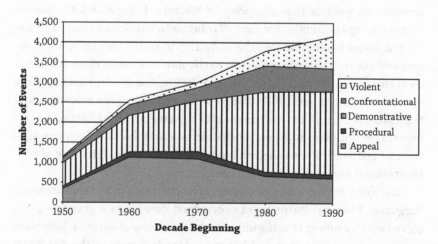

Figure 1.3:
Protest Events in Germany, 1950–1990
Source: Data provided by Dieter Rucht.

period), a net decline occurred in the percentage of routine expressions of claims, what Rucht calls procedural protests and appeals. In contrast, Rucht's evidence shows increases in the proportion of "confrontational" protests in the 1980s and of "violent encounters" in the 1990s. The declines correspond largely to the tactics of the peace movement, while the later increases in violence reflect the rise of right-wing anti-immigrant groups and of the absorption of East Germany. Figure 1.3 summarizes these data for West Germany through 1988 and for the expanded country between 1989 and 1990.

SOURCES OF REPERTOIRE CHANGE

This takes us to the factors that bring about changes in repertoires. We can distinguish two major kinds of process in repertoire change: the effects of periods of rapid political change and the outcome of incrementally changing structural factors. The first are more dramatic, sometimes produce lasting change, but are more easily routinized and repressed as authorities regain control of contention. Incremental changes are less dramatic, depend on factors that evolve more slowly, but can be more enduring.

With respect to periods of rapid political change, during major cycles of contention, the ordinary preference for familiar claim-making routines dissolves in spurts of innovation. American civil rights activists did not simply use the decorous old social movement forms they inherited but deliberately disrupted existing routines. Periods of rapid political change produce sequences of innovation in repertoires, and successive innovations largely account for the ebb and flow of movement activity (Kriesi et al. 1995; McAdam 1983).

During such times of rapid political change, we find both actions and reactions. As each new round of claim making begins to threaten the interests of (or provide new opportunities for) political actors who had previously remained inactive, a spiral of contention ensues. Social movements engender countermovements. Challengers' allies appear and retreat. The state, at first thrown off balance by new forms of contention, eventually reacts and in some cases turns to repression. We will turn to "cycles" and "tides" of contention and to revolutions in chapter 6. The extreme case arrives in a revolutionary situation: a deep split in control of coercive means. During a revolutionary situation, every actor's interest is at risk, and many actors therefore mobilize for action. We saw exactly that shift in the Ukrainian conflicts of 2013–2014.

As we will argue, the major constraints and incentives for contentious politics are *political opportunity structures*, and most of these are local and national. But we think it is important to look beyond the nation-state at processes such as the shift of some kinds of contention to international institutions, the framing of local issues as the results of global problems, and the formation of transnational networks and movement coalitions. In chapter 9, we turn from the local and national patterns of contention that occupy most of our book to transnational diffusion and mobilization. A recent major change is globalization, the increasing economic integration of the planet.

In contrast to the effects of periods of rapid change, incremental changes in repertoires are less dramatic, but more decisive in the long run. The major causes of incremental change sort into three main categories:

- *Connections between claim making and everyday social organization.* For example, mothers bereft of bread for their children gather around the granary whose owner they suspect of hoarding flour. Land-poor peasants who believe that the landlord stole their land sometimes occupy it. And workers, whose one effective tool is the fact that their labor is necessary to make the wheels of production turn, strike to prevent employers from the successful pursuit of profit.
- *Cumulative creation of a signaling system by contention itself.* For example, over the past two centuries, French claim makers have drawn on a dense experience with contention. Three major revolutions, a revolutionary commune, more than a hundred years of strikes, barricades, marches, and demonstrations all lie under the surface of French contention today, to be drawn on, innovated upon, and replayed in endless permutations (Tartakowsky 2005; Tilly 1986).
- *Operation of the regime as such.* Regimes sort performances into prescribed, tolerated, and forbidden categories, dispensing threats and penalties to claimants who move onto forbidden ground. When Clarkson and his colleagues perfected the petition into a tool of mass mobilization, they did so in the context of a parliamentary regime that had recognized petitions as legitimate forms of collective action for centuries. But when French radicalism and Napoleonic arms were threatening Britain, reformers paid the penalty with imprisonment and worse. Chapters 3 and 4 deal in detail with the relations between regimes and forms of contention.

Repertoires draw on the identities, social ties, and organizational forms that constitute everyday social life. From those identities, social ties, and organizational forms emerge both the collective claims that people make and the means they have for making claims. In the course of contending or watching others contend, people learn the interactions that can make a political difference as well as the locally shared meanings of those interactions. The changing interaction of everyday social organization, cumulative experience with contention, and regime intervention produces incremental alterations in contentious performances. At any given moment, however, that interaction promotes clustering of claim making in a limited number of recognizable performances, a repertoire.

Repertoires are the source of tactical performances that combine in protest campaigns. Campaigns can combine strikes, rallies, protest marches, boycotts, sit-ins, and obstructions. "Opposition groups or temporary alliances often piece together campaigns with a unifying set of slogans and specified goals" (Almeida 2014: 6). They sometimes plan organized violence, but, more typically, when violence occurs it is as the result of the interaction of protesters and the "forces of order." Where social movements are sustained—as we will see in chapter 7—campaigns blend into longer sequences of contention, but where movements are weak—as in much of the Global South—campaigns tend to end when a particular policy is implemented or overturned.

WHAT'S COMING

This chapter's comparison of eighteenth century British antislavery with Ukrainian conflicts from 2013 on sent us on a fresh path across bumpy terrain. We have seen how contention, collective action, and politics overlap in contentious politics: interactive, collective making of claims that bear on other people's interests and involve governments as claimants, objects of claims, or third parties. Social movements qualify as a form of contentious politics, but so do revolutions, civil wars, and a wide variety of other struggles this book takes up. In all these forms of contention, distinctive claim-making performances and repertoires vary from setting to setting and regime to regime. Some of those performances are modular; as with the street demonstration, they transfer easily from setting to setting and regime to regime. They build on social bases belonging to the setting or regime.

America's changing contentious politics since 1955, for example, often involved some widely recognizable performances such as street demonstrations. But participants, claims, objects of claims, and forms all grew from particular features of the changing American regime. To explain change and variation in repertoires, we must look at the current pace of political change in the regime at hand, identify incremental changes in the regime's social structure, then figure out how the two affect everyday social organization, people's cumulative experience with contention, and current operation of the regime. With those elements in place, we begin the adventure of explaining change and variation in the forms, participants, issues, objects, and outcomes of contentious politics.

What's next? First, a warning about what this book *does not* do. Despite illustrating its points amply from revolutions, social movements, military coups, civil wars, and other forms of contentious politics, it does not catalog these forms one by one and provide a separate set of generalizations concerning each of them. On the contrary, our aim is to identify parallels in the ways that apparently disparate forms of contention work, and show how their differences result from varying combinations and sequences of mechanisms in contrasting regime environments. Even the later chapters on social movements and large-scale lethal conflict serve mainly to show that similar causes and effects operate in these very different political processes.

The next chapter describes how we propose to study contention and contains a number of hints for students who want to carry out their own analyses. Chapters 3 and 4 connect contention to different types of regimes and the opportunities and threats they proffer, and relate regimes, opportunities, and threats to democratization and dedemocratization. Chapter 5 ("Contentious Interaction") examines how political actors form, change, make claims, and interact with each other. We then move on to political actors' mobilization and demobilization (chapter 6) before applying the analysis to social movements (chapter 7) and lethal conflicts (chapter 8). In chapter 9, we turn to transnational contention, and in chapter 10 ("Contention Today and Tomorrow") to movements against inequality to recapitulate the book's main lessons. The book ends with a reflection on how social media may be transforming contentious politics and with suggestions for how students can use this book as both scholars and citizens.

In an action soon widely adopted elsewhere, African American students from North Carolina A & T College peacefully occupy seats at the previously whites-only lunch counter of an F.W. Woolworth store in Greensboro, North Carolina (1960). (Copyright @ Bettmann/CORBIS).

CHAPTER 2
How to Analyze Contention

Ferguson, Missouri, August 9, 2014, a largely-black suburb of St. Louis. An 18-year-old black man, Michael Brown, is fatally shot by officer Darren Wilson, 28, a white Ferguson police officer. Brown, and his friend, Dorian Johnson, had been up to no good, having stolen several cigars from a convenience store and shoved the store clerk. Wilson, answering a call about the robbery, saw the two young men walking down the street, and blocked their passage with his police cruiser. An altercation occurred through the window of the cruiser, shots were fired, and Brown and Johnson made off down the street. Wilson left his cruiser and fired twelve shots at the unarmed teen, who, the officer claimed, had moved toward him in an aggressive manner, a claim that was contested by several witnesses who argued that Brown was surrendering when he was shot.

What followed was a wave of unrest both in the black community of Ferguson and across the country. Untold numbers of black and non-black protesters marched throughout the St. Louis area and around the country, their hands raised above their heads, chanting "Hands Up, Don't Shoot!" as Brown was said to have done before he was shot. The local police force at first responded with military force, but was ultimately overwhelmed by the complexity and delicacy of the issue, and called in a variety of forces of order. The Governor, Jay Nixon, ordered the local police to cede their authority to the Missouri State Highway Patrol, which tried to de-militarize a situation that threatened to repeat the wave of urban riots that swept the country in the 1960s; and the St. Louis County Prosecuting Attorney, Robert McCulloch, decided to bring the case in front of a grand jury to determine whether there was probable cause to indict Wilson for his actions.

McCulloch's grand jury only complicated an already volatile situation. On November 24, McCulloch announced that the jury had decided not to indict Wilson, who, the jury decided, had had adequate justification for shooting Brown. Legal analysts raised concerns over McCulloch's approach, asserting that the way he presented the evidence could have influenced the grand jury to decide in Wilson's favor, and highlighted significant differences between how a grand jury typically operates and the procedures that McCulloch followed. At the same time, US Attorney General Eric Holder, launched a civil investigation of Wilson's behavior to determine whether the officer had violated Brown's civil rights, an investigation that eventually found no cause to proceed. The grand jury decision brought black anger to a head, and a night of protest and rioting worse than what had been seen before ensued, both in the St. Louis area and around the country.[1]

That was not the end of the Ferguson episode. Black Americans had been complaining for decades that American police forces disproportionately target them for infractions that white Americans escape. In New York City, for example, a "stop-and-frisk" tactic by the police was demonstrated to be so disproportionately aimed at minorities that a Federal District Court Judge banned further use of the practice.[2] In New Jersey, black drivers often complained that they were stopped by state police for "driving while black." In places as far apart as Sanford, Florida, Cleveland, Ohio, Staten Island, New York, and Albuquerque, New Mexico, minorities and young African Americans were being gunned down by police or trigger-happy white citizens when they found themselves in the wrong place at the wrong time. Figure 2.1, taken from data collected from FBI records by the public interest group, ProPublica in October, 2014, gave statistical credibility to the resentment that had long seethed in the black community. It showed, in the words of ProPublica's reporters, that "Young black males in recent years were at a far greater risk of being shot dead by police than their white counterparts—21 times greater" (Gabrielson et al, 2014: 1).

But public protests were not the only outcome of the Ferguson police shooting and the grand jury decision, for—as we will see throughout this book—disruptive protest often leads to policy reactions and sometimes bleeds into violence. On the one hand, these events led to widespread criticism of police practice and to legislative action, both at the state and the federal levels. In the weeks following the grand jury decision, at least five new bills were presented to Congress, and the Justice Department acted to require police in departments that receive DOJ grants to wear body cameras.[3]

On the other hand, the chain of events that began in Ferguson in August produced lethal violence against police: on December 2, 2014, a

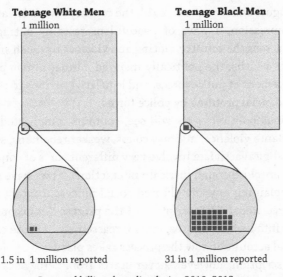

Figure 2.1:
Reported Killings of Black and White Teenage Men by Police, 2010–2012
Source: Ryan Gabrielson, Ryann Grochowski Jones, and Eric Sagara, "Deadly Force in Black and White."
ProPublica, October 9, 2014. http://www.propublica.org/article/deadly-force-in-black-and-white?utm_
source=et&utm_medium=email&utm_campaign=dailynewsletter

deranged black man from Maryland, Ishmael Brinsley, came to New York City and fatally shot two police officers in their squad car, before being killed himself.[4] The double murder led to outrage among police forces around the country, and to the criticism from the police union of New York Mayor Bill de Blasio, who the union's chief accused of having "blood on his hands" for having criticized the police after the Ferguson events. More important, it led to the evaporation of much of the sympathy for the victims of police violence that had grown up in the wake of the Ferguson case and to a siege mentality among the police. When Mayor de Blasio attended the funerals of the two slain officers, hundreds of policemen in uniform turned their backs on him in an act of protest.[5]

CONTENTIOUS EVENTS AND EPISODES

Why begin our voyage through contentious politics with this confused, and contradictory case of a police murder in a suburb of St. Louis? The first reason is that it illustrates that contentious politics involves many different forms and combinations of collective action. In the few months between August and December, 2014, the country saw an isolated incident of police repression, a wave of peaceful protests by outraged African Americans across the country, rioting and violence by much smaller numbers of black youths, the politically-inspired murder of two policemen, a countermovement of police forces, and legislative actions to rein in police violence and racial profiling by police forces.

Contentious politics, as we will see, contains complicated social processes. Vigilante violence, military coups, worker rebellions, social movements, and digital activism involve very different sorts of contention, but all of them unfold through intricate interactions, as we have seen in this episode. Explaining any complicated social process (contentious or not) involves three steps: (1) description of the process, (2) decomposition of the process into its basic causes, and (3) reassembly of those causes into a more general account of how the process takes place.

Good description, however, never starts from zero. Because contentious politics is complicated, any observer who wants to explain contention needs a reliable guide to description. A reliable guide identifies features to look for, features that clearly belong to what we must explain. The concepts laid out in chapter 1—*political actors, political identities, contentious performances, and repertoires*—make up our elementary guide to description of the processes we mean to explain. For explanation, we need additional concepts. This chapter supplies seven of them: *sites, conditions, streams of contention, episodes, outcomes, mechanisms,* and *processes.* We will define and illustrate all of them as the chapter proceeds.

Using many different examples, we locate contention in its varied sites and sketch conditions at those sites. We single out streams of contention and tag some apparent outcomes of that contention for explanation. We describe contentious processes by means of episodes and decompose those episodes into their causal mechanisms before reassembling the mechanisms into more general accounts of the processes involved. Mechanisms and processes sometimes operate within individuals. But the central mechanisms of contentious politics are interactive. We can see them in the interactions between peasant resistance and state violence in Guatemala to which we will return in greater depth in chapter 6.

MASS CONTENTION AND STATE VIOLENCE IN GUATEMALA

"Among the most dreadful aspects of the years of mass contention and state violence in Central America," writes Charles Brockett (2005), "were the many massacres of unarmed civilians." This was especially true in

Guatemala, where a major massacre of civilians "took place on May 29, 1978 in the indigenous town of Panzós . . . when fifty-three unarmed Q'eqchi' Maya were shot down and another forty-seven were injured" (3–4). The Panzós massacre shocked Guatemalan and international public opinion. But it was not an isolated incident. It can help us to analyze the many forms of contentious politics we will encounter in our book.

Brockett first enumerates a series of events that both led to and accompanied the massacre in Panzós. From a string of demonstrations by peasants claiming land in the area starting in 1970, to petitions read on the floor of the national congress, to meetings denouncing the local mayor for complicity with landowners, to peasant resistance against threatened evictions from their lands, he shows how residents of the Panzós valley joined in a wide array of contentious performances (4–5). Similar demonstrations and denunciations were multiplying in neighboring municipalities at the same time. State actors responded with escalating violence. Altogether, these events were raising the scale of contention as they brought national labor organizations, peasant leagues, and political parties into an ever-widening "cycle of protest" against the state and the landlord class it supported.

How can we best characterize a narrative like the one we have just sketched from Brockett's work? We could be satisfied by retelling the story step-by-step, as a good narrative historian would do. We could reduce it to the motivations of the actors and their calculations of gain or loss, as analytically sharp rational-choice analysts would do. Or we could point to the cultural desire for ownership of the land, as sensitive culturally oriented scholars would do. As useful as these approaches can be in describing peasant resistance, all of them miss the *dynamics of contention*. We can capture dynamics by looking for the mechanisms and processes that drive contention.

MECHANISMS AND PROCESSES

By *mechanisms*, we mean a delimited class of changes that alter relations among specified sets of elements in identical or closely similar ways over a variety of situations. Mechanisms compound into processes. By *processes*, we mean regular combinations and sequences of mechanisms that produce similar (generally more complex and contingent) transformations of those elements. Distinct processes involve different sequences and combinations of mechanisms that interactively produce some outcome. Some mechanisms and processes recur frequently in our book; others appear only rarely. This section outlines the logic of the mechanism-process approach, lays out some of the key mechanisms and processes that appear in a wide variety of contentious politics, and illustrates them through cases, both domestic and international.

Many social scientists model their approaches on simple versions of physics or engineering. They ask how output variables such as levels of violence covary with input variables such as ethnic fragmentation, without saying much about the causal chains in between the inputs and the outputs. Mechanism-process explanations come closer in spirit and reasoning to biology. There, mechanisms concatenate into small-scale processes such as reproduction or long-term ones such as evolution. Although these processes' outcomes lend themselves to measurement, the processes themselves are often empirically invisible as such; you don't see evolution happening. Biologists can make headway in identifying crucial processes by correlating outputs with inputs. But for detailed explanations, they soon turn to examination of these processes' constituent mechanisms.

Let's take the process of reproduction of a species as an analogy. Species reproduction is a collective process that depends on a number of interactive mechanisms that occur between individuals—mechanisms like courtship, display, sexual encounter, pregnancy, birth, and, in some species, the nurturing of infants. Biologists cannot directly observe species reproduction, but they can study its mechanisms. First, they can break reproduction into its component mechanisms to better understand its dynamics. Second, they can compare that process in one species to its equivalent in others to see whether or not the same mechanisms are present in all. Third, they can examine which mechanisms co-occur so frequently as to constitute a robust process.

In examining the dynamics of contention, we can follow the same mechanism-process procedures as biologists do:

- We can disaggregate a familiar process, such as mobilization, into its component mechanisms, in order to understand what makes it work.
- We can compare how such a process works in different settings to understand what difference the presence or absence of a particular mechanism makes.
- We can examine whether particular mechanisms coincide so frequently with similar outcomes as to constitute a robust process.
- Larger processes such as democratization or nationalist mobilization can also be examined through a mechanism-process approach (Tilly 2004).

In contentious politics, similar reasoning applies to performances and repertoires. People transmit performances such as the demonstration in pretty much the same shape from one contentious episode to the next. Nevertheless, minor innovations in performances occur all the time, much as minor variations in morphology lead to changes in biological adaptation. As in some evolutionary changes, some innovations lead to dead ends, either because they fail to inspire people or because they are too easily repressed (Margadant 1979: 267). Other innovations stick either because they produce unexpected successes, because prestigious leaders adopt them, or because brokers forward their transfer from one setting to another. Our narratives will repeatedly reveal mechanisms that combine in different settings and situations of contentious politics. Three of the most common are brokerage, diffusion, and coordinated action:

- *Brokerage*: production of a new connection between previously unconnected sites
- *Diffusion*: spread of a form of contention, an issue, or a way of framing it from one site to another
- *Coordinated action*: two or more actors' engagement in mutual signaling and parallel making of claims on the same object

Here is an important example how brokerage, diffusion, and coordinated action came together to revitalize the civil rights movement in the late 1950s.

SITTING IN IN GREENSBORO

The American civil rights movement had an early success in 1954, with the Supreme Court decision to strike down "separate but equal" black and white schools in the South (*Brown v. Board of Education*, 347 U.S. 483). This was an example of what we will call "contained contention"—what students of courts and movements have called "legal mobilization" (McCann 1994, 2006). But a determined effort by segregationist state governments and white supremacist groups successfully limited the scope of the Court's decision (Andrews 2004), and no new strategy had been formulated by the NAACP, which had won the *Brown* decision (Klarman 2004). Across the South, civil rights activists were frustrated at the failure of Congress and the executive branch to follow up the Court's decision with legislation that would force the southern states to comply with the decision.

What happened then? When, in 1960, four black students sat down at a whites-only lunch counter in Greensboro, North Carolina, sit-ins had already taken place in the American South. But these were mostly set-piece performances mounted by civil rights organizations. Here, four well-dressed black freshmen appeared unannounced at a whites-only lunch counter in the heart of a southern city. Before it was over, the Greensboro sit-in led to what Doug McAdam and William Sewell (2001) would call "a transformative event" (see also Andrews and Biggs 2006; McAdam 1999: 138–140). The students staged a deeply transgressive performance, but they carried it out in the most polite, contained manner.

Coordinated action was the first mechanism we see in this episode. One of the students, Franklin McCain, later recalled:

> The planning process began on Sunday night. I remember it quite well. I think it was Joseph [McNeil] who said; "It's time that we take some action now. We've been getting together, and we've been, up to this point, still like most people we've talked about for the past few weeks or so—that is, people who talk a lot but, in fact, make little action." After selecting the technique, then we said, "Let's go down and just ask for service." It certainly wasn't titled a "sit-in" or "sit-down" at that time. (Raines 1977: 76)

Nor did the current state of the civil rights movement predict that the Greensboro sit-in would occur when it did. African American protests had gone into a holding pattern after the flurry of activity generated by the Supreme Court's *Brown* decision in 1954 (Andrews and Biggs 2006: 757). Building on McAdam's (1999) efforts to use the *New York Times* to map the civil rights movement, Craig Jenkins and his collaborators charted events involving the civil rights movement between 1947 and 1997 (Jenkins, Jacobs, and Agnone 2003). As their data in Figure 2.2 figure show, in the wake of the *Brown* decision, the number of both protests and of general civil rights events declined. The concerted action in Greensboro reversed that trend.

Right after Greensboro, sit-ins diffused rapidly across the South. Kenneth Andrews and Michael Biggs (2006) observe, "The protest was repeated, with increasing numbers of students, on subsequent days. A week later, the sit-ins began to spread to other cities. This typically meant students occupying seats at downtown lunch counters at 'five and dime' stores demonstrating their resistance to public segregation and disrupting the normal operating of business" (753).

Scholars have disagreed about the degree of planning versus spontaneity of the student sit-ins and about the role of the media versus civil rights

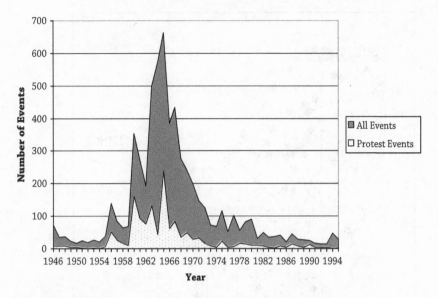

Figure 2.2:
African American Total Movement and Protest Events, 1946–1994
Source: Data provided by Craig Jenkins

organizations in their diffusion (Andrews and Biggs 2006; Killian 1984; Morris 1984; Oberschall 1989; Polletta 1998). But all agree that Greensboro provided a model picked up and rapidly diffused across the South. A week after the initial protest, similar sit-ins appeared in other cities, first in proximity to Greensboro but eventually all over the South (Oberschall 1989: n. 4). By April, sit-in campaigns had occurred in more than seventy cities (Andrews and Biggs 2006: 759). We can see how far the movement spread from Andrews and Biggs' map of where student sit-ins appeared in figure 2.3.

No complex outcome ever results from the operation of a single causal mechanism. Diffusion of the sit-in movement was partly "non-relational"—the result of word spreading across college campuses that the Greensboro protests had taken place. But the Greensboro model also spread through the organizational networks of adult and student civil rights organizations. Both new and old student organizations took up the model of polite, but determined demand for the right to be served at lunch counters across the South. Brokerage, the production of a new connection between previously unconnected sites, caused important changes in contention.

To brokerage and diffusion, suppose we add our third mechanism, coordinated action. In that mechanism, two or more actors signal their intentions to each other and engage in parallel making of claims on the same

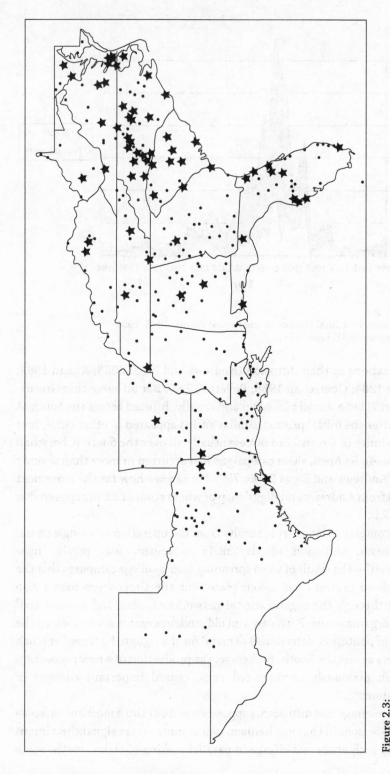

Figure 2.3:
Sit-ins in the American South, February 1 to April 14, 1960
Source: Andrews and Biggs (2006: fig. 2).

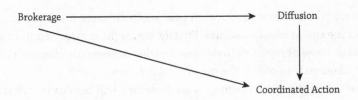

Figure 2.4:
Sites of New Coordination

object. Imagine two neighborhood associations simultaneously erecting signs opposing the construction of a freeway between their neighborhoods. A leader from Neighborhood A talks with leaders of Neighborhood B, persuading them to erect hostile signs on the same day, and supplying appropriately hostile language for the signs.

Mechanisms combine into processes. When we add coordination to brokerage and diffusion, we get coordinated action and have one version of a process we can call *new coordination* (see figure 2.4).

Coordinated action produces further effects, perhaps including creation of new alliances across neighborhood boundaries, attempts by city authorities to tear down the offending signs, and even second thoughts on the part of city council members from the affected neighborhoods. Sometimes it leads to coordination at a higher level as, for example, when different neighborhood groups combine to lobby the state legislature or march on Washington. We call this process *upward scale shift*. Chapter 6 examines that process in detail.

SITES OF NEW COORDINATION

We see the elementary process of new coordination in a wide variety of sites, including the England of 1785, the Ukraine of 2014, and in the national protest wave against the Ferguson police murder of 2014. Yet we have other ways to use this mechanism-process analysis of new coordination. Sometimes we will want to work new coordination into our explanation for a particular stream of contention—for example, the search for allies within the elite on the part of the antislavery campaign in England. In that case, we will also have to take initial conditions into account, including such elements as the institution of the petition and the growing role of a free press as a mechanism of communication.

Sometimes, in contrast, we will want to focus on new coordination itself, asking whether it works pretty much the same across a wide variety of sites, and whether it produces dramatically different outcomes depending on the site in which it occurs. Finally, we might compare contention in different types of regimes, to determine whether new coordination occurs more frequently in one or the other, and if so, why.

Our use of the mechanism-process approach will help us in two ways:

- By taking apart mobilization into its constituent mechanisms, we can see how the process is triggered and how central a particular mechanism is to its fruition.
- By comparing different types of contention—such as social movements and civil wars—we can pinpoint which mechanisms are key to the transition from one to the other.

OTHER MECHANISMS

If contentious politics consisted only of diffusion, brokerage, and coordination, we would see a great deal of contention but very little continuity. In fact, many episodes of contention do trickle away or suddenly stop because they find little support in society or because little remains to sustain them after their initial claims are made. Think of the American urban riots of the 1960s: They caused tremendous damage and triggered state policies to prevent their recurrence, but they left little behind after the rioters had dispersed.

In many of our episodes, however, additional mechanisms and processes will appear to expand the range or extend the life of contentious episodes:

- *Social appropriation*: nonpolitical groups transform into political actors by using their organizational and institutional bases to launch movement campaigns. For example, in the 1950s and 1960s, the previously conservative black churches became sites of social appropriation for southern civil rights groups (McAdam 1999; Morris 1984).
- *Boundary activation*: creation of a new boundary or the crystallization of an existing one between challenging groups and their targets. For example, by defining citizens as members of a particular racial or ethnic group, the census acts as an agent of boundary activation (Williams 2006).
- *Certification*: an external authority's signal of its readiness to recognize and support the existence and claims of a political actor. For example, when the state of Israel was proclaimed in 1948, both superpowers, the

United States and the USSR, lent it certification by voting for its creation in the United Nations.

- *Identity shift*: formation of new identities within challenging groups whose coordinated action brings them together and reveals their commonalities. For example, in 1956, Martin Luther King Jr. framed the Montgomery bus boycott as the source of an identity shift to what he called "the new Negro" (McAdam, Tarrow, and Tilly 2001: 319).
- *Competition:* social movements are seldom unified; they are made up of complementary and sometimes rival organizations with different preferences and different leaders—and often undercut one another (Gamson 1990).
- *Escalation and Radicalization:* Most contention begins in routine interactions and much of it remains routine. But when counter-protesters, the police, or the state respond with vigor, challengers often escalate their tactics and radicalize their claims (della Porta 2013; Alimi et al., 2015). We will see both escalation and radicalization in the cycles of protest we examine in chapter 6.

One particular set of mechanisms that we have already encountered in the Ferguson story and will encounter in almost all our episodes is *repression* and *social control*.

Repression and Social Control

Repression we define as the attempt by a state or its agents against challengers in order to end their challenge by arresting them, harassing them, or destroying their organizations. We saw repression at the beginning of this chapter in the actions of officer Darren Wilson in Ferguson in August, 2014. Repression is only one of a spectrum of modes of *social control*: it is part of what Jules Boykoff (2007) calls "suppression." "In the short run," he writes, "these modes of suppression slow down—or in some cases paralyze—the practice of dissent. In the long run they demobilize dissent by discouraging *future* action (35). Table 2.1 presents a list of different forms of suppression from Boykoff's work. Ranging from mass media underestimation of the power of protest all the way to physical repression—what Boykoff calls "direct violence" (Boykoff 2007: 36).

States not only engage in violent repression of dissent: as Table 2.1 shows, they can use legal prosecution, employment discrimination, surveillance, infiltration, and other forms of harassment that avoid physical repression. We also find repression in extreme form in the attempt to end

Table 2.1. MODES OF SUPPRESSION EMPLOYED BY STATES
AND THE MASS-MEDIA

- Mass Media Underestimation of Challengers
- Mass Media Depreciation of Challengers
- Demonization of Challengers or the Group they Come From
- Mass Media Manipulation
- Extraordinary Rules and Laws
- Harassment and Harassment Arrests
- Creating False Documents Purporting to Come from Challengers
- Infiltration of Challenger Groups and Use of Agent Provocateurs
- Surveillance and Break-ins
- Employment Deprivation
- Prosecutions and Hearings
- Direct Violence [repression]

insurgency in Central America, stamp out the nationalist movements that arose as the Soviet Union disintegrated, suppress the Solidarity movement in Poland, and defeat the forces of violent Islamism by the United States and its allies. But it is important at the outset to understand that violent repression is only one of a differentiated set of tools that a state uses in order to oppose challengers.

Mobilization and Demobilization

We have said that mechanisms congeal into processes. Two major processes will recur in our analyses: mobilization and demobilization (see chapter 6). By *mobilization*, we mean how people who at a given point in time are not making contentious claims start to do so; by *demobilization*, we ask how people who are making claims stop doing so. In chapter 6, we will show how mobilization turned into demobilization in the case of the Italian cycle of contention of the late 1960s and early 1970s. The process of mobilization increases the resources available for collective claim making, while the process of demobilization decreases those resources.

Mobilization often leads to counter-mobilization. We saw this complex relationship in the response of police forces to the sympathy evoked for Michael Brown and his family and in reaction to the murder of two New York City police officers. In that case, the counter-mobilization was peaceful and symbolic; but in other cases we will encounter, counter-mobilization escalates and radicalizes the conflicts between opposing actors and organizations.

EPISODES AND EVENTS

Events we define as visibly coherent interactions among challengers and their opponents, with third parties, including the media, involved in secondary but often crucial roles in communicating information about the event to other actors and other conflicts. *Episodes* we define as bounded sequences of continuous interaction, usually produced by an investigator's chopping up longer streams of contention into segments for purposes of systematic observation, comparison, and explanation. These range from relatively simple episodes—such as the shantytown occupations on American college campuses, all the way to major cycles of contention, revolutions, and civil wars.

How can we capture the complexity and permutations in such large episodes of contention as English antislavery and the Ukrainian conflict since 2013? We can learn a lot from what activists say or later write about their activities. But memory tends to be selective. No single activist, however well placed, joins all the activities in an episode of contention. We will learn more by examining what activists *do* during major episodes of contention. This can be done through a variety of methods, some of them sophisticated but most easily available through newspaper records, archives, and online press releases.

Easiest to access—because officials collect them—are records of workers' strikes. Working with such sources, Edward Shorter and Charles Tilly (1974) examined the shape, the size, and the length of strikes in France from 1830 to 1968. At about the same time, scholars such as Seymour Spilerman (1970) and Charles Perrow (1979) and his research team conducted systematic studies of urban riots and protests that had occurred during the sixties. Their approaches to episodes of contention provided models for the next generation of students. In the 1980s, for example, Doug McAdam (1999) and Craig Jenkins (1985) examined, respectively, the American civil rights and farmworkers' movements. Similarly, Dieter Rucht (2005) carried out the systematic analysis of German protest events that chapter 1 reviewed. In Italy, Sidney Tarrow (1989) and his team read newspapers systematically for the period 1966–1973. In the early 1990s, Susan Olzak (1992) developed a sophisticated model of ethnic conflict. All of these researchers looked for any episode that qualified as a "conflict event" according to a standard set of definitions.

Also readily available—because officials worry most about this form of collective action—are sources of data on violence. Especially in the wake of 9/11, a whole industry involving studies of organized violence and terrorism has developed (Berman and Laitin 2008; Sageman 2004). Although considerable slippage entered the definition of *terrorism* as a variety of scholars and journalists got into the act, its expansion stimulated a broadening from studies of the statistical incidence of violence and its correlation with other variables to its links to nonviolent contention, its rituals, and its forms of performance (Alexander 2004; Collins 2004).

Studies of "waves," "cycles," and particular streams of contention combine attention to strikes, protest demonstrations, sit-ins, organized violence, and even institutional forms of participation, such as referenda. In their study of social movements in France, Germany, the Netherlands, and Switzerland, Hanspeter Kriesi and his collaborators (1995) used a major newspaper in each country to examine the number of contentious events, the magnitude of participation in them, the type of performance involved—demonstrative, confrontational, or violent—the types of organizations that mounted them, the allies they attracted, and the dynamics of the episodes. For the fifteen-year period they studied, they complemented their sweeping comparisons by issue-specific analyses of nuclear energy, gay activism, cross-national diffusion, and the outcomes of the movements they studied. In Kriesi and his collaborators' investigation, the division of streams of contention into episodes did three different kinds of analytical work, all of them crucial:

- It drew from a bewildering, tangled series of events a narrower, more manageable set of public interactions that reasonably represented the overall direction of the complicated whole. They could then compare each national profile of contention to the differences in institutional structure and the dominant political strategies of the actors to produce tentative explanations of why some kinds of contention were more prominent in some countries than in others.
- It facilitated comparison of trends and fluctuations in different kinds of contention. In their findings, "demonstrative" events were far and away the most frequent in all four countries, but marked differences appeared in the incidence of "confrontational" and violent events.
- By distinguishing "new" from "old" actors—mainly the working class—Kriesi and his collaborators could speculate about the directions and dynamics of change.

Suppose you want to do your own study of contentious politics. In a recent review, Sven Hutter provides a "how to" survey of the methods of protest event analysis since the earliest efforts in the 1950s and 1960s to the Web-based analyses of today (Hutter 2014). Hutter's review shows that you need not read newspapers in four different languages, as Kriesi and his collaborators did, to imitate their discipline. Any source that regularly records contentious politics in a relatively uniform way lends itself to the construction of a catalog you can analyze systematically. The next section shows how one scholar at an American university drew from her own experience a protest event analysis that went well beyond description to analysis and evaluation.

Soule on Shantytowns

In early 1985, news reports described government-ordered beatings and shootings of peaceful South African protesters against that country's repressive system of apartheid, or racial segregation. More than five thousand killings had already occurred in South Africa as the result of political violence. By the end of the apartheid regime in the mid-1990s, there would be thousands more. For her PhD research at Cornell University, Sarah Soule (1995) examined the rise and fall of the protest wave of American college students against their universities' investments in South Africa. Soule's interest in the protests she studied arose from observation of protests on her own campus. But she went on to compare Cornell with protests in favor of divestment on many other campuses and analyzed the data over time to evaluate its effect on public policy (Soule 1995, 1997, 1999).

The shantytown performance first emerged in an early protest at Columbia University during April 1985. At Columbia, students blockaded Hamilton Hall, the site of the first historic anti-Vietnam War sit-in in 1967. To establish a presence there, they dragged armchairs and sofas from a nearby dormitory. When night fell, they rigged up tarps and brought in blankets. When the Reverend Jesse Jackson came to speak, participation in their protest grew to over five thousand. Jackson's presence, the large number of African American demonstrators on campus, and the fact that Columbia had helped to start the 1967–1968 protest wave gained national media attention and helped to trigger a diffusion in favor of college divestment in South Africa across the country (Hirsch 1990; Soule 1997: 857).

Columbia's constructions of tarps, blankets, and furniture soon spread with a variety of labels to campuses around the country. At Princeton and Santa Cruz, participants called it a "camp-out"; at Harvard, a "sleep-in"; at Iowa, the students renamed the administration building "Biko Hall," after the murdered South African student leader Stephen Biko. A number of other student groups held what they called "sit-outs." It was only in late spring, when the snow melted in Ithaca, that Cornell students collected scraps of wood, tar paper, and plastic to construct a shack in front of the university's administration building. That shack, notes Soule, "was the first of what later became known as the *shantytown*, "a performance and a name that eventually spread to similar structures around the country" (Soule 1997: 858; also see Soule 1999).

In all, Soule identified forty-six shantytown protests between 1985, when the campaign against investment in South African firms began, and 1990, when it ended. All of these events used roughly the same performance—student activists' building of a makeshift structure to oppose their universities' investments in firms with ties to South Africa. While some made broader claims, all professed clear statements about the necessity of divestment. Figure 2.5 tracks the shantytown protests that Soule found in her database over this six-year period.

Soule moved from description to analysis to evaluation. From personal observation at Cornell, Soule described an event—the "naming" of the shantytown performance. That experience interested her in learning more. But rather than write up a case study that might have given an exaggerated importance to her own campus and reified the innovation, she analyzed a more systematic source: the NEXIS file of hundreds of newspapers. (You will find it in your campus library.) NEXIS offered Soule a search function that made it unnecessary for her to pore over hundreds of

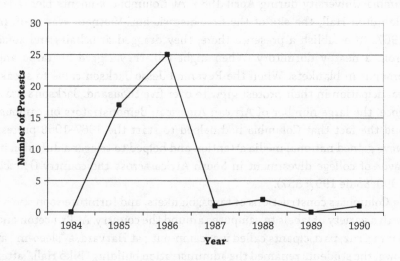

Figure 2.5:
"Shantytown Protests" on American College Campuses, 1984–1990
Source: Data provided by Sarah Soule

newspaper articles as many of her predecessors—including the authors of this book—had done before her (Soule 1997: 864).

NEXIS also made it possible to construct a timeline of the shantytown protests (in Soule's language, an "event history") and relate it to other variables. For example, Soule analyzed what kind of campuses tended to produce shantytown protests—were they more likely to emerge in large private universities, mostly black or liberal arts colleges, or big state institutions? She also studied whether there was a geographic pattern of diffusion from Columbia to nearby campuses in the Northeast, or whether the movement spread through the media, irrespective of location. And she evaluated the effect of the protests: Were those campuses in which shantytowns appeared more likely to divest than those that had seen no protests?

Two kinds of results followed from Soule's procedures. On the one hand, by examining her sources carefully, she discovered that the "invention" of the innovation at Columbia was not deliberate and that it only developed a modular identity as it spread. Indeed, it was only after the Cornell events that the student divestment protesters gave a name to their performance and deliberately modeled their actions on it. Looking back, we can see that the innovation was no more than a symbol-laden variant of the sit-in, with a special symbolism related to the conditions of life of black South Africans.

For that reason, the performance petered out at the end of the divestment campaign. It had no symbolic relationship to other types of claims. As a result, unlike the sit-in or the demonstration, it did not become part of the basic repertoire of contention. People now remember it mostly as a failed innovation (Soule 1999). Shantytown protests against divestment failed in another way as well. When Soule carried out an analysis of the co-occurrence of shantytown protests with colleges' investment policies, she found that it was ineffective in forcing divestment. "Colleges and universities that had shantytowns," she concludes, "actually had slower rates of divestment than those that did not have them" (Soule 1999: 121; see also Soule 1995). Evaluation followed description and analysis.

Soule's research on the diffusion of the shantytown protests provides a simple model for how students can examine streams of contention, sites of contention, and the diffusion of contention, with data that are easily available. Second, it tells us how a new performance can spread—not randomly in a population, like a contagious disease, but among similar social actors. Third, if we are interested in the mechanisms and processes of contention, her work on a particular performance's "career" helps us to understand how particular paths of diffusion that a performance follows affect its longevity. Will it peter out, trigger a sustained social movement, or explode into revolution? For example, the fact that the shantytown diffused mainly through the media probably meant that activists on different campuses did not know each other, did not coordinate their actions, and, as a result, could not build a national organization. In our language, the shantytown performance diffused but did not produce a shift in the scale of the divestment movement. But some events congeal into campaigns and campaigns sometimes explode into cycles and tides of contention capable to challenging, and in some cases liquidating an entire regime, as we will see when we turn to the collapse of the Soviet Union in chapter 5.

OTHER VARIETIES OF EVIDENCE AND ANALYSIS

Collecting catalogs of contentious episodes serves the analysis of contentious politics well in two different ways. First, it clarifies what you have to explain and therefore what might explain it. Second, it focuses attention on the process of contention itself rather than diverting attention to antecedents and consequences. Still, some investigations properly emphasize antecedents or consequences. Sometimes, for example, we want to know whether certain actions by legislatures regularly generate contentious reactions or under what conditions military coups change the distribution of power outside the military. In either regard, contentious events will mark relevant cases, but large catalogs will probably be less helpful than close case comparisons. At other times, we want to understand what the social bases or organizational bases of a particular movement or episode are. For this purpose, the examination of movement networks would serve our purposes better than the study of events (Diani 1995 and 2015; Diani and McAdam, eds. 2003; Osa 2003a, 2003b; Hadden 2015).

Mechanism-process accounts facilitate explanation well outside the world of event catalogs. Think back to British antislavery and Ukraine's conflicts in 2013–2014. Either one would lend itself to constructing catalogs of contentious episodes. But for many purposes, other methods will serve better. In the analysis of British antislavery, we would learn a great deal by tracing changes in the connections among activists both inside and outside contentious events. We would gain from compiling life histories of many, many activists, to see how their social origins, religious affiliations, occupations, and political memberships varied and changed between 1785 and 1835. Content analysis of parliamentary debates, pamphlets, and news reports concerning antislavery would yield valuable information on splits and shifts in public representation of the issues.

This chapter's general lessons would still apply. You would arrive at better explanations by specifying the sites of contention, describing relevant conditions at those sites, identifying the relevant streams of contention, naming the most important outcomes, looking for crucial mechanisms, compounding those mechanisms into processes, and using analogies or direct comparisons with similar processes elsewhere to combine conditions, mechanisms, and processes into explanations of the outcomes. Chapters to come will often follow exactly that pattern: looking closely at the internal workings of contentious events without chopping them up into episodes for comparison.

As we move on, we will return repeatedly to chapter 1's basic descriptive concepts: political actors, governments, political identities, contentious performances and repertoires, social movements, and so forth. And this present chapter's basic concepts—sites, conditions, streams, outcomes, mechanisms, processes, and episodes—will provide a flexible explanatory framework for dealing with such questions as how political actors form, how political identities change, and how streams of contention sometimes congeal into sustained social movements. We will return to some of the mechanisms and processes highlighted in this chapter—in particular, to the mechanisms of brokerage, diffusion, and coordination and to the processes of mobilization and demobilization. Each will serve us well as we move into closer examination of contentious processes. But in order to do this, we will have to place political actors and their forms of contention within their political contexts. We will need to examine political regimes and the different combinations of opportunities and threats they offer or withhold from contentious politics. This task we turn to in chapters 3 and 4.

NOTES

1. "Ferguson Shooting: Protests Spread Across the U.S." *BBC News.* November 26, 2014. www.bbc.com/news/world-us-canada-30203526.
2. Joseph Goldstein, "Judge Rejects New York's Stop-and-Frisk Policy", New York Times, August 12, 2013. http://www.nytimes.com/2013/08/13/nyregion/stop-and-frisk-practice-violated-rights-judge-rules.html?pagewanted=all&_r=0
3. Lauren Victoria Burke, "Turning Action into Law to Stop Police Killings," *The Root*, January 5, 2015. http://www.theroot.com/articles/culture/2015/01/turning_action_into_law_to_stop_police_killings&ei=UTF-8&hspart=mozilla&hsimp=yhs-001
4. Ian Simpson and Jonathan Allen, "Two New York City Police Officers Killed, Gunman Dead," http://www.reuters.com/article/2014/12/20/us-usa-newyork-police-idUSKBN0JY0N820141220
5. You can watch the police turning their back on Mayor de Blasio at https://www.youtube.com/watch?v=CJUy_S8UUfY

PART TWO

Repertoires, Regimes, and Opportunities

Source: *Description **Occupy Wall Street** Anonymous 2011 **Shankbone**.JPG*, accessed at commons. wikimedia.org.

Friday, September 30, 2011. An Occupy Wall Street protester wearing a Guy Fawkes mask favored by "Anonymous" protesters.

CHAPTER 3

Democracy, Undemocracy, and Change in Repertoires

Contentious politics varies and changes in close connection with shifts of political power, and it organizes both inside and outside institutional venues. In this chapter, we examine how democratic and undemocratic political regimes structure and are affected by contentious politics. In the next chapter we will turn to the considerable number of regimes that are neither wholly democratic nor entirely undemocratic. We call these "hybrid regimes." Here are the three terms that will motivate these two chapters:

- *Contentious repertoires* are arrays of contentious performances that are currently known and available within some set of political actors.
- *Regimes* consist of regular relations among governments, established political actors, and challengers, and are perceived and acted upon by outside political actors, including other governments.
- *Opportunity structures* include aspects of a regime that offer challengers both openings to advance their claims and threats and constraints that caution them against making these claims (Goldstone and Tilly 2001).

We will first use the American protest repertoire to map how repertoires change and the opportunities they offer challengers to advance their claims in the period from the civil rights movement to the Occupy movement of 2011–2012. We will then describe the interactions between changing repertoires and regimes, focusing on the difference that democracy and elections make to how people protest. We will then use the transition to democracy in Argentina to show how democratic change affects changes in the repertoire of contention. Our analyses will show that the connections among contention, political power, and institutions appear in both turbulent periods and in the more routine politics of settled democracies. Our central question is, "How do the structures of political power and institutions and the character of contentious politics interact?"

REPERTOIRE CHANGE IN THE UNITED STATES, 1955–2015

The post–World War II years did not begin with the promise of major change in the American repertoire of contention. The Cold War, domestic anticommunism, and satisfactions of the consumer society turned people's attentions away from political contention. When innovations in the repertoire of contention emerged, they arrived from a new and unexpected quarter, the black middle class. African Americans did not enter contentious politics all at once or using any single form of collective action. But the civil rights movement that began quietly in the mid-1950s led to a fundamental change in the American repertoire of contention. Partially released from the grip of southern Jim Crow repression by urbanization, migration to the North, and entry into the middle class, many educated African Americans were growing restive under the effective segregation of American life.

The federal government gave them an assist. Concerned about the contradiction between fighting for freedom abroad and abetting discrimination at home, from the late 1940s on, the government took halting steps to combat segregation. African Americans also drew encouragement from the most institutionalized form of contention that Americans possess: bringing lawsuits. *Brown v. Board of Education* and other landmark cases ultimately brought mixed results (Klarman 2004; Rosenberg 2008). But they encouraged black parents to register their children in formerly white public schools and led black college students to fight to register in once-white universities. Conventional legal battles provided a foundation for the more confrontational contentious politics to come.

Four developments marked a shift in performances that would culminate in the major cycle of protest of the 1960s and early '70s. First was the practice of what came to be called "legal mobilization"—using the courts to advance movement goals (McCann 1994; 2006). Second was the practice of "marching on Washington" in major set-piece demonstrations culminating in rallies before the Lincoln Memorial. Third came the practice of dedicating a period of time—usually the summer—to a particular campaign. The fourth spread the disruptive practice of sit-ins, road blocking, and building occupations: first at lunch counters, then at bus stations, and finally wherever public segregation was practiced.

Taken together, these innovations congealed into a major cycle of contention that many Americans remember—some with nostalgia, others with distaste—as "the sixties."[1] In fact, the period of increased contention lasted well into the 1970s, as we can see from Figure 3.1, which combines the number of civil rights, environment, antiwar, consumer, student, and women's collective actions from the records of the *New York Times* from 1953 to 1980.[2]

Marching on Washington, the second major innovation, descended from forms of contention familiar in the American past. Among other precedents, they stemmed from the veterans' march of the 1930s and from the civil rights march that A. Philip Randolph threatened to organize in 1941, just as the United States was mobilizing for its part in World War II. But in the 1960s marching on—or, rather, "in"—Washington D.C. became a dramatic way of demonstrating a movement's strength and determination that was adopted by a variety of groups, especially after television

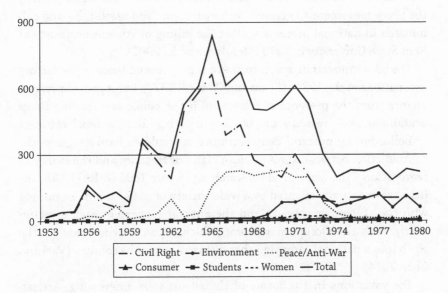

Figure 3.1:
Social Movement Actions in the United States, 1953–1980
Source: Doug McAdam and Katrina Kloos, *Deeply Divided: Racial Politics and Social Movements in Postwar America* (2014):p. 56. The data, provided from Doug McAdam, come from a research project at SUNY Stony Brook, directed by Charles Perrow, from the *New York Times*. For partial reports on the project, see McAdam 1982 and Jenkins 1985.

made it possible for Americans to participate at great distances in dramatic events like Martin Luther King's "I have a dream" speech at the Lincoln Memorial.

Over the decades after the 1960s, marches became more contained, but they also grew in magnitude and in their "made for television" character. Eventually organizers even provided mobile TV monitors for demonstrators who were too numerous or too far away to see the speakers. Organizers set up port-a-potties for the crowds, and the National Park Police offered seminars in how to run an orderly demonstration (McCarthy, McPhail, and Smith 1996). With the routinization of the March on Washington, what had begun as a disruptive performance became conventional while retaining the trappings of contention: banners, chants, serried ranks moving forward in the face of power.

Mississippi Freedom Summer was the most notable example of the third innovation, the choice of a finite period of time to concentrate the energies of militants on a particular goal—in that event, to register African Americans to vote (McAdam 1988). Other seasonal campaigns, such as Vietnam Summer and Labor Summer, followed. The biggest protest demonstrations in this period were aimed at the waging of the Vietnam war, beginning with a march of over 20,000 people on the Pentagon in October 1967. That movement produced national "Moratoriums" in 1969—the name given by the peace movement to massive demonstrations and teach-ins—and culminated in national protests against the killing of student protesters at Kent State University in 1970 (McAdam and Su 2002).

The final innovation, *the sit-in*, had a family resemblance to the factory occupations of the 1930s (Piven and Cloward 1977), but it gained new resonance from the presence of television. If the public saw spitting thugs brutalizing well-dressed young black men sitting calmly at lunch counters or police hosing peaceful demonstrators, it would be hard to ignore the contradiction between the American claim of freedom and the reality of segregation. "The whole world is watching," wrote Todd Gitlin (1980). Sit-ins were eventually adopted by a wide variety of social actors, beginning with the student movement and the antiwar movement and, most recently, with the Occupy movement, which expanded the model of the sit-in into a national campaign that diffused across the country (Vasi and Chan 2014).

The variations in the forms of the sit-ins were interesting. African Americans mainly occupied only sites in which public services were unequally enjoyed by whites and blacks. College student activists sat in at their administration buildings. Antiwar protesters sat in wherever they could disrupt routines and gain media attention. The Civil Rights March on Washington stayed contained and ended predictably at the Lincoln Memorial. But antiwar protesters marched across the Potomac to the Pentagon, which they surrounded in a mock levitation, while African Americans sat in on the Triborough Bridge in New York City to block the opening of the 1964 World's Fair.

After the 1960s, sit-ins diffused widely across American social groups. From their origins in the civil rights movement, sit-ins spread to groups of all kinds who occupied public space on behalf of causes they favored. From students occupying administration buildings in the 1960s, it was a short step to the antinuclear road blockades of the 1970s and the "shantytown" protests of the 1980s (see chapter 2).

The model was expanded over the decades to sit-ins on city squares, streets, public buildings, and college campuses. By the time we reach the Occupy Wall Street protests of 2011, the tactic has become routinized, standardized, and modular and reached almost every sector of the population. The Occupy Wall Street movement of 2011 even tried to occupy the Brooklyn Bridge. Table 3.1 shows how that movement adapted the sit-in to different kinds of sites as it spread around the country.

By no means all of the performances discussed so far in this chapter were new, though in combination they produced the impression of a wave of "new social movements." Alongside them was the strategy that

Table 3.1. TYPES OF OCCUPY SITES, SEPTEMBER 17 TO OCTOBER 1, 2011

Location	Cities	Location	Cities
Park	32	Capitol Building	9
Street	20	City Hall	9
Plaza	13	Bank	7
Square	10	Courthouse	7
Downtown	9	State House	2
Center	4	Federal Reserve Building	2
Common	2	Executive Building	1
Bridge	1	Chamber of Commerce	1
Bell Tower	1	Post Office	1
University Campus	7	Art Institute	1
Other	10		

Source: The table contains information, collected by Chan Suh and Yisook Lin, on the location of OWS protests in 265 Cities from the press and from self-reports by protesters at Guardian (https://docs.google.com/spreadsheet/ccc?key=0AonYZs4MzlZbdGhwWGhTUXphUkw3RldHWUlKZmI5NEE&hl=en_GB#gid=6)

initiated the modern civil rights movement in the 1950s—*legal mobilization*—which began when the Legal Defense Fund of the National Association for the Advancement of Colored People (NAACP) determined to fight segregation in the public schools by bringing evidence to the Supreme Court that segregated school systems were far from equal. In the well-known case of *Brown v. Board of Education* (347 U.S. 483 [1954]), which was argued before the Supreme Court by future Supreme Court Justice Thurgood Marshall, the case launched the legal strategy that dominated civil rights activism until the early 1960s, when more militant tactics by a younger generation of activists entered the fray. Even after African Americans turned to more transgressive protests, seeking redress in the courts continued to be a major weapon of change-seeking movements, including the women's movement's use of the courts to legalize abortion, and the campaign by a coalition of groups that sought legal remedies for discrimination against gay and lesbian Americans (see chapter 10).

Legal mobilization was by no means limited to progressive or liberal groups. Following the model created by "legal liberalism," and assisted by Edwin Meese, Attorney General under President Ronald Reagan, and by the Federalist Society, a spectrum of conservative law firms created a conservative legal movement (Teles 2008; 2009). This movement helped to train a generation of conservative lawyers and succeeded in placing a number of them in highly-placed judgeships, including in the United States Supreme Court. This was a classical case of movement-countermovement interaction (Meyer and Staggenborg 1996).

Two other trends emerged in the 1980s and 1990s. On the one hand, many social movement organizations transformed themselves into public interest groups and shifted their main forms of mobilization from the streets and campuses to direct mailings, educational campaigns, and lobbying. On the other hand, religious groups involved themselves increasingly in contentious politics. These trends came together—or, rather, they clashed—in the growing, rancorous, and apparently endless struggle over abortion. It pitted "choice" advocates—largely organized by public interest groups and using direct mail appeals—against Catholic and evangelical Protestant congregations employing more effective door-to-door proselytizing on behalf of "life" (Ginsburg 1989; McCarthy 1987). Both trends coincided in the 2004 election, when the enormous outpouring of small contributions to the Democratic Party campaign failed to match the capacity of the Republican Party to mobilize supporters among the religious faithful for George W. Bush's presidential campaign.

As the United States entered the new century, it was clear that a new instrument—the Internet—was beginning to transform the nature of contentious politics (Almeida and Lichbach 2003; Bennett and Segerberg 2013). The 2004 MoveOn.org campaign on behalf of Governor Howard Dean demonstrated that through skilled use of electronic media, it was now possible to mobilize thousands of people on behalf of a common cause—if only for brief periods of time. This meant that the elaborate mobilizing structures that previous campaigns had mounted to organize major demonstrations might one day become obsolete (Bennett and Segerberg 2013). The Internet also brought once-parochial American activists into greater contact with counterparts abroad—for example, in the simultaneous protests against the launching of the Iraq War in 2003 (see chapter 9).

The 2008 presidential campaign of Barack Obama expanded the use of the Internet and combined it with a new tool—social media—that may be transforming contentious politics in general (see chapter 10). The same tools helped to diffuse the message of the "Arab Spring" across the Middle East and North Africa in 2011–2012. It also helped to spread the "Occupy Wall Street" movement from a single occupation in downtown Manhattan to a national campaign in a mere few weeks (Vasi and Suh 2014). Through these tools, people who had never met, and might live thousands of miles apart, came to see themselves as parts of an "imagined community" with a common identity (Anderson 1991).

Most of these forms were inherently peaceful but violence frequently occurred as a byproduct of both conventional and confrontational contention. In the late 1960s, as the mainstream of the civil rights movement moved into institutional politics and the New Left faded, minorities of militants, outraged at what they saw as the "sellout" of their values by their more moderate comrades, formed military or underground groups such as the Black Panthers and the (mostly white) Weather Underground. Far smaller than the groups they sought to supplant, these groups used violent performances to catch the attention of the media and add an air of terror to contentious politics. (Most Americans, even today, think of the 1960s as a period of "riots.") Their desperate efforts backfired, because their violent methods gave political elites a justification to meet contention with state violence. Even more violent—and therefore justifying greater repression—were the Islamist movements that began to spread across the globe in the 1990s (see chapter 9). The culmination of both trends arrived with the attack on the World Trade Center and the Pentagon on September 11, 2001, and the Patriot Act, which curtailed Americans'civil liberties on the altar of freedom.

While there were major changes in the repertoire of contention in the United States in the half century between the 1960s and the end of the first decade of the new century, the continuities were also clear:

- First, once a new performance proved viable, it varied little from place to place and from protest to protest.
- Second, protest performances diffused broadly across the country and across the ideological spectrum; unlike the strike, these performances were *not* associated with a particular population group.
- Third, with the exception of the violent groups on the margins of the civil rights and antiwar movements, the new innovations were accommodated by the institutions of American law and administration.

Did the American political regime change between the 1960s and today as the result of the changes in repertoire described above? Clearly, the government responded to the antiwar movement with clandestine and illegal surveillance (Keller 1989; Tarrow 2015: ch. 8) and the Nixon administration even engaged in unconstitutional behavior, both in the Watergate affair and in the repression of dissidents. Yet as the repertoire expanded, there was no major wave of repression, no overturning of elites or institutions, and contentious politics continued to thrive. The suppression of protest took mainly institutional forms, as police and protesters collaborated to prevent demonstrations from leading to violence (McCarthy, McPhail, and Crist 1999).

But this trend was not irreversible: when protest demonstrations became more disruptive, police tactics turned more aggressive (Soule and Davenport 2009). With the rise of the global justice and antiwar protests at the turn of the new century (see chapter 9), police forces turned to a strategy of the "incapacitation" of protesters (Gillham 2011). And in the wake of the Bush administration's "War on Terror," there was a growing militarization of the police, who were increasingly ready to use violence against demonstrators.

REGIMES

Despite these threats to civil liberties, the nature of the American regime changed little and was able to absorb many of the new performances that were born in the 1960s. Not so the response of authoritarian regimes to protest. Regimes vary from one country to the next. Some regime variations across countries are quite subtle. Think about similarities and differences between the US and Canadian political systems. Both feature federal arrangements (states and provinces), national and regional legislatures, formally independent judiciaries, and forms of common law. Yet the United States has an elected president, while the Canadian chief executive is a prime minister drawn from the parliament's dominant party. The US government exercises priority over natural resources, while Canada cedes extensive control over natural resources to its provinces. These subtle differences in regimes have actually produced significant differences in contentious politics—for example, a more robust tradition of social democracy in Canada as against the more centrist "liberalism" of the American Left.

Two big differences among regimes across the world matter most to contentious politics: governmental capacity and extent (or lack) of democracy.

- *Capacity* means the extent to which governmental action affects the character and distribution of population, activity, and resources within the government's territory. When a high-capacity government intervenes in population, activity, and resources, it makes a big difference; it raises taxes, distributes benefits, regulates traffic flows, controls the use of natural resources, and much more. Low-capacity governments may try to do the same things, but they have little effect.
- *Democracy* means the extent to which people subject to a given government's authority have broad, equal political rights, exert significant direct influence (e.g., through competitive elections and referenda) over government personnel and policy, as well as receive protection from arbitrary action by governmental agents such as police, judges, and public officials. A regime is undemocratic to the extent that political rights are narrow and/or unequal, consultation of citizens is minimal, and protections are fragile (Tilly 2007).

Obviously democracy and capacity are relative matters. By these standards, no pure broad, equal, full-consultation, protective democracy has ever existed on a national scale. Nor has any government—not even those we call totalitarian—had absolute control over the population, activities, and resources within its territory. The distinctions still allow us to separate significantly different types of regimes, as in figure 3.2.

As of the early twenty-first century, here are examples of regimes falling into the four quadrants of this regime space:

- *High-capacity undemocratic*: China, Iran, Morocco
- *Low-capacity undemocratic*: Nepal, Somalia, Sudan
- *High-capacity democratic*: Australia, Japan, Norway
- *Low-capacity democratic*: Cyprus, Jamaica

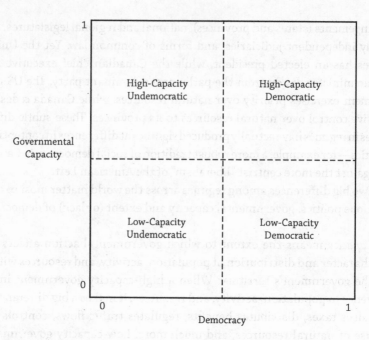

Figure 3.2:
Crude Regime Types

Over all human history, regimes have distributed very unevenly across the four types. The great bulk of historical regimes have fallen into the low-capacity undemocratic sector. Many of the biggest and most powerful, however, have dwelt in the high-capacity undemocratic sector. High-capacity democratic regimes have been rare and mostly recent. Low-capacity democratic regimes have remained few and far between. We will encounter one of them in Argentina later in this chapter.

REGIMES AND REPERTOIRES

On the average, very different sorts of contention prevail in the four corners of this regime space (Tilly 2006). High-capacity undemocratic regimes feature both clandestine oppositions and brief confrontations that usually end in repression. Low-capacity undemocratic regimes host most of the world's civil wars (Fearon and Laitin 2003; Cederman et al. 2013). Low-capacity democratic regimes gather more than their share of military coups and struggles among linguistic, religious, or ethnic groups. High-capacity democratic regimes foster the bulk of the world's social movements. The differences result from dramatic variation in the sorts of threats and opportunities faced by potential claim makers in different regime environments.

Why do repertoires vary systematically from one kind of regime to another? Some of the difference results from accumulated history. Longer-lasting regimes also tend to have higher capacities, which is why they last longer. Over those histories, they accumulate ways of doing political business that authoritarian leaders borrow from each other and help each other perform. Despite its multiple twentieth-century revolutions, China has centuries of experience with centralized rule, and over those centuries, it has traded influences with its East Asian neighbors Korea, Japan, and Mongolia.

History also provides models that future challengers use in advancing their claims. In Russia, for example, protesters in the 1917 revolution built on models of their predecessors in the 1905 revolution; in Italy in the 1960s, workers occupied factories much as their grandfathers had done after World War I; and in the United States, claimants in the same-sex marriage movement in the 2000s went to court, using the modular repertoire of legal mobilization that their predecessors in the civil rights movements had used in the 1950 sand 1960s.

But a significant part of the variations in contention result directly from properties of the regimes in the four quadrants of figure 3.2 and from changes as those regimes evolve. General features of a regime affect the opportunities and threats impinging on any potential maker of claims, and *changes* in those features produce changes in the character of contention. This is what we call *political opportunity structure*.

REGIMES AND OPPORTUNITY STRUCTURES

We can sum up crucial features of regimes with the concept of political opportunity structure. Political opportunity structure includes six properties of a regime:

1. The multiplicity of independent centers of power within it
2. Its openness to new actors
3. The instability of current political alignments
4. The availability of influential allies or supporters for challengers
5. The extent to which the regime represses or facilitates collective claim making
6. Decisive changes in items 1 to 5

Multiple centers of power provide challengers with the chance to "venue shop" for the most welcoming part of the regime. Openness to new actors enables new groups to make claims on elites. From the perspective of a whole regime, the instability of alignments and the availability of allies (items 3 and 4) amount to the same thing. Stable alignments generally mean that many political actors have no potential allies in power. By such a definition, however, political opportunity structure varies somewhat from one actor to another; at the same moment, one actor has many available allies, another few.

Threats also vary in different opportunity structures, and most people who mobilize do so to combat threats or risks (Goldstone and Tilly 2001). The prolife movement in the United States sees a threat to Christian values in the legal availability of abortion. The xenophobic National Front in France sees itself struggling against the threat to national integrity represented by Muslim immigrants. Even Islamist suicide bombers are responding to what they see as the threat of the occupation of their countries by Western forces (Pape 2003). In both democratic and undemocratic regimes, most people who engage in contentious politics see themselves responding to threats they perceive to their interests, their values, or their identities.

But threats and opportunities co-occur, and most people engaging in contentious politics combine response to threat with seizing opportunities. For example, in Iraq under the American occupation regime from 2003 to 2010, the Sunni population saw construction of a new constitution as a threat to its power. This change brought about an intensification of Al Qaeda-affiliated-groups' tactics (Alimi et al. 2015).

Rapidly shifting threats and opportunities generally move power holders toward rigid repertoires and challengers toward more flexible ones. Power holders cling to proven performances, including repression of challengers. Meanwhile, challengers seek new means to outwit authorities and competitors. Rivalry among power holders often leads some of them to form alliances with challengers, which can induce a challenger to shift its repertoire from transgressive to contained contention. Shifting threats and opportunities thus introduce more uncertainties into the relations between claimants and objects of their claims. Programs, identities, and political standing all shift more rapidly.

Opportunity structures shaped contention in many of the episodes of contention we have encountered so far in this book. To recall just a few:

- British antislavery drew guidance in its development from the parliamentary practice of receiving petitions from concerned citizens' groups and gained easier access because of the division within the British elite that resulted from the failed attempt to keep the American colonies in the empire.

- Russian-speaking nationalists in the Crimea and then in eastern Ukraine took advantage of the disorganization of the Ukrainian regime after President Yanukovych's fall to seize territory and call in Russian assistance.
- In response to the increasing violence against black demonstrators by South Africa's apartheid regime, American college students in the 1980s took advantage of the open opportunity structure on their campuses to pressure their administrations to divest from South African stocks.

But on the other side of opportunities lie threats:

- Indigenous groups in the Panzós valley that Charles Brockett examined in Guatemala, faced by troops that had shown themselves willing to massacre unarmed peasants, had no choice but to retreat or to engage in armed struggle.
- In Ferguson, Missouri, the threat of militarized repression drove peaceful protesters from the streets, leaving the field open only to those who were willing to use violence.

The very character of opportunities and threats varies dramatically from one kind of regime to another. That point takes us to different types of regimes and to the institutions that constrain and condition contentious politics.

REGIMES AND INSTITUTIONS

In general, regimes and their institutions grow up together and accommodate to each other. Where kinship groups organize much of social life, for example, they usually intertwine closely with government or even run the state. Where capitalist firms, labor unions, schools, political parties, and private associations prevail, in contrast, they shape the regime to fit their needs. A given firm, union, school, party, or association may oppose current governmental policies, but on the whole these institutions and others like them depend on a measure of governmental toleration and support. On the other side, no government that rides roughshod over all existing institutions lasts very long.

Yet regimes also shape institutions. Regimes exert significant control over institutional operations in three complementary ways: by *prescribing* institutions (e.g., by requiring people to belong to mass associations or political parties or to marry only with people of the opposite sex), by *tolerating* others (e.g., by allowing different sorts of religious groups to gather so long as they stay out of public politics), and by *forbidding* still others (e.g., by banning private militias). In a parallel way, regimes prescribe, tolerate, and forbid different sorts of claim making performances—perhaps prescribing mass pledges of allegiance, tolerating religious processions, but forbidding armed gatherings except by the government's own military forces. Of course, low capacity regimes can forbid all they want but their lack of capacity inhibits their capacity to limit contention.

On the whole, high-capacity undemocratic regimes prescribe an exceptionally wide range of ritualized performances. For example, in the former Soviet Union, citizens were expected to vote, even though the Communist party was unwilling to tolerate opposition. But they tolerate only a narrow range of institutions and performances, while forbidding many institutions and performances. At the opposite end of the range, low-capacity democratic regimes feature extensive toleration of institutions and performances, but they can neither prescribe nor forbid very many. Think about differences between Morocco (currently a high-capacity undemocratic regime) and Jamaica (currently a low-capacity but relatively democratic regime). This variation from one sort of regime to another has an interesting effect on locations of contention.

CONTAINED AND TRANSGRESSIVE CONTENTION

We have made a rough distinction between contained and transgressive contention. *Contained* contention takes place within a regime, using its established institutional routines, while *transgressive* contention challenges these routines and those it protects. *Transgressive* contention crosses institutional boundaries into forbidden or unknown territory. It either violates standard arrangements or adopts previously unknown forms of claim making. It sometimes teaches citizens to stage collective action and turns it into a more tolerated form of claim making by disguising transgression within institutional routines—for example, through protests at funerals or during election campaigns.

In democratic regimes, we find a great deal of contention, most of it contained by institutions created to structure and contain conflict; in authoritarian regimes, there is much less open contention, but what there is takes largely transgressive forms because the regime regards so many forms of expression as dangerous. In particular, authoritarian rulers may fear *organized* collective contention even more than temporary protestors who lack an organizational basis. For example, the Chinese state has a repertoire of tools to effectively absorb popular protests that erupt without the support of a formal mobilizing vehicle such as a nongovernmental organization (NGO), but it fears protests organized by NGOs because such contention signals an underlying organizational infrastructure. In response to the high risks of organized contention, some Chinese activists have devised innovative tactics such as "disguised collective action" (Fu 2015).

Some regimes also tolerate behavior from some groups that they forbid from others. For example, the Communist Chinese regime tolerates thousands of demonstrations from workers and neighborhood groups that it does not tolerate from religious sects or ethnic minorities. The French state, in fear of the growth of Islamist terrorism, bans women from wearing full-face headdresses, but has no objection to Jewish stars or Christian crucifixes. The Turkish state encourages free expression from citizens of Turkish ethnicity, but not from the Kurdish or Armenian minorities.

Contention helps to shape institutions and vice versa. The co-occurrence of social movement development and institutional development in the democracies of the West, for example, produced movement-style claim making within institutions; movement-style claim making against institutions; institutionalization of some movements, participants, and organizations; accompanied by radicalization of other movements, participants, and organizations. Movements hover at the gates of institutional politics, sometimes entering, sometimes rejecting, but always in an uneasy relationship with institutions (Tarrow 2013).

ELECTIONS AND CONTENTION[3]

Elections offer opportunities for contention in both democratic and authoritarian regimes.

In democratic systems, movements interact with elections in several ways:

- *First*, movements can transfer their activism to support friendly parties in elections, as the American trade union movement did with the Democratic party in the 1940s and 1950s; this was also the pattern of the "Tea Party" in the United States, which arose as a grassroots movement in 2010 and transferred its activism to the Republican party (Skocpol and Williamson 2011).

- *Second*, movements can react to disputed elections or leadership decisions they oppose.
- *Third*, movements can bring about changes in parties' electoral fortunes. If we consider major turning points in electoral politics in the United States (i.e., the election of Abraham Lincoln in 1860 and of Franklin D. Roosevelt in 1932) they were mainly the result of the intrusion of social movements into electoral politics.
- *Fourth*, movements can induce parties to shift to the extremes in order to satisfy their demands, thus producing greater polarization in the political system (McAdam and Kloos 2014).
- *Fifth*, elections can weaken or strengthen movements when they become involved in election campaigns or align themselves with parties' programs. Michael Heaney and Fabio Rojas found that the congressional campaign of 2006 and the election of Barack Obama in 2008 drew so many activists from the antiwar movement that had arisen against the Iraq War in 2003 that the movement was weakened (Heaney and Rojas 2015).

But elections are features of undemocratic systems too: authoritarian regimes use elections to legitimate their rule, identify opponents, and reward allies with political patronage. But these elections can offer opposition movements a legitimate institutional umbrella for activism, often around the theme of electoral corruption. (Bunce and Wolchik 2011). When dictator Slobodan Milošević tried to steal local elections in Serbia in 1996, opposition was widespread but remained largely uncoordinated. Between that year and 2000, when Milošević tried to steal a national election, the opposition was ready. Inspired by a national student-led movement called "Otpor," militants used a variety of performances to oppose the regime. Otpor developed a sophisticated strategy of targeting Milošević using comic and theatrical tactics instead of mass demonstrations that police could attack. For nearly two months, demonstrators marched, sang, blew whistles, listened to speeches, alternately heckled and fraternized with the police, and went to court to keep the pressure on Milošević. Otpor, the broker, diffused these tactics across the country to bring down a dictator (Bunce and Wolchik 2011).

Between 2000 and 2004, the Otpor model diffused from Serbia to Georgia. In November 2003, President Eduard Shevardnadze rigged a parliamentary election to provide a sure victory for the parties that supported him. Shevardnadze was no Milošević. But like the dictator in

Serbia, his attempt to foil the electoral process brought down the government. Three weeks of peaceful street protests culminated in a "March of the Angry Voters," led by Mikheil Saakashvili, leader of the opposition coalition and the country's president after Shevardnadze had to step down. For months, activists led by the student group Kmara engaged in graffiti, leaflet, and poster campaigns against corruption and police brutality, and for university reform and media freedom. This was no spontaneous demonstration; it was a coordinated plan for tens of thousands of citizens to converge by buses, cars, and trucks on the capital, Tbilisi.

Where had the opposition learned such tactics? In the months before the election, Saakashvili had traveled to Serbia to contact the former organizers of the anti-Milošević movement. He returned with a plan for nonviolent action modeled closely on the success of Otpor. Ex-Otpor activists traveled to Georgia, where they led training sessions for Georgian reformers. The Georgians, in turn, trained a cadre of grassroots activists. Brokerage combined with diffusion through electronic communication.

An important tool in the Georgian campaign was the American-made documentary on the fall of Milošević, *Bringing Down a Dictator*, which was supported by the Washington-based International Center for Nonviolent Conflict. "Most important was the film," said Ivane Merabishvili, general secretary of the National Movement party that led the revolt. "All the demonstrators knew the tactics of the revolution in Belgrade by heart because they showed . . . the film on their revolution. Everyone knew what to do. This was a copy of that revolution, only louder" (*Washington Post*, November 25, 2003, A22). In Georgia, as in the spread of most new movements, diffusion through the media and brokerage through intermediate agents combined to produce new coordination (Tarrow and McAdam 2005). These anti-election fraud protests helped to bring about democratization in several of these regimes.

DEMOCRATIZATION AND DEDEMOCRATIZATION

To look more precisely at democratization and dedemocratization, we can borrow a leaf from the New York-based democracy-monitoring organization Freedom House.[4] Since 1972, Freedom House has been recruiting experts to rate all the world's independent regimes along two dimensions: political rights and civil liberties. The raters fill in two questionnaires for each regime they examine. The political rights questionnaire includes such items as these: Is the head of state and/or head of government or other chief authority elected through free and fair elections? Do the people have the right to organize in different political parties or other competitive political groupings of their choice, and is the system open to the rise and fall of these competing parties or groupings? The civil liberties questionnaire asks, among other things: Is there freedom of assembly, demonstration, and open public discussion? Are property rights secure? Do citizens have the right to establish private businesses? Is private business activity unduly influenced by government officials, the security forces, or organized crime? (Karatnycky 2000: 584–585) An elaborate scoring system groups answers to such questions in two sets of seven rank levels, from low to high political rights, and from low to high civil liberties.

Roughly speaking, Freedom House's political rights scale covers our breadth, equality, and consultation, while its civil liberties scale rates protection. The two scales actually smuggle in some judgments about governmental capacity as well: Higher ratings on political rights assume that the government can actually enforce those rights, and higher ratings on protection assume that the government actually delivers promised protections. Without some hidden judgments about capacity, the whole rating process would fail, since almost every government in the world declares itself democratic on paper. With that qualification, the Freedom House ratings provide a convenient worldwide look at degrees of democracy.

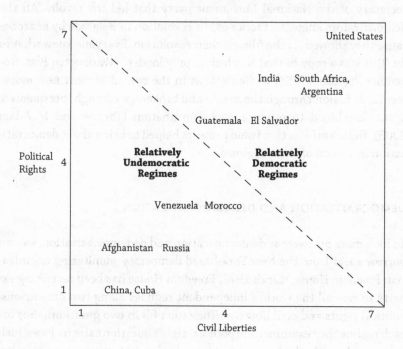

Figure 3.3:
Freedom House Rankings for Selected Countries, 2012

Figure 3.3 locates twelve regimes in the Freedom House space of political rights and civil liberties as of 2012. The diagonal dotted line marks a rough distinction between democratic and undemocratic regimes. In the diagram's lower left-hand corner, we see China and Cuba with the lowest possible ratings on both political rights and civil liberties. Others in that corner (but not in the diagram) are Burma,[5] Libya, North Korea, Saudi Arabia, Sudan, Syria, and Turkmenistan. All of them clearly qualify as undemocratic regimes. Most of them also qualify as high-capacity regimes.

The United States anchors the diagram's upper right-hand corner, with the highest possible ratings on political rights and civil liberties. It has plenty of company in the corner: Andorra, Australia, Austria, Bahamas, Barbados, Belgium, Canada, Cape Verde, Chile, Cyprus, Denmark, Dominica, Finland, France, Germany, Iceland, Ireland, Italy, Kiribati, Liechtenstein, Luxembourg, Malta, Marshall Islands, Micronesia, Nauru, Netherlands, New Zealand, Norway, Palau, Portugal, San Marino, Slovenia, Spain, Sweden, Switzerland, Tuvalu, the United Kingdom, and Uruguay.

In this set appears a mixture of very high-capacity democracies (e.g., Germany and Iceland) with some relatively low-capacity democracies (e.g., Barbados and Cyprus). Although any of these countries could dedemocratize under some conditions, we would expect the high-capacity and low-capacity democracies to do so differently. In the case of high-capacity democracies, a vast shock to governmental capacity, military conquest, or ruthless internal takeover of the existing governmental apparatus might do it. In the case of low-capacity democracies, undermining of the regime by criminal activity, externally supported subversion, military coup, or intergroup conflict would be more likely to produce dedemocratization.

Despite its high ranking, the United States still fails to offer equal protection to all its ethnic and racial groups. Plenty of citizens in the other 7 + 7 countries listed earlier also have justified complaints about inequality of rights, consultation, and protection. Freedom House ratings simply tell us that on the whole India doesn't provide as much democracy as, say, Finland and Uruguay.

One feature of the diagram that immediately strikes the eye is the clustering of regimes along the diagonal from 1 + 1 (Cuba) to 7 + 7 (United States). Regimes that receive high ratings on political rights also tend to receive high ratings on civil liberties, while low ratings also go together. Some of the correlation probably results from raters' "halo effects"; that is, if a regime's civil liberties look good, raters most likely give it the benefit of the doubt on political rights. But on the whole, political rights and civil liberties reinforce each other. When a regime de-democratizes, denial of protection to targeted minorities also undermines the breadth and equality of political participation and consultation. Our final example—the transition to democracy in Argentina—illustrates the impact of regime change on the repertoire of contention.

REGIME AND REPERTOIRE CHANGE IN ARGENTINA

If ever there was a contrast to the stability of the political regime in the United States, Argentina would be that regime. It illustrates that a regime can rank high in political and civil rights (see Figure 3.3, where it ranks close to the United States in both respects) but still be highly contentious. It also shows how contention intersects with the process of democratization (Auyero 2002; 2007).

Founded as a Spanish colony in 1776, Argentina had an independence movement (1810–1818), followed by a long civil war that ended only in 1861. A long period of relative stability and prosperity followed, until the 1930s, when the country began to be wracked by a series of coups, counter-coups, and military governments, punctuated by brief periods of representative politics. Between 1930 and 1983, Argentina experienced twelve such coups. With each coup, "the ferocity of the military regimes escalated throughout the period" and "their recurrence established a pattern of civil-military relations characterized by a lack of military subordination to civilian rule, an increase in the political autonomy of the military actor and the internal politicization of the armed forces" (Smulovitz 2012: 65).

The only modern period of political stability was the establishment of a hybrid regime under the charismatic leadership of Juan Perón, which lasted from the end of World War II until he was ousted by a coup in 1966. Perón was the first in a long line of "elected authoritarians" who found a novel synthesis between charismatic leadership and "free" but managed elections. In chapter 4 we will see how widespread this synthesis has become in the new century. Perón, who came from the military but enjoyed broad working class support, governed informally with his wife Evita, who was the main character in a future Broadway musical. When Perón was exiled by yet another coup in 1955, a new period of instability transpired, until a final military coup, in 1976, put an end to representative government until the fall of the generals in 1983.

The decades of political instability after Perón's fall were a catalyst for the radicalization of contention. In addition to military coups, there were major strike waves led by Argentina's well-organized labor unions, a vital student movement, and the rise of two left-wing extremist movements, the *Montoneros* and the People's Revolutionary Army (ERP), and the rise of an extreme right-wing movement, the Argentine Anticommunist Alliance, to combat them (Finchelstein 2014). This produced a spiral of movement-countermovement interaction that led to an atmosphere of tension and violence.

In this clash of extremes, Perón returned from exile, was elected President in 1973, with his third wife, Isabel, as Vice-President, but died of natural causes before his promise to bring back political order could be tested. After signing a secret decree to allow the destruction of the extreme left, Isabel was ousted by a military coup led by General Jorge Videla, beginning a decade of repressive military rule worse than anything before experienced. A national commission later estimated the number of "disappeared" victims during this period as 8,900, a figure that was almost certainly too conservative (Smulovitz 2012: 66).

In the "Dirty War" that Videla and his *junta* launched against guerillas and political opponents, the country was rapidly dedemocratized. Congress was shut down, the judges of the Supreme Court were removed, political parties and unions were banned, and a clandestine campaign of torture, disappearances, and executions was launched. By the end of 1976 the *Montoneros* had been destroyed; by 1977, the ERP was defeated, and the country sank into a period of "bureaucratic authoritarianism" (O'Donnell 1973). Only the most courageous actors, like the *Madres de Plaza de Mayo*—mothers whose children had been "disappeared"—continued to protest by appearing in the main square of Buenos Aires to demand information on their loved ones (Guzman Bouvard 1994). When the regime collapsed in 1983, it was not because of the success of protest, but because of international and church condemnation and a failed attempt to take over the *Malvinas* (Falklands) Islands. Their legitimacy destroyed, the generals were convinced to return the country to civilian rule.

The end of the dictatorship and the return of democracy was prolific with new and revived forms of contention. Newly-liberated labor unions began to go out on strike; unemployed workers organized pickets in demands for jobs (Rossi 2011); and marches and demonstrations filled the streets. A whole vocabulary of new forms of contention was coined, by a populace that had always been contentious and how had the opportunity to express its claims. Even organized violence returned, as a Jewish center was bombed—probably with the connivance of foreign terrorists—in which eighty-four people died.[6]

Much of the mobilization after the fall of the dictatorship was organized around the desire of victims, relatives of victims, and the human rights groups that supported them to prosecute the crimes of the dictatorship. Before leaving power, the generals and their legal defenders had attempted to prevent future prosecution by passing a "self-amnesty" law and by destroying records of their crimes (Smulovitz 2012: 66–67). A new government, under Raúl Alfonsín, was elected in 1983; but despite his promise to ignore the self-amnesty law, the new President "hoped for a self-cleansing of the military that would allow both the juridical punishment of a limited and symbolically prominent group of human rights violators and the fulfilment of electoral promises, without the government becoming an enemy of the armed forces" (67). A truth commission (CONADEP) was created to receive evidence of disappearances and send them to the justice system and track down the whereabouts of children who had been taken from condemned prisoners.

In this "movement" of opinion demanding transitional justice, courts, lawyers, and international human rights groups began to play an important role (Smulovitz 2002, 2012; Sikkink 2005). When it appeared that the armed forces were unwilling to "cleanse themselves," the Federal Appeals Court of Buenos Aires condemned junta leaders to terms ranging from four years to life in prison; lawyers who had defended victims of the repression during the dirty war went to court to demand redress; and international human rights groups who had opposed the dictatorship continued to shine an international light on the government's hesitant policies (Sikkink 2005). "In sum," writes Catalina Smulovitz, "between 1982 and 1990, the treatment of past human rights violations became a central topic of the transition agenda and was characterized by the initial success of the judicial strategy" (2012: 70). But the decision to prosecute would not have been made if not for the pressure of contentious and legal actions by an array of social actors, ranging from the *madres* and the *abuelas* of the plaza, to human rights groups like the CELS (Center for Legal and Social Studies), the political parties, the media, and international human rights groups (Sikkink 2005). Democratization opened the opportunity structure for contention, and contention—combined with legal and political action—helped to bring about the return of rule of law, without which no democracy can be established on stable grounds (O'Donnell 2004).

REGIMES AND CONTENTION

What does all this mean for the relations between regimes and contentious politics? As we will see in chapter 7, with democratization, social movements become more frequent. Why should that be? Think again about the elements of democracy: broad, relatively equal political participation, combined with binding consultation of political participants on governmental personnel, resources, and policy; plus protection of political participants from arbitrary action by governmental agents. Broad, equal participation does not qualify as democratic in itself. After all, high-capacity authoritarian regimes such as the European fascist regimes of the 1930s and state socialist regimes before the 1980s commonly institutionalized broad, equal, even compulsory political participation.

When breadth and equality combine with consultation in the form of elections, referenda, opinion polls, press discussion, interest group formation, and rule of law, however, the combination gives citizens both incentives and means to band together for demands and complaints. Effective breadth, equality, and consultation also depend on protection from arbitrary governmental action, especially when it comes to minorities. When breadth, equality, consultation, and protection join in the same regime, they provide a favorable environment for social movement activity. In general, they guarantee a more open political opportunity structure than their opposites.

An across-the-board increase in breadth, equality, consultation, and protection counts as democratization. On the whole, low-capacity regimes face serious obstacles to democratization. In those regimes, the opening of political opportunity structure provides too many opportunities for ruthless opportunists such as warlords to seize control of the government and turn its activity to their own advantage. High-capacity regimes regularly resist democratization because it means that whoever currently runs the government must share power, and runs the risk of losing it entirely. Still, a high-capacity regime that democratizes at least has the means of providing protection and enforcing the results of binding consultation.

Nothing guarantees that democratic institutions will stay in place forever. European governments that lost capacity through losses in World War I became especially vulnerable to dedemocratization. With losses in war, disciplined strongmen could seize the instruments of government and even gain popular appeal by comparison with their discredited predecessors. Many of Europe's fascist and state socialist regimes overturned relatively extensive democratic institutions on their way to high-capacity undemocratic rule. The histories of Italy, Germany, and Hungary after World War I all illustrate strongman dedemocratization.

Increases in state capacity can tilt the balance of largely democratic regimes toward hybrid regimes even in regimes that are largely democratic. When war, terrorist threat, or natural disasters create the conditions for expanding state capacity, even established democratic regimes may erode guarantees of protected consultation by expanding state capacity. Think of the passage of legislation allowing the US government to invade people's privacy after the September 11 massacres. Dedemocratization can occur by lethal coup, as it did in Argentina, or by an incremental ratcheting up in state capacity. With dedemocratization, political opportunity structure generally narrows, and overall levels of contention usually decline after the new regime overcomes resistance to its rule.

Here is the most general point: A regime's relations, institutions, opportunities, threats, and repertoires combine to shape its popular contention. The deep processes of democratization and dedemocratization strongly affect relations, institutions, opportunities, threats, and repertoires. Contention feeds back. It also reshapes political relations, institutions, opportunities, threats, and repertoires, and thereby promotes democratization or dedemocratization. Only a dynamic analysis of contentious politics will capture these connections.

But recent experience has shown that the most common alternatives to democracy are not fully-fledged authoritarian regimes. Over and over—especially after the fall of the Soviet empire—promises to create democracies have led to combinations of democratic and undemocratic institutions—what we call "hybrid regimes." Some of them—like South Africa under apartheid—offer both political and civil rights to a dominant minority, while denying them to the majority of citizens; others— like Israel today—have high ratings on political rights, but civil liberties are compromised by substantially unequal protections for different segments of the citizenry. In many of the post-Soviet regimes, at least one minority suffers some sort of legal handicap. We will examine the consequences of hybrid regimes for contentious politics in the next chapter.

NOTES

1. For the best existing analysis of "the sixties" and their impact on the future of American contention, see Doug McAdam and Katrina Kloos, *Deeply Divided: Racial Politics and Social Movements in Post-War America*, Oxford University Press 2014.
2. I am grateful to Doug McAdam and Katrine Kloos for allowing me to reproduce this figure from *Deeply Divided*, (2014: ch. 2).
3. The following section draws on two articles with Doug McAdam: McAdam and Tarrow 2010, 2013.
4. The Freedom House website (https://freedomhouse.org/) is free and easy to use and is a precious resource for scholars and students alike.

5. Note that Burma's democracy rating has improved since its 2012 reforms from 6 to 7 and its civil liberties rankings have been moved from 5 to 6, even though Freedom House still describes the country as "not free."

6. The inquiry into the perpetrators of the bombing dragged on for decades and led indirectly to the apparent murder of a state prosecutor who was on the point of releasing material that accused the government of complicity in the cover-up in early 2015. Jonathan Gilbert and Simon Romero, "Puzzling Death of a Prosecutor Grips Argentina" New York Times, January 19, 2015 at http://www.nytimes.com/2015/01/20/world/americas/alberto-nisman-found-dead-argentina-amia.html?_r=0.

During the Hong Kong "Umbrella Revolution," protesters turn their umbrellas against the police. (Photo by Bobby Yip/Reuters).

CHAPTER 4
Contention in Hybrid Regimes

In the last chapter, we focused mainly on two types of political regimes—democratic and undemocratic ones (See figure 3.2). These we have divided into low-capacity and high-capacity variants. But of course, our typology of regimes is based on what social scientists call "ideal types"—abstractions at the poles of variation. Between these extremes, there are a range of regimes that combine elements of democracy and undemocracy. Figure 3.3 placed a number of these states near the border between democratic and undemocratic states, based on the intersection of civil liberties and political rights. In Africa, Asia, Latin America, and in many of the countries that emerged from the former Soviet sphere, there are systematic segments of democratic and undemocratic rule operating side by side within the same regime. They are what we call "hybrid regimes."

Political scientists have long been aware of regimes that combine authoritarian and representative mechanisms of rule. Some have called them *competitive authoritarianism* (Levitsky and Way 2002), while others have called them *anocracies* (Fearon and Laitin 2003). We prefer the term *hybrid regimes* (Rocha Menocal, et al., 2008), because they include some regimes with strong rule of law traditions, as well as some that lean more toward the authoritarian side. What has remained unspecified is whether these regimes produce forms of contention that are distinct from both their authoritarian cousins and from true democracies. In this chapter we will see that hybrids have particular combinations of contention, which combine violent and nonviolent conflicts and produce unpredictable outcomes.

"DEMOCRATIC" HYBRIDS

As figure 3.3 and a large body of research shows, such combinations are mainly found in the Global South and in the former Soviet area. But they can also be found on the democratic side of the ledger: regimes that vacillate between more democratic and less democratic regimes or employ constitutional means for the majority alongside the repression of minorities. This produces combinations of transgressive and contained contention and peculiarly unstable and unpredictable outcomes.

Such was the case for the United States before the Civil War (some would say it is still true today), as black people were denied the rights of citizenship even as whites were gaining manhood suffrage (women were another matter). Although this uneasy balance was maintained for more than a half-century, a savage civil war was fought to bring the nation under something resembling unitary rule. Even afterwards, the South continued to be governed as a one-party region, while African Americans were denied the right to vote and lived under conditions of quasi-feudalism. A second—and even longer-lasting—case of a constitutional regime that ruled part of its territory through repressive means was the United Kingdom.

Five Centuries of Irish-English Violence

The English presence in Ireland goes back to the assimilation of Anglo-Norman conquerors and colonists, after which Ireland settled into several centuries of competition among indigenous chiefs and kings. Beginning with Henry VIII, however, Tudor invasions generated a new round of armed resistance. Thus began almost five centuries during which some group of Irish power holders was always aligned with Great Britain, and multiple other power holders aligned against Great Britain. The colonization was overlaid between conflicts between mostly-English Protestants and the Catholics who made up the bulk of the population. Most Catholics were poor, but between the 1690s and the 1780s, even propertied Catholics lacked any rights to participate in Irish public politics. From the 1780s to the 1820s, they still suffered serious political disabilities. Since the sixteenth century, Ireland rarely moved far from virulent, violent rivalries. The island has repeatedly careened into civil war.

During the nineteenth century, demands for Irish autonomy or independence swelled. In 1801, largely in response to the rebellion of 1798 and the threat that rebellion posed to Britain's pursuit of its great war with

France, Great Britain (England, Scotland, and Wales) incorporated Ireland into a United Kingdom (UK). That move dissolved an exclusively Protestant Irish parliament and a hundred Irish Protestants joined the House of Commons in distant London. With Catholic Emancipation (1829), propertied Catholics acquired the right to vote and hold most public offices.

These regime changes connected Irish contention more closely to the British political opportunity structure, which was opening erratically as the nineteenth century proceeded; independent centers of power were multiplying, the regime was becoming somewhat more open to new actors, political alignments became a bit more unstable, influential allies and supporters became more available to organized Irish Catholics, and the overall repressiveness of the United Kingdom government declined. But Protestant-Catholic and British-Irish distinctions retained much of their political force. This was becoming a hybrid system.

Over the nineteenth century, conflict between tenants and landlords exacerbated, and public shows of force on either side repeatedly generated street violence in Northern Ireland (Tilly 2003: 111–127). A campaign for home rule brought disestablishment of the previously official Church of Ireland in 1869. Despite the eventual backing of Prime Minister William Gladstone, however, home rule itself failed to pass the UK Parliament. Irish Protestants rallied against such measures to the theme that "Home rule is Rome rule" (McCracken 2001: 262). The Franchise Act of 1884, simultaneous with Great Britain's Third Reform Act, awarded the vote to most of the adult male Irish population and thus greatly expanded the rural Catholic electorate. By that time, however, each major party had attached itself to a single religious segment. Catholic-based parties had committed themselves decisively to Irish autonomy or independence. A combination of civil war, deadly ethnic-religious conflict, and revolution was in the making.

After multiple anti-British risings over the previous sixty years, the question of military service on behalf of the United Kingdom split Ireland profoundly during World War I. At first Irish people collaborated with the war effort. To be sure, Ulster's Protestants collaborated much more enthusiastically than the rest of the Irish population. The prewar Ulster Volunteer Force, a Protestant paramilitary unit opposing Irish home rule that organized in 1913, joined the British army en masse. Meanwhile, the British maintained twenty thousand troops and police in the rest of the island to contain popular militias of Irish Catholics that started forming in 1914.

By that time, Ireland contained five distinct armed forces: not only the British army and the Ulster Volunteers but also their opponents: the Irish Volunteers, the Citizen Army, and the Irish Republican Brotherhood. Still, serious opposition to the British cause did not crystallize until the war had been going on for almost two years. The abortive Easter Rebellion of 1916—organized in part from New York, supported by German agents, backed by German bombardment of the English coast, and suppressed brutally by British troops—slowed the cause of Irish independence temporarily. Nevertheless, Irish nationalists began regrouping in 1917.

The parliamentary election of 1918 brought a victory for Sinn Féin, a party popularly identified with the Easter Rebellion and the republican cause. When the UK government decreed military conscription for Ireland in April 1918, all Irish members of Parliament (MPs) except the Protestant representatives of the North withdrew from the UK Parliament. Returned MPs led organization of opposition back home. In December 1918, Irish nationalists won southern Ireland's votes in a parliamentary election handily, with thirty-four of the sixty-nine successful candidates elected while in prison. The newly elected MPs decided to form their own Irish parliament instead of joining the UK assembly. On meeting in January, 1919, they chose New York-born Eamon De Valera, then still in prison, as their parliamentary president. De Valera soon escaped from prison, but after four months of activity in Ireland, he left for the United States.

Soon the British government was actively suppressing Irish nationalist organizations. Nationalists themselves mobilized for resistance and attacked representatives of British authority. By the end of 1919, Ireland reached a state of civil war. As Peter Hart (1998) sums up for County Cork:

> Sinn Fein won and guarded its new political turf with the obligatory minimum of street-fighting and gunplay. However, in the course of the revolution the familiar exuberance of party competition turned into killing on an unprecedented, unimagined scale. The political arena was transformed into a nightmare world of anonymous killers and victims, of disappearances, massacres, midnight executions, bullets in the back of the head, bodies dumped in fields or ditches. Over 700 people died in Cork in revolutionary or counter-revolutionary shootings or bombings between 1917 and 1923, 400 of them at the hands of the Irish Volunteers—soon rechristened the Irish Republican Army. (50)

The British painfully established military control but also began negotiating with Irish representatives. Within two years, the negotiations led to an agreement: partition of Northern Ireland (Ulster less Counties Cavan, Donegal, and Monaghan) from the rest, and dominion status similar to that of Canada and South Africa for a newly created Irish Free State outside the North. Although hard-line Irish republicans refused to accept the settlement and raised an insurrection in 1922, the arrangement lasted in roughly the same form until the 1930s.

Within Northern Ireland, anti-British forces never gave up. Partly inspired by the example of American civil rights, a new round of conflicts began with Catholic marches in 1968, violent confrontations with police, struggles with Protestant counterdemonstrators, and more scattered attacks of each side on the other's persons and property. In 1972, British paratroopers trying to break up an unarmed but illegal march through Derry by the Northern Ireland Civil Rights Association fired on the demonstrators, killing thirteen of them. The uproar following that "Bloody Sunday" induced a worried British government to take back direct rule of the province.

After a bilateral cease-fire declared in 1994, raids and confrontations (including some quite outside Ireland) actually accelerated. A further treaty in 1998 (the so-called Good Friday agreement) initiated serious talks among the major parties and terminated most public standoffs between the sides, but it did not end guerrilla action by all paramilitary units or produce full disarmament of those units. Even as negotiations proceeded, paramilitary groups on both sides repeatedly broke the peace. Support of Catholic militants by the well-armed Irish Republican Army (IRA), based in independent Ireland and extensively supported by Irish overseas migrants, certainly sustained the conflict. But militant Catholics native to Ulster repeatedly challenged equally militant Ulster Protestants. One of Europe's longest runs of large-scale intergroup violence continued into the new century.

The toll has been serious. Between 1969 and 1982, Northern Ireland's collective violence laid down the following records: 2,268 persons killed, including 491 military, 187 police, and 1,590 civilians; 25,120 persons injured; 29,035 shooting incidents; 7,533 explosions; 4,250 malicious fires; 9,871 armed robberies; 153 tarrings and featherings; and 1,006 kneecappings (Palmer 1988: 2). The numbers bespeak political actors at each other's throats. Although the intensity of violence waxed and waned with the more general rhythms of intergroup struggle in Northern Ireland, mutual attacks continued into the 1990s. Even the tentative settlement of 1998 did not end them.

Yet Britain/Northern Ireland remained a hybrid system with composite forms of contention: All through the post-World War II conflicts, elections continued to be held, Orange (Protestant) supporters marched, the families of victims demonstrated, and political dialogue continued in some forms. Even at the height of the violence, British agents were meeting secretly with representatives of the IRA to try to work out an accommodation. By the time of the Good Friday accord, political parties were slowly asserting their power over their paramilitary allies. The 2005 declaration of the IRA that it would abandon collective violence largely ended lethal conflicts, but we cannot yet be sure.

British people, Irish people, and observers of British-Irish conflict have often described relations across the Irish Sea as the outcome of fierce, ancient, irreconcilable hatreds. The actual history of the long conflict, however, reveals that such apparently ancient hatreds are negotiable. Once most of Ireland became independent, the levels of ethnic and religious conflict declined, and the sites of violence concentrated in Northern Ireland. Even the Northern Irish struggle narrowed, became less violent, and showed signs of settlement after 2000, as the IRA began to disarm, its leaders became internationally recognized negotiators, and even Northern Ireland's Protestant leaders searched for paths to a longer-term settlement (Maney 2006).

The political processes that produced changes in British-Irish relations did not come from a separate realm unique to ancient hatreds and ethnic-religious conflict. On the contrary, the story of Ireland shows us familiar effects of shifting political opportunity structure, mobilization, polarization, brokerage, and repression—in short, of contentious politics at large. It also shows us how ordinary politics continues to be played alongside the lethal conflicts that dominate the headlines.

Settlers into Nationalists

England/Ireland became a hybrid regime because the British "planted" Protestants in its Irish colony and then found they had to use repressive means to protect their survival in a largely Catholic society. Settler colonies are inherently hybrid and unstable. We can see this in an even more intractable conflict that combines democratic practices with repressive rule: the Israeli-Palestinian conflict, in which rival nationalist movements took root in the same territory, each with an equally credible claim to the land, and both with significant support from abroad (Avineri 1971).

The violent history of the relations between the predominantly Jewish population of the state of Israel and the Muslim/Christian population of the territories west of the Jordan River is very different from the history of sectional conflict in the United Kingdom. Yet here too, a structural disjuncture between the regions' politics and peoples has produced a stalemate in their political relations, and created a composite between contained electoral contention and social movement politics in Israel proper, and political violence on its fringes. We cannot review the long and tortured relations between these two peoples here, but the evacuation of Jewish settlers from the Palestinian enclave of Gaza in 2005, the election of the militant Islamist group, Hamas, in 2006, and the repeated military invasions by the Israeli Defence Force (IDF) after that takeover, reveals the parallels between the two cases.

Homeless in Gaza

In 2004, Prime Minister Ariel Sharon, who had masterminded the planting of Israeli settlements among the Arab populations of the West Bank in the 1980s, announced the evacuation of some seven to eight thousand settlers from Jewish enclaves in the Gaza strip, home to over 1.3 million Palestinians. These Israeli citizens responded to Sharon's move with a wide array of actions from what we have called "the social movement repertoire." Their actions intersected with the forms of lethal politics more typical of the authoritarian and semiauthoritarian regimes we studied in the last chapter.

Jewish settlements emerged in the West Bank and in the Gaza Strip after 1967 as an extension of the pre-independence Zionist practice of "planting Jews" strategically amid the majority Arab population. But private motivations were at play as well: Families that could not afford the high living costs in Israel proper and religious Zionists who were uncomfortable living in Israel's largely secular society were eager to accept the generous subsidies that the Israeli state offered to take up residence in the territories. Under increasing international pressure and in the face of the ruinous financial and military cost of maintaining isolated settlements, Prime Minister Sharon decided in 2004 to evacuate Gaza's approximately eight thousand Jewish settlers.

While the creation of the state of Israel resulted from a policy of "settlement" that qualified as a social movement, Gaza was unusual in this respect: Israel had wrested the region from Egyptian control in a 1967 war. Israel settled it largely with religious Zionists, inspired both by the desire for subsidized housing and by the desire to bring redemption to the land of Israel. Most were farmers who hired Palestinian labor to produce fruits and vegetables for urban markets along the Mediterranean coast. Israeli authorities surrounded those prosperous enclaves with barbed wire and protected them against the surrounding Arab population with a substantial military presence. Periodically, violent Palestinian groups, both secular Marxists and Muslim activists such as Hamas and Islamic Jihad, set off bombs and lobbed mortars into the Jewish enclaves, which led to retaliation from the IDF. These militants also used the southern boundary of the Gaza Strip to bring arms and ammunition across from Egypt.

By the turn of the new century, the Gaza settlements had become a running sore for Israeli rulers and for their relations with Egypt and the Palestinians. Sharon's government sympathized with the settlers' plight. But the government wanted to find a way to break the regional stalemate without giving up its claim to the West Bank—what it had come to call by the historic Hebrew names "Judea" and "Samaria." As relations with the weak and divided Palestinian Authority stalled and the prospect of a general settlement retreated, the evacuation of a small number of Jewish families from the seething slum of Gaza seemed a sensible way of showing progress in relation to the Palestinians and lowering the tension between Israel and its allies.

Composite Contention in Israel/Palestine

The evacuation of the Jewish settlements in the Gaza Strip was embedded in a hybrid regime. Listen to what longtime left-wing critic of the Israeli occupation Uri Avneri had to say about it:

> The present struggle is a kind of civil war, even if—miraculously, again—no blood will be spilled. The Yesha people [i.e., the settler movement] are a revolutionary movement. Their real aim is to overturn the democratic system and impose the reign of their rabbis. Anyone who has studied the history of revolutions knows that the role of the army is the decisive factor. As long as the army stands united behind the regime, the revolution is condemned to failure. Only when the army is disintegrating or joins the rebels, the revolution can win. (Avneri 2005)

Civil wars, revolutionary movements, armies? Avneri's prognosis makes it sound as if Israel had begun to resemble a revolutionary situation. Yet on Freedom House's rankings, Israel ranks in the highest category for political rights and in the third category for civil rights. Of course, these rankings exclude the occupied territories, where the rankings were close to the bottom for both political and civil rights. And it ignores the fact that the Israeli government used the national security regulations of the former British colonial power to govern its Palestinian subjects (Berda 2013). The disjunction reminds us that regimes can vary internally in terms of their degree of democracy. That internal variation leads to variations and intersections between their forms of contentious politics. In the Gaza settler's movement we find a social movement campaign overlapping with civil strife.

Let's put this analysis in terms of explanations from earlier chapters. Israel/Palestine's political opportunity structure divides sharply between Israeli citizens and Palestinian subjects. (The Arab population of Israel proper stands somewhere in between, but this may be changing as an increasingly rightwing Israeli regime insists more and more on the "Jewish" nature of the state). Gaza's settlers occupied an uneasy transition zone between two kinds of politics: the civil politics that regularly produce robust social movement campaigns among Israelis and the uncivil politics that produce lethal conflict both within Israel and in the West Bank and Gaza. If this is not the revolutionary situation that Avneri predicted, it did produce a composite politics of contention in response to the Sharon government's plans to evacuate Gaza in 2004–2005.

In its factual details, the settlers' campaign had little in common with the actors, the performances, and the targets of the social movements we will examine in chapter 7. But it embodied many of the properties of the politics we have seen elsewhere. The settlers used nonviolent performances from the inherited repertoire of contention. But they innovated around its edges. For example, some of them—notoriously for survivors of the Holocaust—marched out of their settlements wearing yellow stars of David on their clothing. That gesture scandalized most Israelis by hinting that the IDF soldiers accompanying them resembled Hitler's SS.

The stars of David were no mere costume ornaments. They drew on Israeli's founding myth to maneuver between the majority of Israelis who supported Sharon's move and the intense minority who opposed it. Their campaign followed a clear trajectory of mobilization and demobilization, first bringing in supporters from outside the borders of Gaza to organize resistance and then losing steam as the IDF and the government combined facilitation of resettlement with careful repression of those who refused to leave.

The settlers also built on a social movement base: the organizations of West Bank settler communities and their religious Zionist supporters both in Israel and the United States. Their actions could not hope to stop the evacuation, but they were successful in furthering the split in the ruling party. In the midst of the evacuation, Finance Minister Binyamin Netanyahu, Sharon's rival for power, made a dramatic move. Supported by a majority of the Likud Party, Netanyahu resigned from the cabinet and prepared to try to wrest control of Likud from Sharon. As settlers and their allies demonstrated at the Wailing Wall and used the imagery of the

Holocaust to protest their government's actions, they were innovating in the repertoire of contention and helped to influence the country's institutional politics.

As their differences from Prime Minister Sharon sharpened, the settlers also activated a new boundary between religious and realist conservative Zionism. They sought certification for their cause by identifying it with the traditions of frontier Zionism and with the horrors of the Holocaust. West Bank militants who filtered into the Gaza Strip brokered the settlers' alliance with far-right elements in Israeli politics. Their resistance shifted upward in scale to Israeli national politics when thousands flocked to the Wailing Wall to protest the evacuation.

Reciprocal Polarization

But no social movement operates in a vacuum. Creation of Israel as a state had produced a vast Arab refugee population, part of it living in refugee camps in the West Bank and Gaza. Another part dispersed in a broad diaspora that fed what Benedict Anderson (1998) calls "long-distance nationalism." At first secular Arab leaders, inspired by conventional Marxist and nationalist models, led the liberation movement this displacement fed. After the Iranian revolution in 1979, however, Islamist groups became more influential, both at home and in the diaspora. As the Palestine Liberation Front, which had piloted the violent resistance to Israeli rule through the 1980s, turned into the institutionalized Palestinian Authority, the movement to liberate Palestine took on an increasingly apocalyptic tone. In 1981, militants started using suicide bombing in Lebanon. During the 1990s, it became a preferred tool of religious militants in authoritarian situations (Berman and Laitin 2008; Gambetta 2005; Pedahzur and Perliger 2006). From that point on, suicide bombers killed increasing numbers of Israelis and provided a model for the wider Islamist movement that gave birth to Al Qaeda and other clandestine groups (See chapter 9).

Polarization infested both communities. After the death of longtime Palestinian Liberation Organization leader Yassir Arafat, a new Palestinian Authority government in the West Bank began to seek accommodation with Israel. But the Israeli government demanded more—a retreat from violence to advance the peace process. For this to happen, Palestinian president Mahmoud Abbas would need to suppress Hamas and the other Islamist groups, a capacity he lacked. Lethal violence recurred within the Palestinian community, culminating in shoot-outs in Gaza during and after the evacuation (Usher 2005).

The radical fringe of the Palestinian resistance had no monopoly of violence. In part in reaction to that resistance, but in part as an offshoot of the military nature of the settlement process, a growing strand of apocalyptic religious Zionists emerged, both in the settlement communities and in Israel proper (Lustick 1988; Sprinzak 1999). In the course of the 1990s, attacks on Palestinians by Jewish militants multiplied. Conflicts sharpened between them and the secular majority of Israeli society. This process of mutual radicalization culminated in the assassination of Prime Minister Yitzhak Rabin by a religious fanatic at a Tel Aviv peace rally in 1995 (Peleg 2002; Sprinzak 1999). In the same period, attacks by Jewish militants on West Bank Arab farmers increased. Lethal politics had migrated from the occupied territories to Israeli society itself.

By the time Israel evacuated its settlers from Gaza, this double radicalization had hardened relations between Arabs and Jews as well as within both communities. While the majority of Israelis had wearied of living in a state of civil war, the pro-settlement minority moved inexorably toward extremism (Hirsch-Hoefler 2008; Alimi and Hirsch-Hoefler 2012).

Not only that: the much-vaunted restraint of the Israeli Defense Force hardened into vicious violence as it retaliated for unselective mortar attacks on Jewish communities coming from the Gaza strip (Levy 2012).

Simultaneously, while the Palestinian Authority under Abbas reluctantly accepted the necessity of coexistence with Israel, the religious militants of Hamas and Islamic Jihad intensified their attacks on them and on Israel. Hamas, which won the first elections in the Gaza Strip after the settlers' evacuation, itself became a hybrid—trying to govern both as a political party and as a militant movement, bringing in arms through tunnels from Egypt and using home-made mortars to bombard Israeli communities in the Negev.

As often occurs when the possibility of peace appears, after the Gaza evacuation, tensions developed within Israeli and Palestinian politics. On the one hand, as the Palestinian Authority prepared to take control of Gaza, Hamas militants were taking credit for the pullout and looking forward to governing the "liberated" territory (Usher 2005). In response, increasingly nationalistic Israeli governments punished Hamas for militants' mortar attacks on Israel proper with military invasions in 2008–2009, 2012, and 2014. Each operation inflicted deadly destruction on the civilian population, left the Palestinian Authority helpless, and made the chances of a peace agreement look increasingly impossible. The hybrid nature of the Israeli regime produced two kinds of contentious politics: the social movement politics we saw in the Gaza evacuation and lethal politics within and between the two communities.

HYBRID DICTATORSHIPS

Despite the lethal politics found in these two hybrid regimes, Great Britain and Israel are nevertheless constitutional democracies. But in the decades since the end of World War II—and especially after the fall of the Soviet dictatorship in 1991—hybrid rule has been experienced in the majority of countries of "the global South." Some of these uneasy hybrids vacillated between more democratic and less democratic mechanisms of rule and shifted back and forth between contained and transgressive forms of contention, while others are divided between autorititarian and participatory forms of contention. Consider Venezuela as an example of the first type and Hong Kong's conflicts as exemplary of the second.

Venezuela Vacillates

From 1972 to 2000, Venezuela never entered the zone of the highest rankings on civil liberties and political rights, but according to Freedom House, it vacillated constantly between the two poles. Between 1972 and 1976, political rights expanded. The two-party system continued to operate, with some openings in political opportunity structure. In that period, the government was simultaneously benefiting from OPEC-backed oil price rises, taking steps toward nationalization of the industry, engaging in large public works projects, and making concessions to organized workers and peasants. Then came the *caracazo*, a wave of unrest which took its name from the country's capital, in 1989, as the result of falling oil prices and government reform efforts (López-Maya 2002).

Between those events and 2002, there was a rapid decline in political rights, and an attempted coup by Hugo Chavez, a popular general who was jailed but eventually freed and who took power by electoral means. A slight revival of political rights appeared between 1992 and 1996, and held through 1997 and the election year of 1998. After 2000, according to Freedom House, civil liberties declined to a record level, even as political rights were climbing slightly. When Chavez died in 2012, his successor, Nicolás Maduro, responded to heightened opposition by jailing opponents and reducing civil rights still further. Figure 4.1 tracks the changes in political rights and civil liberties there between 1972 and 2010.

The *caracazo* was not the only time when contained contention burst its bounds in Venezuela. The research by Margarita López-Maya and her team adopted the same methods for Venezuela that had been used by

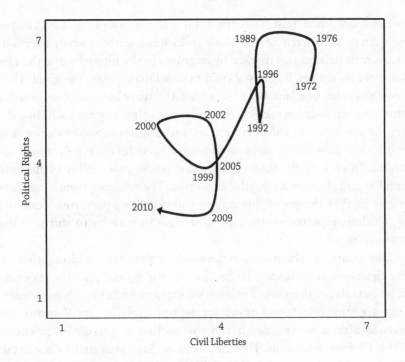

Figure 4.1:
Freedom House Rankings for Venezuela, 1972–2012
Source: Freedom House (2012)

Charles Brockett in Guatemala, Hanspeter Kriesi in four European democracies, Sarah Soule on American campuses, and Mark Beissinger in the former Soviet Union. The López-Maya team looked at the situation in Venezuela from 1983 to 1999 and encountered these sorts of episodes:

- *Legal*: assemblies, caravans, press releases, concentrations of people, strikes, marches, rallies, collection of signatures
- *Illegal but tolerated*: go-slows, civil servant strikes, national go-slows
- *Illegal but sometimes tolerated*: street closings, building invasions, land invasions, invasion of businesses
- *Repressed*: disturbances, sackings, sequesterings
- *New*: turning off of lights, banging pots and pans in the streets, human chains, whistling, taking off of clothing in public (Lopez-Maya, Smilde, and Stephany 2002: 50)

Altogether, over the seventeen years that their research covered, they counted 1,219 conventional events, 1,108 confrontational ones, and 708 violent encounters. That yielded 178 per year, or 3 to 4 per week.

But more important than the total numbers were the fluctuations over time. Each turn of the clock from quasi-authoritarian to quasi-democratic politics was marked by increases in the intensity and the violence of contention. Figure 4.2 tracks these fluctuations. The graph's top line shows the total number of episodes; the space between the lines the number of episodes in each category. Violent episodes grew each time the regime was entering a shift from more authoritarian to more democratic politics and gave way to more conventional episodes during election campaigns. In each crisis, confrontational episodes rose visibly in absolute number and share of all public contention. The evidence from Venezuela shows us that the prevailing mix of claim-making performances—the contentious repertoire—changes over time in resonse to shifts in the national regime.

Like many hybrid states, Venezuela's regime was held together by the charisma of its leader, Hugo Chavez, and by the massive revenues of its petroleum reserves. But both oil exports and charismatic leadership are unstable foundations for regime stability, as Venezuelans learned after Chavez's death and the decline of petroleum prices in 2014. Chavez' successor, Nicolás Maduro, has struggled to maintain the country's economy faced by falling oil prices, galloping inflation, and an enraged middle class encouraged by the political opportunity offered by Chavez's passing. Since Chavez's death, he has maintained the institutions of democracy, but has increasingly cracked down on opponents.

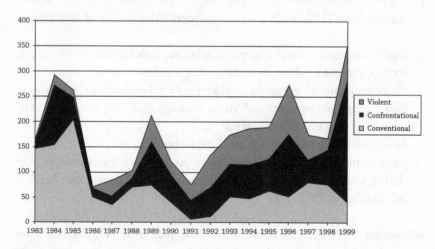

Figure 4.2:
Protest Events in Venezuela, 1983–1999

Enduring Hybrids

Unlike Venezuela, many countries in the Global South and in the former Soviet space have developed enduring hybrid practices. Why? For one thing, international institutions like the World Bank and the United Nations pushed them to adopt the rule of law and democratic practices. For another, citizens have demanded the right to vote and to be represented by governments of their choice. But for another, dictators have learned that providing opportunities for electoral participation helps them to identify supporters, isolate enemies, and distribute patronage to those who turn out to support the regime.

These regimes are unstable compounds of democracy and undemocracy. Their authoritarian elements lead them to periodically crack down on dissent, but their democratic institutions give challengers opportunities to continue to make claims on the regime. Some of these regimes survive in this uneasy compound for decades, while others ultimately transition in one direction or the other. One territorially-divided hybrid regime is the largely authoritarian Communist Chinese state and its quasi-democratic enclave, the city-state of Hong Kong.

The "Umbrella Revolution," 2014

Settled by British imperialists in the nineteenth century, Hong Kong evolved from an outpost of British imperialism to a key economic actor linking China to international markets. Using the term "One Country, Two Systems" to describe its ambivalent status in relation to China, the British government signed a treaty with the People's Republic, maintaining for the city a separate status and the political privileges and civil liberties that Britain had granted it over the previous decades. In return, Beijing agreed to universal suffrage for the region by 2017. But by 2014, although some of the members of the legislature were elected directly, only a limited number of Hong Kong citizens could participate in the election of the Chief Executive.

Decolonization was never a smooth process. Following the Chinese revolution, which ended in 1949, waves of riots, beginning in 1956 and culminating in 1967, convinced the British that they needed to provide welfare benefits and political participation to the residents of the city-state. The result was that when the British decided to give up their claim to control of the island and its surrounding territory, residents had both the habit and practice of political participation, and a legislative council to represent their interests.

In the meantime, the island's elite was using its proximity to China to develop its economy into one of the "Asian tigers." By the 1980s, it formed an integral link in the emerging Asian economic miracle, serving as an outlet for Chinese manufactures and a financial center for international capital. But while Hong Kong's development spawned a generation of millionaires, it also produced great inequality between rich and poor. While 8.5 percent of Hong Kong's population has an annual income of over a million dollars, its Gini coefficient, which measures the ratio between the richest and the poorest citizens, is one of the most unequal in the developed world. The population also possesses a high level of education, levels of Internet usage that surpass that of the United States, and a dense fabric of political parties and NGOs (Lam 2014).

The combination of rapid economic development, an educated middle class, a poorly-paid working class, political and civil rights and a lively press all under the ultimate control of authoritarian China was bound to produce a high level of contentious politics. In 2003, when the Beijing government tried to impose a rigid national security law that would have constricted civil liberties, thousands filled the streets and succeeded in persuading the Legislative Council to retract the bill. In 2011 there were mass protests against a new education law that was intended to instill Chinese patriotism in Hong Kong children. In 2013 there were even greater protests against the Chief Executive and in favor of universal suffrage, which the island's residents had been promised by the British.

But none of this equaled either the massive level of participation or the conflict that broke out in 2014, first on the part of dock workers striking for higher wages and better benefits; and then by students and a group calling itself "Occupy Central for Peace and Democracy" calling for universal suffrage. The protests were triggered by an announcement by the legislative body of the Chinese government that the promised universal suffrage for Hong Kong would be qualified by two caveats. First, the region's Chief Executive would be an individual who "loves the country and loves Hong Kong," and, second, that the Chief Executive would be nominated by a nominating committee whose composition would mirror the existing electoral college, which heavily favored elites close to Beijing. The protesters felt that these stipulations would overturn Beijing's promise of universal suffrage for Hong Kong by 2017.

In August, the Chinese government had promised to accord the city-state universal suffrage in 2017 with one hand, but with the other they limited candidacies to candidates vetted by the committee of notables approved by Beijing. In September, Occupy Central and two different student groups converged on the downtown business district with encampments that recalled the repertoire used by the Occupy Wall Street movement in the United States two years earlier. The police at first responded with violence, which enraged the protesters and expanded their ranks. At one point, a large majority of the Hong Kong public approved of the occupation. In response, the authorities took a more placatory tone and invited a delegation of students to meet with them in a well-publicized meeting in October. The problem was that the Hong Kong Chief Executive, while he was the elected face of Hong Kong's political authority, ultimately answered to Beijing.

The problem for the Chinese authorities was a double one: they could not engage in the kind of violent repression they had used in the Tienanmen Square massacre of 1989 without scaring off international capital; and they could not accord meaningful rights of universal suffrage to Hong Kong without risking the diffusion of the movement to cities in the mainland. Already in October, Beijing was straining to prevent news of the protests from spreading on social media to China's increasingly astute generation of Internet users, The students, their adult allies, and the authorities, both local and in Beijing, remained locked in a political stalemate until the end of 2014, when the Hong Kong police gradually dismantled their protest sites.[1] Figure 4.3 traces the rise and decline of the protest wave through the number of Google searches for these events from August 24 to December 23, 2014.

There are plenty of reasons why you might be interested in this explosive episode of contentious politics on the border of authoritarian China: the role of students at the heart of the protests; the parallels with the Occupy Wall Street movement in 2011; the centrality of social media in mobilizing the protesters; and the tug-of-war between the Internet-savvy Hong Kong population and the censors of the People's Republic. But what is most interesting from the standpoint of contentious politics was the relationship between the throbbing democratic politics of the city-state and the authoritarian politics of the People's Republic. In the contentious relations between Beijing and Hong Kong there was a structural disjunction that led to an unstable mix of conventional, confrontational, and violent behavior, which made resolving the conflict especially resistant to solution.

CONCLUSION

What do British/Irish conflicts, the enduring conflict in Israel/Palestine, elective authoritarianism in Venezuela, and the Hong Kong/Beijing relationship have in common? All four, of course, combined social movement politics with lethal conflict. All four involved institutional elites and

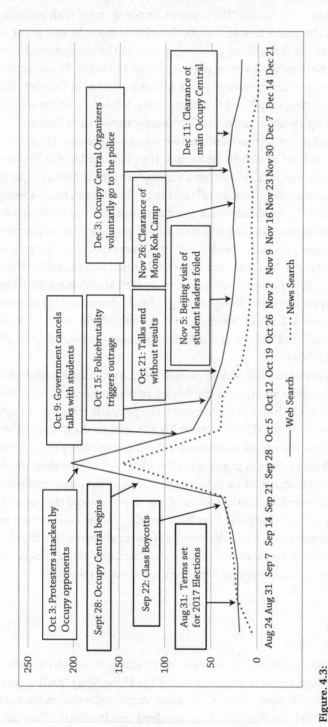

Figure 4.3:
Hong Kong Protests and Political Responses, August–December, 2014

Note: The trend lines represent the volumes of Web and news searches using Google. The Google Trends program was used to compute these numbers. The following four key words were used: "umbrella revolution," "occupy central," "occupy hong kong," and "hong kong central" (The results are available at: http://www.google.com/trends/explore?q=umbrella+revolution#q=umbrella%20revolution%2C%20occupy%20central%2C%20occupy%20hong%20kong%2C%20hong%20kong%20central%20central&geo=HK&date=8 per cent2F2014 per cent205m&gprop=news&cmpt=q).

ordinary people. And in all four, the mechanisms we have emphasized earlier—diffusion, boundary activation, brokerage—could be seen. All four also exhibited a process we have seen before—*polarization*—that is difficult to reverse once it takes hold.

Polarization had particularly devastating effects in antebellum America because it was buttressed by the doctrine of states' rights that was enshrined in the Constitution. While Whig and Democratic politicians in antebellum America tried to keep the Union together by balancing the entry of slave and free states to the Union, ultimately, the structural differences between the regions and the polarization of their political forces drove the two regions apart.

Similarly, polarization between Irish Catholics and the mostly Protestant British and their Irish allies made the English/Irish conflict difficult to resolve, not only because of "ancient hatreds," but because there were electoral incentives for political leaders to seek support from the extremes. Under situations of polarized hybrid regimes, "contained" politics worked to support the transgressive politics of the militants.

The same has been true in Israel/Palestine, where both the Zionist and Palestinian movements believe with equal justice that they have a claim to the same land. As a result, each time the moderates appeared close to a convergence, radicals in one or both communities seized the opportunity to repolarize the situation.

Venezuela's and Hong Kong's hybrid politics are still in flux as this book goes to press. In the former, it is the country's dependence on the international economy that will bring about a resolution in one direction or another and, in the latter, the vast weight of the People's Republic against the tiny island enclave the produces a more stable outcome. As we write, in early 2015, there are breadlines in a Venezuela with a galloping rate of inflation, and the veterans of the "Umbrella revolution" are trying to restart their movement. If the other cases of hybrid regimes we have sketched are any precedent, the conflict will endure for years—perhaps generations.

NOTES

1. This brief examination of the Hong Kong protests is based largely on the reporting of the *South China Morning Post*, Hong Kong's daily newspaper of record, which maintains a timeline of "Occupy Central" events called "How Occupy Central's democracy push turned into an Umbrella Revolution," available at http://www.scmp.com/news/hong-kong/article/1612900/timeline-how-occupy-centrals-democracy-push-turned-umbrella?page=all. Also see Victoria Tin-bor G=Huim "Hong Kong's Umbrella Movement: The Protests and Beyond" at http://live-jod.pantheon.io/article/hong-kong%E2%80%99s-umbrella-movement-protests-and-beyond.

PART THREE

Interaction and Mobilization

Parisian demonstrators supporting free speech after the murder of the French journalists of "Charlie Hebdo" by Islamist radicals in January 2015. (Photo by AP Photo/Thibault Camus).

CHAPTER 5

Contentious Interaction

As we pointed out in chapter 1, this book takes an interactive approach to contentious politics. Instead of studying "protest," "collective action," or "social movements," we examine the interaction among challengers, their opponents, third parties, the media, and more. So far, we have focused on the forms of collective action that people use (performances and repertoires), the contexts of their action (different regimes), and the opportunity structures that encourage or constrain them. We have also introduced some key mechanisms, including brokerage, diffusion, and coordination, that link challengers to others. But we have not yet delivered on our promise to connect challengers to the other actors in contentious politics. This chapter begins that task. We start where many people have found the heartland of contentious politics—in the city of Paris.

PARISIAN CONTENTIOUS INTERACTION

In any given year, writes Olivier Fillieule (1997), Parisians protest over practically everything, from war, civil rights, and racism to wages, employment, and working conditions, all the way to the weight of the *baguette* produced by neighborhood bakers. Although Parisians' repertoire is wide and deep, the street demonstration—*la manifestation*, in French—is their favored instrument. Regularly, but most often on weekends, Parisians assemble in habitual venues such as the square in front of the Gare de l'Est. Organized by the parade marshals of their *services d'ordre*, they array themselves behind colorful banners proclaiming the names of their organizations and their goals. Often chanting, they march down a broad avenue to a prearranged destination where prestigious speakers stir them.

Well-organized marchers representing parties, interest groups, and particular localities are not alone among the demonstrators. Although most demonstrations organize around a central claim, they often attract sympathizers, makers of cognate claims, curious onlookers, occasional opponents, and others with private axes to grind. From their interactions within the enthusiasm and solidarity of the demonstration, a unified "we" may even emerge.

Interaction does not occur only among those who demonstrate. On the margins of demonstrations appear onlookers, sympathetic, hostile, or indifferent. In an important sense, the task of the demonstrators is to turn sympathizers into participants, neutralize opponents, and turn indifferent onlookers into sympathizers. At a discreet distance, and often in civilian clothes, stand the police. Snapping photos and taking interviews are reporters from the press and television. Leading the parade are often celebrities, local officials, and party leaders. Bringing up the rear are lines of bright green garbage trucks sent to clean up the debris of pamphlets, handouts, and fast food that participants and spectators will leave behind. Officials of the prefecture who are responsible for public order and public officials at whom demonstrators direct their claims remain out of sight but keep themselves informed.

So modular has the demonstration become in France that it was publically organized by the French government after the "Charlie Hebdo" and "Hyper Casher" murders by Islamist terrorists in December, 2014. We will return to this massacre in chapter 9, but here it is enough to point out that it brought together advocates of free speech, opponents of Muslim immigration, opponents of anti-Semitism, and many French people who were simply appalled by the cruelty of the attacks. So widespread was opposition to the murders that it led to a surprising upward jolt in the popularity of the President, to police sweeps against those who had expressed sympathy for Islamism, and to a new set of measures aimed at Islamist sympathizers but also threatening other Muslims.[1]

Pierre Favre (1990) made the demonstration the subject of his book, *La Manifestation*. The book offers an interactive portrait of the demonstration; the actors include not merely the demonstrators but those who join them, oppose them, and observe their progress. Figure 5.1 reproduces Favre's schematic map of the actors in and around a typical demonstration. Favre's diagram separates those on the side of the demonstrators (e.g., organizations, ordinary participants) from those who oppose them (e.g., the targets of protest, the forces of order) and from various third parties (e.g.,

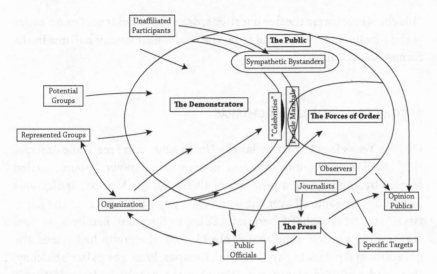

Figure 5.1:
Typical Actors in a Demonstration
Source: Favre (1990:19)

unaffiliated groups, the press). The important point is that, for Favre, the demonstration is not just an action but a collective *inter*action among all these different actors. The same is true of contentious politics in general. That is this chapter's organizing theme.

As in the demonstration, other sorts of contentious episodes often bring together actors who know little or nothing of one another at the outset, yet sometimes emerge from their participation as a unified actor with an identity, with boundaries separating them from others, and with a set of unified claims that they put forward against significant targets. In doing so, they become collective political actors (McAdam et al. 2001: ch. 11). This constitution of collective actors is the most remarkable feature of contentious politics.

How do such things happen? Let us unpack that big question into five smaller, more manageable ones:

- How do political actors form, change, and disappear?
- How do they acquire and change their collective identities?
- How do they interact with other political actors, including holders of power?
- How do existing institutions promote, inhibit, or shape all these processes?
- What kinds of effects do collective claims produce, and how?

This chapter answers the five questions, drawing on evidence from a major social rebellion in Mexico and from the rise of ethnic nationalisms in the former Soviet Union.

ACTOR CONSTITUTION IN CHIAPAS

On New Year's Day 1994, the day the North American Free Trade Association (NAFTA) went into effect, a previously unknown group startled Mexico by announcing a program of liberation for Mexico's indigenous people. Soon people all over the world were paying attention to the Zapatista Army of National Liberation (EZLN in Spanish). Led by a masked man calling himself Subcomandante Marcos, the group had seized the governmental palace in San Cristóbal, Chiapas. From the palace's balcony, they read a vivid declaration to the Mexican people. It declared that a long-suffering people had endured centuries of oppression and deprivation, but, finally, *hoy decimos ¡basta!* (today, we say enough). At various points in the declaration, the authors identified themselves in these terms:

- A product of five hundred years of struggle
- Poor people like us
- People used as cannon fodder
- Heirs of our nation's true makers
- Millions of dispossessed
- "The people" as described in Article 39 of the Mexican national constitution
- The Zapatista Army of National Liberation
- Responsible, free men and women
- Patriots

They denied that they were "drug traffickers, or drug guerrillas, or bandits, or whatever other characterization our enemies might use." They opposed themselves explicitly to these groups:

- The dictatorship
- The political police
- A clique of traitors who represent the most conservative and antinational groups
- The Mexican federal army

- The party in power (PRI) with its supreme and illegitimate leader, Carlos Salinas, installed in the federal executive office (Salinas was then president of Mexico)

Announcing a revolution on behalf of Mexico's poor, dispossessed, indigenous people of Mexico, they called for "us" to rise against "them."

The revolution did not take place. But the Zapatistas soon made an impact on Mexican politics. Within Chiapas, they held off threatened suppression by the army and forced the national government to start negotiations over peasant property rights. On a national scale, they started a much more general campaign for indigenous rights. During the spring of 2001, they staged a colorful march from Chiapas, Mexico's southernmost state, to Mexico City itself. The march publicized demands for enforcement of the local autonomy laws that the legislature had passed in response to concerted pressure from organizations of indigenous people, backed by international activists.

The Zapatistas quickly acquired an impressive international reputation and following. Electronic web sites and mailing lists, operated mainly by foreign supporters, broadcast their messages across North America and Europe. Those connections brought activists, funds, and enthusiastic statements of solidarity to Chiapas from as far away as Western Europe (Hellman 1999). Many outsiders interpreted the Zapatista mobilization as a form of resistance to the recently enacted NAFTA. For that reason, they saw it as a welcome addition to worldwide antiglobalization efforts. In 1996, the Zapatistas drew thousands of supporters to a "First Intercontinental Encounter for Humanity and against Neoliberalism" in the jungle of Chiapas. One observer argued that "the interest and attraction generated by the EZLN beyond its national borders is matched by no other movement in the post-Cold War period" (Olesen 2005: 12).

Constitution of a Zapatista identity did not come out of the blue; it built on what chapter 1 called a social base. Indigenous identity is hardly a new idea in a country such as Mexico, which has literally hundreds of indigenous groups. Many of its military and political heroes came from indigenous roots. Its 1905 revolution was, in part, the struggle of indigenous peasants to assert their rights to the land. It was no accident that the leaders of the Chiapas rebellion named their organization after revolutionary leader Emiliano Zapata (Womack 1971). Though of mixed background, Zapata became best known as the representative of indigenous peasants.

But the mobilization of an identity does not follow automatically from the existence of a social base to which it corresponds; if it did, indigenous uprisings would have occurred constantly throughout Latin America. The fact that such uprisings are sporadic and usually short-lived turns our attention from their social bases to their constitution as actors. Mexico's native peoples have still not achieved the liberation their Zapatista advocates called for in 1994. Still, they have gone from near-invisibility to significant political prominence. They have become a weighty interest in national politics, an internationally recognized model for political mobilization, and frequent participants in contentious interaction throughout Latin America, where governments in Bolivia and Ecuador came to power with significant indigenous support. The Zapatistas created a significant political actor on regional, national, and international stages. Their success in doing so leads us to the first of our five questions: How do political actors form, change, and disappear?

FORMATION, CHANGE, AND DISAPPEARANCE OF POLITICAL ACTORS

Remember how chapter 1 described *political actors*: recognizable sets of people who carry on collective action in which governments are directly or indirectly involved, making and/or receiving contentious claims. Political actors include governments and agents of governments, such as presidents and police. But they also include a wide range of nongovernmental actors, from neighborhood groups to worldwide organizations. They qualify as political actors by making claims, receiving claims, or both. Political actors regularly form, change, and disappear. How does that happen?

The most general answers are quite simple. Political actors form through mobilization, by increasing the resources available for collective making of claims. They change by participating in contention. They disappear by demobilizing. Of course, the complexities start there—in exactly how mobilization, participation, and demobilization work and produce their effects.

Chapter 2 introduced the simple process of *new coordination*, in which the mechanism of *brokerage* activates the mechanism of *diffusion*, and the two mechanisms jointly produce *coordinated action*. We saw a similar process with different actors in Argentina, as human rights workers, lawyers, courts and international human rights groups converged to pressure the government to take seriously the prosecution of military criminals in the Dirty War.

Zapatista brokers brought together a motley coalition of indigenous communities, religious activists, urban radicals, and guerrilla fighters in a coordinated large-scale actor that announced itself as the unitary Zapatista

Army of National Liberation. Its language, symbols, and practices then diffused widely among opponents of the current Mexican regime. The new actor then collected allies elsewhere in Mexico for even larger-scale making of collective claims. The Zapatistas of 1994 and afterward combined brokerage with diffusion, ultimately creating a coalition of participants, supporters, and sympathizers at a much higher scale than the jungles of Chiapas (Olesen 2005, Tarrow 2005: ch. 7).

The Zapatistas benefited from a mechanism we met briefly in chapter 2: certification. *Certification* occurs when a recognized external authority signals its readiness to recognize and support the existence and claims of a political actor. If the authority has international visibility and heft, its signal broadcasts the likelihood that the authority would intervene to support the new actor in future claims. Certification thus changes both the new actor's strategic position and its relation to other actors that could become its oppressors, rivals, or allies. (The opposite process of decertification withdraws recognition and commitments of future support, while often threatening repression.) The Zapatistas gained leverage within Mexico both from the country's long *indigenista* tradition and from their extensive certification by external organizations—NGOs, the foreign press, even some governments urging the Mexican government to avoid a bloodbath. Those external organizations could and did exert pressure on that government to recognize and bargain with the Zapatistas.

Here is another way of seeing the same point. Remember the components of political opportunity structure from chapter 3: (1) the multiplicity of independent centers of power within the regime, (2) the regime's openness to new actors, (3) the instability of current political alignments, (4) the availability of influential allies or supporters for challengers, (5) the extent to which the regime represses or facilitates collective claim making, and (6) decisive changes in items 1 to 5. Changes in political opportunity structure shape the ease or difficulty of mobilization, the costs and benefits of collective claim making, the feasibility of various programs, and the consequences of different performances in the available repertoire. In all these ways, changes in political opportunity structure affect the attractiveness of different collective action strategies.

Activist groups rise, fall, and change as a function of political opportunity structure, of their programs' success or failure, and of their effectiveness in mustering support from patrons, allies, and social bases. As a result, political actors spend some part of their time and energy doing other things than making collective claims. They build on existing resources and gather new ones, maintain solidarity, manage internal disputes, recruit followers, provide services to members, and so on, through a wide variety of sustaining activities. Even ferociously activist groups devote plenty of effort to building, maintaining, and repairing their organizations.

Making collective claims always depletes available resources in the short run, even if it attracts new resources in the longer run. Because of that, political organizers necessarily balance two kinds of activity that sometimes contradict each other: on one side, making collective claims; on the other side, building up their organization and its access to sustaining resources. Struggles among activists often spring up over precisely that division of labor: Are our leaders spending too much time raising money for themselves and too little on forwarding our interests? Have they destroyed our activist group by spending all their energy making claims and not enough energy on recruiting new members and drumming up financial support?

By identifying different kinds of political actors, you can untangle complicated contentious episodes. You can detect the arrival and departure of actors from contention, trace how their claim making changed, look for coalitions and divisions among them, and see whether they moved up or down the continuum from intermittent actors to established interests to activist groups. You can even understand why groups that appeared to be insignificant at one point in time seem unstoppable at the next and shrink to a small cadre at a third. Changes in political opportunity structure often return intermittent activists to their ordinary lives, give pause to established interests, and turn activists into a small but militant sect. In the simplest version, you make a list of the major political actors at point 1 in time, sketch connections and divisions among them, do the same thing for point 2 in time, and then try to explain the appearances, disappearances, and realignments from time 1 to time 2.

Nationalism in the Former Soviet Union

Here is a simplified example from Mark Beissinger's (2002) work on nationalist activism in the former Soviet Union. An experienced analyst of Soviet politics, Beissinger wanted to explain the enormous rise of separatist nationalism in the Soviet Union after 1986. Successful bids for independence on the part of former Soviet republics blew the union apart by 1991. Using methods very similar to those we saw in the study of "shantytowns" in Chapter 2, Beissinger centered his analysis on two large catalogs of episodes from the beginning of 1987 to August 1991: one of 5,067 protest demonstrations with at least one hundred participants, the other of

2,173 incidents in which at least fifteen people attacked persons or property. In preparing those two catalogs, he and his collaborators consulted 150 different sources, including Russian-language newspapers, wire services, compilations by Soviet dissidents, émigré publications, and reports of foreign monitoring services. Figure 5.2 shows how contention rose and fell in the Soviet Union and its successor states around the collapse of the Soviet regime in 1991.

Beissinger's data show several other things as well: that as contention rose, the proportion of violent events rose as well, a phenomenon we will turn to in chapter 8. It also reveals how a growing proportion of the events were organized by many regionally organized nationalities across the USSR who used the opportunity of the crumbling regime to make collective claims for autonomy or independence. By 1992, fifteen of them had managed to secede from the union and gain international certification as sovereign states.

The Soviet Union had built these categories and their boundaries into its governing structure, for example by treating Ukraine and Lithuania as distinct units of rule with some degree of autonomy on such questions as language and cultural expression. As a result, all existed as established interests. They easily created activist groups claiming to speak for all Ukrainians, all Lithuanians, and so on, down the list. Brokerage brought together different clusters within a given nationality into a temporarily unified actor. On the union's edge and supported by powerful neighbors,

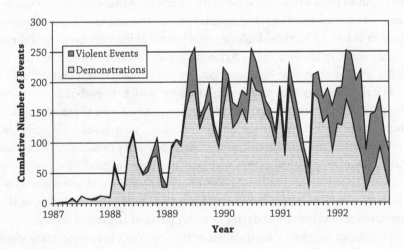

Figure 5.2:
Demonstrations and Violent Events in the Soviet Union and its Successor States, 1987–1992
Source: Data supplied by Mark Beissinger.

Armenians and Estonians acted early and successfully, securing quick outside support for their claims to become independent states. Then the rush began. It peaked at the end of 1990. Of these major actors, all but the Tatars of the Crimea (who ended up inside Ukraine) eventually won independence.

If we looked closer, we would distinguish many more actors and begin to see crucial realignments among them. Within Estonia, for example, we would find a group of ethnic Russians who feared and resisted Estonian independence. We would also see multiple alliances and divisions. Starting in 1987, before either Armenia or Azerbaijan came close to independence, Armenians and Azerbaijanis were engaging in violent confrontations over the disputed territory of Karabakh, geographically inside Azerbaijan but with about three-quarters of its population ethnically Armenian (Beissinger 2002: 64–69, 342–347, 375). In 1992, newly independent Armenia invaded the territory between its border and Karabakh. A 1994 cease-fire left Armenia in de facto control of the territory, but without international certification of its claims. This takes us to our second key question: How do actors acquire and change their collective identities?

POLITICAL IDENTITIES

Once we turn the magnification up far enough to see individual episodes, we begin to notice that crude categories such as "Armenian" and "Azerbaijani" do not capture the self-presentations of the actors or their relations to each other. In Karabakh alone, activists of Armenian heritage did not simply identify themselves as Armenians but as Karabakh Armenians. In order to deal with that complication, we need a better understanding of political identities and the boundaries on which they build. Us-them boundaries play crucial parts in contention. Boundaries themselves commonly take shape outside contentious politics, as a result of a complex, consequential process we call, accordingly, *boundary formation*. Once they exist, however, political actors regularly use them as part of contentious politics. Then the mechanisms of boundary activation and boundary deactivation come into play. Once formed, they are difficult to dislodge, as the persistence of ethnic boundaries in many parts of the world shows.

You bump into social boundaries every day. You observe or participate in boundaries that separate news vendors from newspaper buyers, students from teachers, owners from employees, and patients from doctors or nurses. Every one of these boundaries identifies a social relationship you have little trouble recognizing and, if necessary, negotiating. In all these cases, the combination of a boundary with relations inside and across it always generates some shared sense of the boundary's meaning on one side and the other. Workers and bosses may not see eye to eye on the meaning of the boundary between them, but they negotiate some common recognition of the boundary's existence and importance.

When activated, the combination of boundary, relations, and understandings attached to them constitutes a social identity. Seen from one side of the boundary or the other, it provides varying answers to the questions "Who am I?," "Who are we?," "Who are you?," and "Who are they?" The political identities that concern us here always involve plurals, especially "us" and "them."

The word *identity* sounds tones from very interior to quite exterior. At the interior extreme, we find our sense of yourself as someone unique, complicated, and secret, not completely known by anyone else. At the exterior extreme, we discover the identity of data banks and identity theft, where some stranger needs no more than a name and number to place you. In contentious politics, most of the social identities that count lie between these extremes. They depend on and give meaning to relations with other people. Political identities include boundaries, relations across the boundaries, relations *within* the us and within the them, plus accumulated meanings assigned to the boundaries and relations.

Identities center on boundaries separating us from them. On either side of the boundary, people maintain relations with each other: relations within X and relations within Y. They also carry on relations across the boundary: relations linking X to Y. Finally, they create collective understandings about the boundary, about relations within X and Y, and relations between X and Y. Those understandings usually differ from one side of the boundary to another, and they often influence each other. Together, boundaries, cross-boundary relations, within-boundary relations, and shared understandings make up collective identities. Changes in any of the elements, however they occur, affect all the others. The existence of collective identities, furthermore, shapes individual experiences—for example, by providing templates for us "good" Karabakh Armenians and distinguishing us from those "bad" Karabakh Azerbaijanis.

Identities, then, have four components: (1) a boundary separating me from you or us from them, (2) a set of relations within the boundary, (3) a set of relations *across* the boundary, and (4) shared understandings of the boundary and the relations. Through the Soviet Union's history, Karabakh Armenians and Karabakh Azerbaijanis had maintained distinctive everyday identities despite sometimes settling together, working together, and intermarrying. As the USSR fell apart, however, the paired identities politicized. As of 1992, Karabakh Armenians and Karabakh Azerbaijanis each had extensive internal relations, fought each other across the boundary between them, and offered competing accounts concerning the history of their region as well as the territorial rights that history implied.

Identities become *political* identities when authorities become parties to them. In Karabakh, the governments of Armenia and Azerbaijan backed the people they claimed as their countrymen and denied the opposing claims.[2] As late as 2015, lethal conflict persisted between Armenians and Azerbaijan over the Nagorny-Karabakh area and both government were piling up munitions to use against the other side.[3] Leaders of both regions manipulated and controlled permissible answers to the questions "Who are you?," "Who are we?," and "Who are they?"

These questions do not arise in remote corners of the world alone. After the Al Qaeda attacks of September 2001, the US government activated a boundary that already existed but now became more salient. Identities of Americans as patriotic or subversive became more political as the US government became a party to us-them boundaries separating patriots from terrorists and their sympathizers (Margulies 2013). This affected the thousands of Arab-Americans who live in places like Brooklyn, New York, or Dearborn, Michigan (Akbar 2013). But the first to feel the bite of boundary-erection were several hundred Arab immigrants in the New York area who were locked up in the New York City Metropolitan detention facility well beyond the statutory limit for immigration investigations. Many were physically abused and their religion ridiculed by their jailors.[4]

Europeans maneuver around similar questions, not only in deciding whether to align with US military policy but also in deciding whether Turks are Europeans and whether Muslims in general lie on the opposite side of the us-them boundary. The November 2005 wave of riots triggered by youths of North African Muslim origin deepened that boundary in France. It was rendered almost impassable by the murder of twelve people in the offices of the humor magazine, *Charlie Hebdo*, which had satirized Islam, in January 2015, and of four Jewish shoppers in a kosher supermarket the next day. The war against terror, Europe's open borders, and mass immigration have activated new boundaries and deactivated others.

Boundaries change and new boundaries form largely as a result of processes outside contentious politics—for example, the reorganization of work and the migration of major populations. Most contention does not create and activate new boundaries. On the contrary, most contentious politics activates or deactivates existing boundaries. Think of the conflicts that exploded over the police murder of Michael Brown in Ferguson, Missouri, in 2014 (see chapter 2): it did not create a new boundary but activated the deepest cleavage in American society—the one between blacks and whites.

Boundaries between social classes, ethnic groups, religious faiths, neighborhoods, and other categories organize some of routine social life. But contention typically activates one of these boundaries while deactivating others that could have been relevant. The Zapatista rebellion activated the broad boundary of indigenous identity while deactivating boundaries of the distinct ethnic groups that uneasily cohabit in the state of Chiapas (Hellman 1999). That activation also brought ethnicity into play, while pushing other differences, such as gender, locality, class, or occupation, into the background. Once that happens, conflicts between ethnic groups are almost sure to follow. As both the savage wars in the Balkans after the collapse of communism, and the Islamization of the Palestinian resistance showed, nonethnic identities commonly give way to ethnic identities as ethnicity X and ethnicity Y begin attacking each other (Johnston and Alimi 2012).

The overthrow of Saddam Hussein's regime in Iraq in 2003 had a similar effect on identities. As long as the dictator and his Baath Party were in power, religious and ethnic conflicts remained mainly in check within Iraqi society. Once coalition forces destroyed the repressive regime that had held Iraq in its grip and launched the process of constitution making, the identities of Shia, Sunni, and Kurds activated both in institutional politics and through intersectarian violence. The same occurred in Syria after the outbreak of the Arab Spring. What had begun as a democratization movement degenerated into a civil war, with Christians, different sects of Muslims, and Kurds lining up on different sides.

Many people regard identity claims primarily as a form of self-expression or even self-indulgence—what others do when they are too comfortable, too confused, or too distressed for serious politics. On the contrary, identity claims and their attendant stories constitute serious political business. At various points in US history, social movements helped to establish opponents and supporters of slavery, teetotalers, women, African Americans, gays, Vietnam veterans, survivors of 9/11 victims, families of children with cancer, and indigenous peoples as viable political actors. When they mobilized effectively and made successful claims, they received certification from authorities and from other political actors. Throughout American history, the shift toward established interests and activist groups promoted the emergence of general, indirect, and modular claim-making performances.

Political analysts often describe identities as if they were essential properties of individuals, but other scholars reject this essentialism. They see identities as infinitely malleable. We, too, think identities shift, as should by now have become obvious. But individuals cannot adopt a new identity as simply as they put on a new suit of clothes or change their hairstyle; identities appear and mobilize through interaction (Viterna 2013). This takes us to our third key question: How do political actors interact with other actors, including holders of power?

CONTENTIOUS INTERACTIONS

Political identities take their meaning from contentious interaction: we make claims on them. They (whoever "they" are) often respond with counterclaims: We demand our rights, but the government replies that we have no such rights and, in fact, that we do not even constitute a recognized identity. In the conflict between Armenians and Azerbaijanis, Armenians claimed they had rights to political autonomy or even to annexation by the Armenian state. But Azerbaijan's leaders replied that Karabakh and its populations belonged to sovereign Azerbaijani territory. Later, the Armenian army bid up the claim making by occupying the part of Azerbaijan between Armenia and Karabakh. It remains there under the terms of the 1994 cease-fire, with both countries claiming ownership of the border strip and of Karabakh. At the Armenia-Azerbaijan border, contentious interaction continues.

Collective claims fall into three categories: identity, standing, and program.

- *Identity* claims, as we have seen, declare that an actor exists. That actor may have existed as a recognized actor before the episode began (e.g., the category of indigenous groups is a traditional one in Mexican politics), or it may be *constituted* in the course of the episode. Actor constitution is a crucial part of contentious politics (McAdam et al. 2001: 315–321).
- *Standing* claims say that the actor belongs to an established category within the regime and therefore deserves the rights and respect that members of that category receive. The Zapatistas made a number of standing claims, but the most salient was to be valid representatives of Chiapas's indigenous people. (In fact, some indigenous leaders in Chiapas itself later disputed that claim.) They underlined their standing claims, furthermore, by denying that they were drug traffickers, or

drug guerrillas, or bandits, or whatever other characterization our enemies might use.

- *Program* claims call for their objects to act in a certain way. The Zapatistas called on the Mexican government not only to recognize their identity and their standing as valid representatives of indigenous people but also to change its policy toward indigenous people by protecting their land and defending them against rapacious outsiders. In other kinds of contentious politics, programs range across an enormous variety of claims, such as the following:
- Overthrow the present government.
- Support our candidate for city council.
- Don't build that road through our neighborhood.
- Give our starving people food.
- Make our bosses pay us a living wage.
- Exterminate our enemies.

Although political actors often emphasize one type of claim over others, we see few "pure" cases of identity politics, a politics of standing, or programmatic politics. The Zapatistas first caught international attention by their simple claim to existence. In the elaborate declaration of New Years Day 1994, they said, in effect, "Pay attention to us, because we're a new actor, we mean business, and the boundary between you and us matters." Soon they were also making standing and program claims. But, of course, they made all those claims by speaking concretely—and often negatively—about Mexican institutions. Claims and counterclaims do not occur randomly; they take their shape from surrounding regimes, cultures, and institutions. They respond to a regime's opportunities, threats, and constraints. This takes us to our fourth key question: How do existing institutions promote, inhibit, or shape processes of actor constitution, identify activation, and contentious interaction?

INSTITUTIONS AND CONTENTION

Every regime limits possible claims in three ways. First, every regime's political opportunity structure affects what claims resonate with people and can be transformed into programs. It does so by determining whether established political actors are or are not available as allies for new political actors such as the Zapatistas. If multiple independent centers of power exist within a regime (which means that political opportunity structure is more open in that regard), the chances increase that at least one power center will support and certify a set of identity, standing, or program claims. If political alignments are changing fast, a claimant has more opportunities to join coalitions and to escape repression.

Second, every regime divides known claim-making performances into prescribed, tolerated, and forbidden. A regime's government and other authorities enforce the prescribed performances, facilitate or at least do not block the tolerated performances, and act to suppress forbidden performances. Contained contention occurs within the limits set by prescribed and tolerated performances. Transgressive contention breaks out of those institutional limits into forbidden or previously unknown territory. Like the Mexican state, almost any state of medium or high capacity forbids the formation of actors having autonomous military power such as warlords' militias and guerrilla bands.

In most regimes in most periods, any group that decides to make independent claims by force of arms soon faces repression. Regimes also channel claims at the prescribed end of the range. Any government that makes its citizens assemble for patriotic ceremonies, for example, runs the risk that some hardy soul will disrupt the proceedings by shouting seditious slogans or assaulting a political leader. Since regimes also vary greatly in what forms of claim making they tolerate and forbid, top-down channeling of claims occurs all the time.

Third, from the bottom up, the available repertoire strongly limits the kinds of claims people can make in any particular regime. No one knew how to stage a street demonstration before social movements became standard forms of contentious politics. Although these days the news media have made the demonstration a familiar image across most of the world, even now suicide bombing only belongs to the repertoires of very small terrorist circles in a few world regions. Like the demonstration, suicide bombing depends on shared knowledge of a complex set of relations and routines. Contentious interaction takes place within limits set by political opportunity structure, regime controls, and available repertoires.

Political strategists themselves do not think in terms of political opportunity structure, regime controls, and available repertoires. But they do commonly take existing institutions into account. Within any particular regime, institutions include established, organized, widely recognized routines, connections, and forms of organization employed repeatedly in producing collective action. If you initiate politically contentious interaction in a parliamentary democracy such as France or Japan, you will almost certainly have to consider the presence of a legislature, an executive, and a judiciary, but also think about the relation of your claim making to political parties, labor unions, voluntary associations, economic organizations, religious congregations, and educational institutions, as well as to such routines as electoral campaigns, national holidays, television watching, and sporting events. Every one of them establishes some kind of audience, opportunity, or threat for your contentious claims.

In a theocracy such as today's Iran, in contrast, potential claim makers face quite a different institutional environment. There, they have to make their way through complex religious hierarchies and divisions but give less weight to voluntary associations and labor unions. Still other institutions prevail and channel contention in oil sheikhdoms such as Kuwait, military regimes such as Myanmar (formerly Burma), and fragmented warlord regimes such as Somalia. Both inside participants and outside analysts need institutional maps to navigate a regime's contentious politics.

Identity, standing, and program claims and their certification all vary tremendously as a function of prevailing institutions within one regime or another. In Iran, Baha'is once constituted a substantial religious minority. The Muslim victors of the 1979 revolution slaughtered some of them, sent others into exile, and drove the rest underground. These days some Iranian Baha'is surely exist and connect in private. But in a regime dominated by Shiite Muslims, Baha'i activist groups would have no chance of recognition for their distinctive identity, much less opportunity to firm standing within the regime or advancement of programs for religious reform.

The institutional context for identity, standing, and program claims looks quite different in the United States. In the United States, the (partial) successes of women's rights and civil rights advocates institutionalized the recognition of excluded populations as being deprived of rights to equal treatment. That model eventually facilitated identity and standing claims on behalf of gay and lesbian rights, Indian rights, rights of the disabled, and rights of those not yet born. It also promoted program claims on behalf of remedial action in recognition of minority rights. To be sure, in the United States, programs based on rights claims never succeed fully, often fail, and sometimes generate fierce counterclaims. For example, demands for the rights of animals have largely hit the brick wall of livestock producers and processors. Claims to abortion rights and the right to life clash every day. The point is not that regimes automatically grant certain kinds of identity, standing, and program claims. Instead, what sorts of identity, standing, and program claims are even possible varies remarkably from one regime to another. This variance occurs because institutional contexts differ so dramatically from regime to regime.

HOW CLAIMS PRODUCE EFFECTS

Now we can address our fifth question: What kinds of effects do collective claims produce, and how? Identity, standing, and program claims produce their effects in different ways. In each case we must distinguish between immediate and longer-term effects. Identity claims announce a boundary, a set of relations within the boundary, a set of relations across the boundary, plus some meanings attributed to relations and boundary. Contentious interaction frequently triggers attempts to change those boundaries. The American civil rights movement did not simply produce a wave of policy changes; it also triggered a process of identity reassessment in the black community. After the Montgomery Bus boycott, Martin Luther King asserted a new definition of Montgomery's "Negroes." Said King, "In Montgomery we walk in a new way. We hold our heads in a new way" (Burns 1997: 244). This was but the first in a broad process of claiming not only new boundaries between whites and blacks, but creating a new African American identity distinct from old white-enforced stereotypes.

The implication was clear: The civil rights movement was more than an instrumental effort to change bus seating laws, establish voting rights, or improve educational access for African Americans; it was the expression of a new collective identity among southern blacks, a clear and highly consequential example of identity shift as an outcome of contentious interaction (McAdam et al. 2001: 319–320).

Standing claims generally produce their effects on a smaller number of actors that have some power to certify. Members of the general public may have opinions about the claims of an actor to membership in an established political category, and individual politicians may oppose or support those claims. However, in most cases a limited number of elite actors actually have effective power to certify the claim.

Since World War II, for example, thousands of self-identified spokespersons for different peoples around the world have made standing claims for recognition of their populations as distinctive nations deserving political autonomy. But only about a hundred of them have actually received certification from the United Nations as recognized independent states. As state recognition illustrates, successful standing claims can produce serious effects, including authorization in such weighty matters as creating armies and contracting international loans.

Program claims take very diverse forms. For that reason, tracing their effects takes us into the heart of analyzing contentious politics in general (Giugni, 1998, 1999; Meyer et al. 2005). The effectiveness of program claims depends in part on the prior effectiveness of identity and standing claims: Is this a recognizable, credible actor that has the right to make such demands? If the answer is yes, the struggle has just begun. Could and would the objects of program claims actually make the changes or yield the resources the contentious actor is demanding? How will third parties, including governments, react to the claims? These questions take us into the thick of contentious negotiation.

Notice what has been going on in this chapter. It has provided more detail on the basic descriptive concepts of political actors and political identities, which you first met in chapter 1. At the same time, it has brought into play all the other descriptive concepts: government, contentious performances, contentious repertoires, social movements, regimes, institutions, and political opportunity structure. From the book's basic explanatory concepts, it has drawn especially on mechanisms and processes, such as certification and mobilization. But it has also connected these concepts with:

- *sites of contention*—for example, Armenia and Azerbaijan
- *conditions*—for example, relations of Armenia and Azerbaijan to the disintegrating Soviet Union
- *streams of contention*—for example, interactions among the Zapatistas, their domestic allies, their international supporters, and the Mexican government between 1994 and 2001
- *outcomes*—for example, the success of the Zapatistas in maintaining a previously forbidden form of organization
- *episodes*—for example, the occupation of western Azerbaijan by Armenian troops

In a very preliminary way, the chapter has also tried out the basic steps in the mechanism-process approach to explaining contention: describing sites of contention by means of the major descriptive concepts, describing conditions at those sites in the same terms, identifying the streams of contention that need explaining, specifying which outcomes of those streams deserve attention, breaking the streams into episodes of contention, searching the episodes for crucial mechanisms, reconstructing the processes containing those mechanisms, and (using analogies or comparisons with similar processes elsewhere) combining conditions, mechanisms, and processes into explanations of the specified outcomes. The small sketches of Parisian demonstrators, of Mexico's Zapatistas, of nationalist mobilizations in the disintegrating Soviet Union, and of Armenian-Azerbaijani struggles over Karabakh give no more than a forecast of the more extended explanatory work of later chapters. But at least they recall our basic explanatory strategy.

Two opposite processes have repeatedly shown up in the chapter's analyses: mobilization and demobilization. They matter so much to contentious politics, however, that they deserve a special discussion of their own. That is the next chapter's mission.

NOTES

1. Claire Adida, David Laitin, and Marie-Anne Valfort, "Terror in France: Implications for Muslim Immigration," *The Monkey Cage*, January 14, 2015. http://www.washingtonpost.com/blogs/monkey-cage/wp/2015/01/14/terror-in-france-implications-for-muslim-integration/

2. In Ukraine, where many people spoke a hybrid version of Ukrainian and Russian before the events described in chapter 1, the Russian nationalist movement in the East and the separatist civil war that followed led to a hardening of linguistic lines between the two regions. Peter Pomerantsev, "Do You Speak Surzhyk?" *LRB Blog*, January 29, 2014, at http://www.lrb.co.uk/blog/2014/01/29/peter-pomerantsev/do-you-speak-surzhyk/

3. David M. Herszenhorn, "Clashes Intensify Between Armenia and Azerbeijan Over Disputed Land," *New York Times*, January 31, 2015. http://www.nytimes.com/2015/02/01/world/asia/clashes-intensify-between-armenia-and-azerbaijan-over-disputed-land.html.

4. (*Turkmen v. Ashcroft*, Synopsis and Third Amended Class Action). See http://ccrjustice.org/Turkmen-v-Ashcroft.

Young antigovernment protesters wave flags as they pose for photographs on top of an army vehicle at Tahrir Square in Cairo, February 12, 2011. (Photo by Dylan Martinez/Reuters).

CHAPTER 6
Mobilization and Demobilization

Wae begin this chapter with a little-known episode: occupation of a church in the French city of Lyons by a group of irate sex workers whom the police were badgering. We use it to describe the most central process in contentious politics—mobilization—taking that process apart to examine its component mechanisms, especially interactive ones that connect challengers to opponents, third parties, and the public. Next we turn to more complex episodes of contention: first to the protest cycle of Italy in the 1960s and the 1970s, and then to civil war cycles in Central America, before turning to the revolutionary upsurge in the Arab world beginning in 2011.

Let us start with some key definitions which will serve us in this chapter and the next one:

> *Cycles of contention* consist of many episodes in the same or related
> polities, some of them intersecting, but many responding to the
> same changes in opportunities and threats. In most such cycles,
> contention begins moderately and in interaction with institu-
> tions. (Almeida 2003; Brockett 2005; Koopmans 2004; Kriesi et
> al. 1995; Mueller 1999; Tarrow 1989). Although it sometimes
> produces reform, and sometimes revolution, it usually ends with
> the main challengers being reintegrated within the system.
> *Civil Wars* we can define, with Michael Doyle and Nicholas Samba-
> nis, as armed conflicts within the boundaries of a recognized
> state between that state and a group that challenges its sover-
> eignty, and produces at least 1,000 battle deaths (Doyle and Sam-
> banis 2000)[1];

Revolutions we define as uprisings that transform economic and social structures as well as political institutions, such as the French Revolution of 1789–1799, the Russian Revolution of 1917, or the Islamic Revolution in Iran in 1979 (Tilly 1993: 16).

Composite Contention: the above forms sometimes merge in waves of contention that combine individual campaigns, cycles, civil wars, and revolutions. The world experienced such a "tide" of contention in Europe during 1848–1849 (Weyland 2009); a second, during and after the Russian Revolution of 1917; a third in the late 1960s; and a fourth in the breakup of the Soviet empire in 1989–1991 (Beissinger 2002). We will see a recent example in the "austerity" protests following the 2008 financial breakdown and in the so-called "Arab Spring" of 2011–2015, with which we will end this chapter.

Mobilization we define as an increase of the resources available to a political actor for collective making of claims; *demobilization* is a reduction of this aggregation of resources.

Each one of these episodes began with processes of mobilization. The successful ones were driven by a key process that distinguishes these major episodes of contention from local ones like the sex workers' protest in Lyons—*scale shift*. They end with demobilization. Here too, we find many differences in the scale, the impact, and the outcomes of contention. But despite the differences, we find a surprising number of common mechanisms among (1) simple streams of contention like the Lyonnais protest in France, (2) cycles of contention like those that occurred in Italy, (3) civil war cycles like those in El Salvador and Guatemala, (4) and major tides of contention like the one that has upended the entire Muslim world from Turkey in the Northeast to Tunisia in the West.

A FAILED OCCUPATION IN LYONS

Sex workers would seem to be an unlikely group from whom to expect mobilization into contentious politics. Working illegally and under the "protection" of procurers, they maintain tense relations with the police and public authorities. Much of the public, furthermore, shuns them. Indeed, even when they organize on behalf of their claims, sex workers remain vulnerable to repression and defection—and ultimately to demobilization. Lilian Mathieu's (2001) analysis of the occupation of a church in Lyons emphasizes the unusual properties of sex workers' protests, but it also reveals modal patterns of contentious trajectories that we will find elsewhere.

Following the exposure of a clamorous case of police corruption involving prostitution in Lyons in August 1972, French police ratcheted up the level of suppression of sex workers and closed down the *hôtels de passe* to which they took their clients, some of which were owned by corrupt police officers. In response, a small group of sex workers organized a march against the penalties, which they claimed had more to do with cleaning house in a corrupt police force than protecting the morals of the public. In a hallowed routine from the Lyonnais repertoire, the march was supposed to end at the state prefecture. But the unsuspecting women, led by an apparently friendly squad of police, allowed themselves to be led to the police station instead. Dispersion, recrimination, and humiliation at the hands of the media followed (Mathieu 2001: 110).

For several reasons, it was hard for the Lyonnais sex workers to gear themselves up for public protest. First, like many other unpracticed actors, they suffered from what economist Mancur Olson (1965) calls the "collective action problem." Olson holds that, except in small groups, most people with claims prefer to leave it to those with a larger stake in those claims to represent them. Our more relational way of putting this is that their protest triggered neither brokerage nor diffusion, and led to very little new coordination. It takes strong organization (McCarthy and Zald 1977), determined leadership, or the onset of new opportunities and threats for ordinary people to overcome their collective action problem. The Lyonnais women possessed none of these.

Second, many social actors face cultural, economic, and social impediments to engaging in public politics. Think of the Saudi Arabian women who tried, and failed, to gain the right to drive a car by actually doing so after the Gulf War of 1991. Police sent them home and warned their husbands to keep their women under tighter control. Sex workers work in the shadow of the law, their profession frequently hidden from families and friends, and their lives closely controlled by their procurers. Participating in a public march or demonstration would expose them to the ridicule of the press, the condemnation of public authorities, and possibly beatings from their pimps.

Nevertheless, when police pressures on the Lyonnais sex trade intensified after the failed protest, a group of the women created an informal collective. They gained the support of a progressive Catholic group, "Le Nid" (the nest)—what John McCarthy and Mayer Zald (1977) would call "conscience constituents." By this term, McCarthy and Zald mean those who support a group or a cause, not because they would profit if its claims were realized, but out of sympathy, solidarity, or ideological commitment. Le Nid offered legal services and helped to legitimate and publicize their cause. Encouraged by the recent appointment of two prominent women to the national government, they also sought the support of France's fledgling feminist movement. Braced by the support of these allies and by the favorable publicity it brought them, the Lyonnais women moved from contained to transgressive contention.

That transition occurred gradually. Like many claim makers, the sex workers first approached public authorities with a letter. But the Prefect of the Rhône rebuffed them. When some of their number received prison sentences, a small group decided to abandon institutional channels and chose a more transgressive performance—the occupation of a church (Mathieu 2001: 115). For members of a despised minority, the church constituted a free space in which to build solidarity. Second, it allowed the women to demonstrate their claims without revealing their identities. Such a performance had achieved success in France when illegal migrants used it a few years before. Nevertheless, the occupation of the church of Saint-Nizier failed. Breaking with long-standing precedent, the police burst into the building without the prior permission of the local bishop and escorted the occupiers out.

Once outside the "free space" of the church, demobilization came rapidly and bitterly. Despite efforts at concealment, the identities of many of the occupants became known, tensions with their pimps rose, and several of the leaders used their newfound notoriety to leave the profession. The episode also divided the fledgling feminist movement between those who wanted to defend the rights of exploited women, whoever they are, and others who opposed prostitution for its exploitation of women. Soon the allies who had sustained and guided the occupation moved off into more conventional causes, and most of the women were back on the street. As in many episodes of contention, what began with enthusiasm and solidarity ended in disillusionment and recrimination (Mathieu 2001: 129; Zolberg 1972).

In this brief episode we find several of the mechanisms with which you are already familiar: brokerage and diffusion were *not* present, but new coordination was, as the women moved from the streets to the church, where they enjoyed the protection of a sympathetic group of Catholics; competition emerged between different sectors of the women's movement; and one key mechanism—repression—was selectively employed here, but not in all episodes of contention, as we will see below.

The occupation of the church of Saint-Nizier did not fail completely. First, a national conference on the rights of sex workers took place in a renowned Parisian meeting hall, and the women met with a magistrate who had been charged by the government to write a report about their problems. What was really new was their newfound capacity to frame their status as exploited workers instead of as social parasites. In doing so, they slightly shifted the boundary that divided them from the rest of society. Subsequent protests like these in France and elsewhere would all be framed as claims on behalf of workers.

THE PROTEST CYCLE IN ITALY, 1966–1974

Italy in the 1950s experienced a period of rapid economic growth as the result of possessing reservoirs of labor with a high level of skills, entrepreneurial abilities, and proximity to European markets, where its low labor costs gave it a strategic advantage. It had Communist and Socialist parties that both claimed the mantle of Marx, neither of which was interested in violent revolution, but participated in parliamentary and electoral politics. It also had a strong labor movement, which was, however, divided among Communist, Catholic, and Social Democratic unions. But by the early 1960s, as its supply of cheap labor dried up and labor costs increased, Italy's postwar political-economic miracle began to implode. Its Christian Democratic political leaders won a brief reprieve by bringing the Socialists into the government, leaving their communist allies isolated in opposition (Ginsborg 1990: ch. 8). Reforms followed, but each attempted reform either triggered a conservative backlash (as did the nationalization of electricity) or opened the floodgates to broader contention (as did the passage of a modern industrial relations law).

When, in the late 1960s, the explosion came, it came from the middle-class student movement, surprising those who had feared a communist-led working-class onslaught. It was significant of the new identities emerging in the Italian student population that the earliest outbreaks took place in both the secular Universities of Turin and Pisa and at Catholic centers of learning in Milan and Trento. Reflecting the remaining potency of Italy's Marxist subculture, the insurgents framed their demands in "workerist" terms. But their links to the industrial working class remained more symbolic than real.

By 1969, the main force of university-based rebellion had subsided (Tarrow 1989). But a second wave of contention began even before the first had spent itself. Stimulated by the students' example, by a tight labor market, and by a new industrial relations law, contention spread to the factories (Franzosi 1995). The "Hot Autumn" of worker insurgency first stayed concentrated within the North's large factories. Then it became especially violent among the new wave of semi-skilled mass workers who had entered the workforce in the miracle years of the 1950s. Skilled and white-collar workers who had enjoyed higher wages responded to the successes of these mass workers by demanding the preservation of wage differentials. Militant workers used a variety of new forms of contention that the unions had not dared to employ. The unions, anxious not to be outflanked, quickly took hold of working-class insurgency and moved sharply to the left in their demands and their ideology.

In the Italian cycle, we find many of the mechanisms of mobilization we saw on a smaller scale in earlier episodes: challengers perceiving and seizing political opportunities, appropriating organizations and social networks, and innovating in the inherited repertoire. They also formed alliances across the secular/religious divide, shifting boundaries and forging new collective identities. New organizations, such as *Potere Operaio* and *Lotta Continua*, tried to broker ties between worker and student contention. Occupation of university buildings mimicked performances that the students had observed in Berkeley and at Columbia, but it also revived an Italian tradition of factory occupations (Spriano 1975). When students went home on vacation in the summer of 1968, they diffused the message of their claims to others, including younger brothers and sisters in the secondary school system, who started their own acts of protest during the following academic year.

Of course, students and workers interacted in different ways within the structure of political opportunities. For both, splits in the elite created opportunities for contention. And the presence of allies within and outside government helped to convince both groups that their claims might be well received: The Socialist Party in government restrained police repression, while the communists in opposition tried to profit from the new climate of contention by putting reform proposals on the agenda. For the students, opposition to the Vietnam War and debates about educational reform opened up opportunities. For the workers, inflation and full employment expanded their leverage. But these factors alone do not explain why contention in Italy lasted as long as it did. Why, for example, did it not simply diffuse from city to city as the student lunch counter sit-ins we saw in chapter 2 did? Our concept of "scale shift" helps us to see the differences between a simple episode of contention of diffusion, and more substantial cycles of contention.

SCALE SHIFT

Most episodes of contention begin locally. If some process were not expanding contention upward, there would be no national or international waves of contention. *Scale shift* is a complex process that not only diffuses contention across space or social sectors, but creates instances for new coordination at a different level than its initiation. *Downward scale shift* is the coordination of collective action at a more local level than its initiation. In contrast, *upward scale shift* involves coordination of collective action at a higher level (whether regional, national, or even international) than its initiation. A general strike touched off by a dramatic or successful local action is a common example of upward scale shift. Another was the expansion of suicide bombing in the Middle East from a local tactic of insurgents in Lebanon to an important weapon of Islamist militancy (Pedahzur and Perliger 2006). We saw upward scale shift in the British antislavery campaign, when thousands of local petitions were forwarded to Parliament.

Upward scale shift is one of the most significant processes in contentious politics. It moves contention beyond its local origins, touches on the interests and values of new actors, involves a shift of venue to sites where contention may be more or less successful, and can threaten other actors or entire regimes. In the France of May 1968, arrest of a small group of student activists from the University of Nanterre triggered a major national explosion of strikes and protests that threatened the stability of the republic. In Latin America, there has been an almost constant shift in the scale of contention between the local, national and transnational levels (Silva 2013). In chapter 5 we saw how contention in the Soviet Union shifted in scale from Armenians and Estonians in 1988 to Moldavians in 1989, Crimean Tatars, Ukrainians, Latvians and Lithuanians, and Russians themselves in 1990s, to Georgians, and to the breakup of the entire Soviet space in 1991.

Figure 6.1 describes two main routes through which upward scale shift can operate: a *direct diffusion* route that passes through individuals and groups whose previous contacts or similarities help to spread mobilization, and a *mediated route* through brokers who connect people who would otherwise have no previous contacts. We saw an example of the first route in Ukraine, where pro-Russian nationalists took over the east of the country following the Russian takeover of the Crimea. We saw the second route when Clarkson connected local antislavery groups in England into a national movement through the press. Both examples of scale shift began with local actions; each ended with new coordination at higher levels of the polity (Tarrow and McAdam 2005).

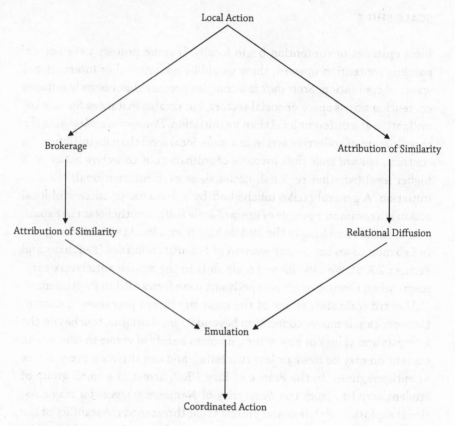

Local Action

Brokerage   Attribution of Similarity

Attribution of Similarity   Relational Diffusion

Emulation

Coordinated Action

Figure 6.1:
Alternative Routes to Upward Scale Shift
Source: Tarrow and McAdam (2005: 128).

Scale shift involves many of the mechanisms we have met before: diffusion, as people learn about episodes of contention elsewhere and adopt their methods; brokerage, as movement missionaries or opportunistic political entrepreneurs make connections among groups that would otherwise be isolated from one another. It also involves two new mechanisms: emulation, as people imitate the performances that early risers have invented, and the attribution of similarity among people who did not know one another earlier or may have seen each other as strangers. In other words, scale shift can create new identities.

Contentious actors often deliberately "venue shop" in order to seek coordination at a level more favorable to them. In Italy, as wildcat strikes spread from large factories in the North to smaller ones and to central and southern Italy, coordination shifted upward to collective bargaining within entire industrial sectors and to the national level. As student occupations spread from major universities in the North to the rest of the country and to the high schools, the parties of government and opposition pieced together a new educational reform. The factory occupation, the university sit-in, and the assembly in the place of work were eventually routinized. But some trends within the movement organizations engendered by the 1967–1969 period escalated the scale of contention and exacerbated conflicts between groups.

The Italian events were part of a broader cycle of contention in Europe, which had its epicenter in what came to be called the "Events of May" in France in 1968. The French events arose suddenly, paralyzed the whole country, and were rapidly reversed by the regime of President Charles de Gaulle. In both countries, demobilization followed the peak of contention in the late 1960s. Demobilization came quickly in France and was complete; by 1969, the country was back in the hands of the autocratic de Gaulle and his center-right party. But in Italy, the process of demobilization was more long-lasting. The state, networks of clandestine militants, and groups of institutionalized movements intersected as the cycle wound down through mechanisms of demobilization. Using the Italian case as our example, we turn to these mechanisms of demobilization.

MECHANISMS OF DEMOBILIZATION

From decades of research on social movements, we know a great deal about the conditions and dynamics of mobilization, but we know far less about how contentious actors demobilize. Do they simply disperse after their claims are made, from either satisfaction or disillusionment? Do governments repress them or co-opt them into tranquility? Or do internal divisions lead to factional splits and to polarization? How inevitable is demobilization? Do claim makers inevitably give up when the enthusiasm of the struggle wanes or when political opportunities disappear? Or do they turn to more institutional forms of participation when the initial flush of enthusiasm has passed (Piven and Cloward 1977)?

Most mobilization processes eventually reverse themselves. How, and how soon they do so depends on the initial conditions of mobilization, on the strategy of elites and authorities in response to challengers' claims, and on the degree to which they provide themselves with enduring structures to maintain their solidarity. The Italian case illustrates these factors with particular force because of the great degree of scale shift that the cycle of contention had reached by the early 1970s.

Three facts about Italian student and worker mobilization made a difference to demobilization, especially when compared to the contemporary French Events:

- The Italian May started earlier, lasted longer, caused greater mayhem, and brought about more death and destruction than in any other western country, with the exception of Northern Ireland (see chapter 5).
- While the French Events of May had the indirect effect of eroding the republic's tight central control and ushered in the fall from power of the Gaullist party, Italy's more volatile and longer period of disorder left the Christian Democratic Party in power until it lost out in the political earthquake of the 1990s.
- By the mid-1970s, little was left of the initial enthusiasm, solidarity, and utopianism typical of initial episodes of contention—what the late Aristide Zolberg called "moments of madness"(1972).

What explains this pattern of longer duration and less political impact of the Italian cycle? When Tarrow disaggregated the Italian cycle into its component performances, he discovered some striking differences in the incidence of different kinds of performances over the near-decade from 1966 to 1974. The majority of the events he uncovered were *conventional*. They included routine performances of petitions, audiences, strikes, marches, and demonstrations—the latter often performed in ways calculated to attract the attention of the media (Tarrow 1989). But systematic analysis of Italian events over a period of years also showed that large minorities of the events were *disruptive*— innovative direct actions intended to inhibit or upset the lives of targets, objects, and third parties. Another minority were deliberately *violent*—attacks on property, on opponents of the claimants, state actors, or third parties.

Figure 6.2 traces the trajectories of these three forms of Italian contention through the years of the "long Italian May." It shows data on all forms of contention gathered from Italy's major newspaper of record, the *Corriere della Sera*, from 1966 through 1973. Notice how, at its emergence in 1968–1969, the Italian cycle contained a relative majority of disruptive events—creative, "in your face" performances designed to draw attention to the protesters, enhance their solidarity, and gain new adherents. The typical disruptive protest was the faculty or factory occupation—exactly the sort of eye-catching performance we saw in Lyons during 1975. This was the period in which students and workers attempted to construct new collective identities, formed loosely coupled informal organizations, and

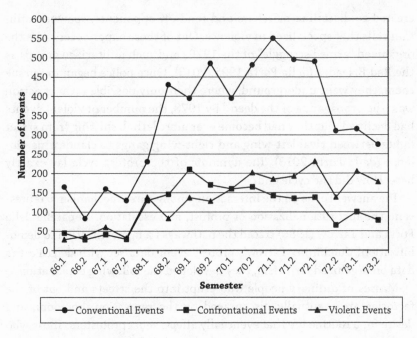

Figure 6.2:
Italian Contention, 1966–1973
Source: Tarrow (1989: 70).

challenged authorities with demands that could not easily be negotiated but could not be ignored (Pizzorno 1978).

The disruptive part of the cycle soon gave way to a wave of more conventional events and to the routinization of 1968's innovative performances. Conventional events reached a peak of more than five hundred events during the first half of 1971, only to fall off significantly during the next two years. Many involved the heirs of the 1967–1968 period, but they were more organized, more routinized, and aimed at achieving specific programmatic claims. This infuriated the extreme sectors of the former student movement, which led them to form new extraparliamentary groups that sought to outflank the institutional parties of the left. It also outraged right-wing youth groups, which began to organize clandestinely to oppose what they saw as the threat from the left. From this mutual radicalization, violent clashes between extreme left-wing and extreme right-wing groups resulted.

The tempo of these violent events started slowly but reached over four hundred per year by 1970. Violence first appeared in clashes with the police and wars over turf between rival groups of left-wing and right-wing students. The extraparliamentary groups' "services of order," created to discipline marchers and fend off opponents, spawned militant cells that specialized in violence. Out of these experiences came the organized "armed struggle" of the 1970s and such militarized groups as the Red Brigades (della Porta 1995, 2013). Once police began to pursue them, they went underground, where their only possible form of action was "the propaganda of the deed." By 1973, the number of violent events had declined. But they had become ever more lethal, shifting from street fights between rival left-wing and right-wing gangs to clandestine violence (della Porta 2013). The dynamic of the protest cycle lay exactly here: How did the cycle end?

The answer turns on the interaction among three mechanisms: repression, the institutionalization of protest, and escalation. Donatella della Porta and Tarrow (1986) traced the pathways from mobilization to demobilization. Combining Tarrow's protest event data set with della Porta's data on organized terrorism, they developed the following explanation:

Masses of ordinary people who erupt into the streets and out of the factories are eventually discouraged by the repression, boredom, and desire for a routine life that eventually affects most protesters. Those who lead them respond in one of two opposing ways:

- By *institutionalization*: the substitution of the routines of organized politics for the disorder of life in the streets, buttressed by mass organization and purposive incentive
- By *escalation*: the substitution of more extreme goals and more robust tactics for more moderate ones in order to maintain the interest of their supporters and attract new ones

In Italy, institutionalization turned off those whose interest in public life was unsatisfied by the routines of everyday politics, leading to alienation from politics or defection to the extremes. Escalation, inevitably met by repression, scared off timid souls and motivated them to move into institutional politics or the relative safety of private life. The result was *polarization*—increasing ideological distance between the wings of a once unified movement sector, divisions between its leaders, and, in some cases, terrorism. The Italian protest cycle ended in a paroxysm of organized violence but it also ended in the institutionalization of protest in the form of political party, trade union, and interest group activism.

Notice the role of *repression* in this bifurcation: the Italian state was brutal towards the more extreme agents of contention, but it reacted more moderately to those who used less aggressive forms of action. What this meant was that the state's actions divided the protest movement into an extreme minority which sank deeper and deeper into clandestine violence (della Porta 1995, 2013), and the more moderate majority whose members either ended up in more pacific forms of contentious action or disappeared into the party system or into private life, disillusioned with the risks and costs of life in the streets (Tarrow 1989: ch. 9).

In the United States, there was a similar bifurcation, though with less escalation and more targeted repression. Critics of the "sixties" like to tell stories about former activists who turned into pillars of the establishment. But major cycles of contention lead to much more than disillusionment and defection. First, many who earned their spurs in the "high-risk activism" of the civil rights and anti-Vietnam movements entered more conventional activist careers (McAdam 1988). Second, the themes of the cycle imprinted the routines of future activists with the frame of "rights"— expanding its meaning in the process (Snow and Benford, 1992). Third, a small minority of both white and black militants entered the shadowy world of clandestine violence, where they were sysematically repressed. It is through such processes of demobilization, reintegration, and sometimes violence, that major protest cycles end.

CENTRAL AMERICAN CIVIL WAR CYCLES

Not all protest cycles end with reintegration as in Italy: in some, especially where autocratic regimes employ indiscriminate and brutal repression, cycles of contention escalate into civil wars.

Charles Brockett's (2005) study of Guatemalan contention reveals this process dramatically. Between 1974 and 1981, as we saw in chapter 2, a cycle of protest arose across Guatemalan society, culminating in a major rural insurgency and in organized violence by and against the Guatemalan regime.

Figure 6.3 combines Brockett's data for four broad types of contention: strikes and student strikes, peaceful demonstrations, occupations and other illegal acts, and organized violence.[2] Brockett's data show that, under some conditions, what begins as a cycle of mobilization can escalate into a civil war. What explains the difference between these central American civil wars and Italy's more contained cycles of contention? Guatemala's neighbor, El Salvador, experienced a similar cycle that widened into civil war too. Between 1927 and 1930 and again between 1962 and 1982, Paul Almeida has shown that what began as reformist labor and peasant protest

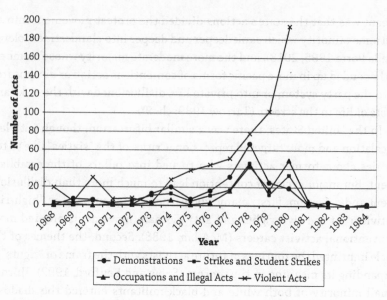

Figure 6.3:
Different Forms of Contentious Politics by Year in Guatemala, 1968–1984
Source: Brockett (2005:176–183)

escalated into wholesale insurgencies against the state (Almeida 2003, 2008). Almeida's work provides an explanation that turns on different state responses to contention. In El Salvador in the early 1960s, conflict began when the government was engaged in tentative reforms that opened the opportunity structure to peasants, middle-class reformers, and urban workers. Using largely nonviolent protest performances, a plethora of reformist organizations arose to take advantage of these opportunities. But the elite took fright at the loss of power it might suffer if reform went too far, and reversed the process. The result was indiscriminate repression, professionalization of dissidence, and a wholesale radicalization of the movement sector that had developed in response to the opening of the regime. By 1981, the spiral of violence and counter-violence that followed led to a civil war. Figure 6.4, drawn from Almeida's reconstruction of Salvadoran contention, shows that the reformist organizations that had developed early in the cycles were transformed into—or were replaced by—more radical groups that turned the protest cycle into a civil war.

Of course, there were major differences between the underlying conditions leading to conflict in Italy and Central America. Italy in the 1960s was a developed capitalist economy with a sophisticated ruling group that represented a coalition of social forces, well established unions and parties, and modern political institutions. El Salvador, in contrast, was a largely

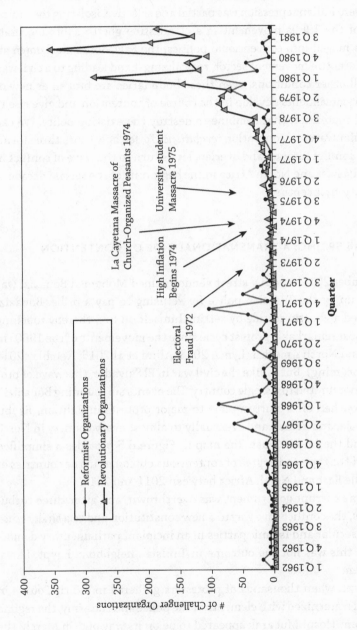

Figure 6.4:
Quarterly Presence of Reformist and Revolutionary Challenger Organizations in El Salvador's Protest Events, 1962–1981
Source: Paul D. Almeida, 2003. "Opportunity Organizations and Threat Induced Contention: Protest Waves in Authoritarian Settings." *American Journal of Sociology* 109: 345–140

agrarian country with an unenlightened ruling class and an authoritarian government that reflected the narrow class interests of the elite. But what mattered most was the political interaction between protesters and the state: where Italian repression was partial and selective, isolating the radical branch of the 1960s movement in a clandestine ghetto as its moderate branches moved into conventional politics, the Salvadoran crackdown attacked the entire movement sector, radicalizing it and leading to a civil war.

In still other conditions, even these boundaries are broken as new or resurgent movements develop in the course of contention and give rise to waves of contention that combine to destroy the existing polity. We call these major waves of contention *revolutions*. To see how those three forms of lethal conflict interact and overlap, let us turn to the wave of conflict in the Middle East and North Africa in the beginning of the second decade of the twenty-first century.

THE ARAB SPRING: A TRANSNATIONAL TIDE OF CONTENTION

In December 2011, a young street vendor named Mohamed Bouazizi was roughed up by the Tunisian police for refusing to pay a bribe. Bouazizi committed a ghastly suicide by setting himself on fire, thereby touching off the most remarkable protest cycle since the movements of the 1960s in Europe and North America (Lynch 2013; Alimi et al.2015; Ketchley 2014 and forthcoming). But unlike the civil war in El Salvador, this wave of protest was not limited to a single country. The events surrounding Bouazizi's suicide touched off a shift in scale to major protests in Bahrain, Egypt, Libya, Syria, and Yemen and eventually to almost every country in North Africa and the Middle East. The map in Figure 6.5 provides a simplified picture of the type and degree of contentious outcomes in the countries of the Middle East and North Africa between 2011 and 2014.

Tunisia's corrupt government was overthrown, and after three turbulent years, the conflict gave way to a new constitution and to a shaky truce between secular and Islamic parties in an incipient parliamentary democracy. But this was not the outcome in Tunisia's neighbors, Egypt, Libya, and Yemen:

In Egypt, when thousands of protesters gathered in Tahrir Square in Cairo and fraternized with elements of the police and the army, the regime of President Hosni Mubarak appeared to be on its way out. In March, the Prime Minister, Ahmed Shafik, resigned following continued protests. Under pressure from the protesters and the army, in June the Mubarak regime fell, and Mubarak himself was arrested. (Ketchley 2014)

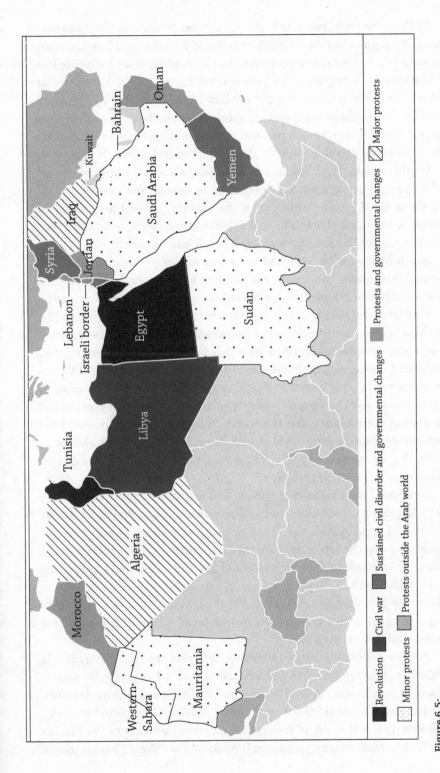

Figure 6.5:
Rough Guide to the Pathways of the Arab Spring, 2011–2012
Source: The Bench Jockeys (available at: http://thebenchjockeys.com/2011/11/20/careful-what-you-wish-for/#more-1236).

At the same time, protests broke out against Muammar Gaddafi's personalistic regime in Libya. Gaddafi employed his elite guard and African mercenaries to defeat the protesters but in August, after he refused to step down, they organized as an insurgent army and seized control of Tripoli. Fear for the lives of the civilian population and the growing number of refugees brought western intervention in the form of air strikes against Gaddafi's forces and, in June, Gaddafi was captured and summarily murdered by a group of rebels. His son and some loyalists fought on.

In June President of Yemen, Ali Abdullah Saleh, was forced out by an urban insurgency against his corrupt government. The presence of Al Qaeda in the Arabian Peninsula in the country, as well as Shia tribal unrest, led the United States to urge Saleh to step down in favor of his Vice President, after an assassination attempt left him wounded.

In 2012, contention appeared to be slowing, as political parties were formed throughout the region, elections were held in Egypt and Libya, a new constitution came into force in Tunisia and contention appeared to be moving from the streets to the party system. Some of these parties—like the Muslim Brotherhood in Egypt or Ennedi in Tunisia—were seasoned campaigners whose leaders had been jailed under the previous regimes, while others—especially the secular liberal parties favored by the West— were new and inexperienced. In Egypt, in June, Mubarak was sentenced to life in prison and the Egyptian people voted in the first free presidential election in their history. But the secular forces that had empowered the January revolution were divided and disorganized, and the electorate chose the inexperienced and divisive Muslim Brotherhood leader, Mohammed Morsi as their president.

Soon there were signs that the joy and solidarity of the Arab Spring were dissolving into conflict and violence. In February, President Bashar al-Assad of Syria blamed the Syrian uprising on foreigners and called for Syrians to stop the rebels. In July, the army carried out a massacre in the village of Tremseh and the International Red Cross declared the uprising to be a civil war. By September, the rebels had taken over the city of Aleppo, and the largest rebel group, the Free Syrian Army, had moved its command post from southern Turkey, which had taken up the opposition to al-Assad, to northern Syria.

The year 2013 brought more worrying signs that the spring was turning colder. In January, massive protests developed all over Egypt against Morsi; in July, he was deposed by an army coup, followed by armed clashes. The army, which had aided the rebel cause by easing Mubarak out of power, now emerged as the core of the regime, attacking activists of the Muslim Brotherhood and clearing protesters from the square. The military launched a dual campaign of elimination against both the Brothers and many of the liberal and secular forces that had played a key role in the January revolution. In the year following the coup, there were 40,000 arrests and 3,000 killed, as well as the passage of a draconian protest law. Supporters of the Muslim Brotherhood tried to protest against the growing repression, but they were forced from the squares and boulevards to lightning protests in the back streets to avoid the assaults of the restored power of the security police (Ketchley forthcoming, ch. 5).

The year 2014 marked the almost complete reversal of the Arab Spring. As the Egyptian army leader took over the Presidency in a doctored election and restricted civil liberties, Libya eruped into conflict between the weak government and Islamic militias that had emerged from the fight against the Gaddafi dictatorship, and the government of Yemen fell to insurgents. In September Islamic militants attacked the American diplomatic mission in Benghazi, killing Ambassador Chris Stevens and three other members of the mission. This led to a more cautious American role in the country as President Obama and his Secretary of State, Hillary Rodham Clinton, were accused of failing to protect their representatives in Libya. In mid-2014, a group of Houthi rebels took over capital of Yemen, Sana, ejecting the weak President, Abed Rabbo Mansour Hadi. Hadi set up a temporary government in Aden before fleeing, in March 2015, to Saudi Arabia, as the Houthis advanced southward. Almost immediately, Saudi Arabia and other Gulf nations intervened, turning Yemen into an internationalized civil war.

But the most sustained fighting raged in Syria, where conflict erupted within the rebel coalition between the secular opposition and the expanding "Islamic State of Iraq and the Levant" (ISIL). By the middle of the year, that group had joined forces with Jihadi groups in Iraq, where they rapidly overpowered the corrupt Iraqi army and took over important sectors of the country and important oil installations, before taking advantage of the chaos in Syria to establish a foothold in that country, too. By September ISIL had declared itself to be the Islamic Caliphate, beheaded British and American prisoners, and began to build a government that included parts of both Syria and Iraq. Only the panicked decision of the United States and its allies, and the determined resistance of the Kurdish Peshmurga fighters from Northern Iraq and Syria, held back the jihadist onslaught.

Of the high hopes and transnational solidarity that were triggered across the region and in the West three years before, only little Tunisia remained as a holdout of the hopes of the Arab Spring. At the end of 2014, new parliamentary elections brought a secular coalition to power under a liberal constitution and the Islamic Ennahda party that had played a key role in the overthrow of the old regime seemed willing to accept a role as the loyal opposition. The Arab Spring ended where it began—in little Tunisia—while most of the region either remained under authoritarian control or was convulsed by violence and chaos.

READING THE ARAB SPRING

The western press quickly dubbed what was happening in the region "the Arab Spring," recalling the uprisings that had swept across Europe in the "Springtime of Peoples" in 1848. But no one was quite sure what to call the forms of contention that emerged: the terms "protest," "riots," "demonstrations" did not quite suffice; they soon gave way to "revolution," in part because of the aspirations of the protesters who filled the streets to overthrow their oppressive regimes; in part because many of these uprisings soon gave rise to violence; and in part because reporters were looking for a story line that would make sense to western readers. But by now, as students of contentious politics, you should be able to detect familiar political mechanisms and processes at work in the escalating struggles of the Arab Spring.

> *First*, behind vague words such as rioting, marauding, and unrest, we can detect innovation by members of different groups. At first, the prevailing claim-making repertoire resembled contemporary Western social movement campaigns for dignity and against inequality. But with the governments of the region responding with repression, and lethal weapons widely available, organized political actors regularly deployed them, and set up a logic of radicalization (Alimi et al. 2015);
> *Second*, we witness the operation of a fluctuating political opportunity structure with diffusion to different states in the region and multiple independent centers of power within the territories of the North African and Middle Eastern states;
> *Third*, there was a process of actor constitution, as established political actors proved incapable of managing the transition and solidarity grew out of contention;
> *Fourth*, there was an availability of influential allies and supporters (both inside and outside the country) for challengers and defection from within the regimes;
> *Fifth*, there were day-to-day changes in all these regards.

Together, these circumstances amounted to a volatile, open political opportunity structure. They offered huge incentives and opportunities for mobilization on the part of the regions' challengers but they also offered opportunities for struggling opposition parties and to defecting elements within the tottering regimes of the Middle East. At a dizzying pace, political actors mobilized and demobilized by means of such mechanisms as diffusion and brokerage. External actors such as the United Nations and the United States intervened in those processes by certifying some of the domestic actors and decertifying others. Us-them boundary activation occurred repeatedly as Muslims and non-Muslims coalesced against repressive governments, producing temporary unity within normally fragmented populations, unity that came apart as one group or the other took power. Through combinations of brokerage and diffusion, actors on both sides created new forms of coordination—for example, the now-legendary encampments in Tahrir Square in Cairo, but also, the terrible destruction wreaked on the Syrian population caught between the government of Bashar al-Assad and the rebels who tried to depose him. Finally, polarization between the two sides scooped out the middle ground between them over and over, snapping the fragile strands of collaboration that had begun to form in the heady atmosphere of 2011.

Behind these processes, notice the signs that we are dealing with low-capacity undemocratic regimes. More so than any other set of conflicts we have looked at with any care so far, most of the Middle East's regimes involved military organizations that formed the core of central states but did not rule consistently and effectively across the national territory. The only regimes that consistently held their ground against the rising tide of contention were those—like Saudi Arabia, the Gulf States, Jordan, and Morocco—that were ruled by traditional monarchies. Except for Tunisia, and briefly in Egypt, contentious politics did not resemble the social movement politics we have seen in Western Europe and the United States.

Notice too that the Arab Spring was a study in radicalization: it began with a low-level conflict between corrupt police and a street vendor and escalated as first neighbors, then student and reform groups, took up his cause, and shifted its scale to the national—and then to the transnational level. The Arab Spring culminated in civil strife across the region, but it wasn't born that way: it escalated into organized civil strife through the interaction between and among protesters, the citizens groups that supported them, vacillating governments, and repressive militaries (Aronson et al. 2014).

Notice, finally, that although the map in figure 6.5 gives different pathways distinct labels, the reality was much more mixed. Take the case of

Syria, where peaceful protest gave way to civil war, passing through conflicts among Alawites, Christians, and Sunnis, Arabs, and Kurds, and ultimately the resurgence of Islamist insurgency in the form of the self-declared Islamic State that—at this writing—controls important parts of the north of the country as well as parts of Iraq and is attempting to spread its influence across the same region that engendered the Arab Spring. Despite the way scholars have divided them up, there are no solid lines separating "civil wars," "ethnic or religious strife," or "revolutions." Each of these lethal forms developed out of less lethal forms—like the social movements we saw in the last chapter; each one grew through the process of radicalization that we saw in Italy, with the difference that once contention crosses a line into armed insurgency, challengers come to think of themselves as warriors and seldom wish to turn back until stalemate or defeat stares them in the face (Aronson et al. 2014).

CONCLUSION

Let us pause briefly to summarize the broad range of cases and mechanisms we have seen in this chapter. First, we saw that a number of the same mechanisms appeared in contentious episodes of increasing scope and significance. Minor episodes such as the occupation of the church of Saint-Nizier, major cycles such as the Italian protest wave, civil war insurgencies as in Central America, and continental cataclysms such as the conflicts in the Middle East and North Africa resembled each other in many ways. In all four, people used preexisting networks and identities, developed new ones to express their claims, build solidarities, and challenge opponents. In all four episodes, we saw diffusion, brokerage, and new coordination. In all of them demobilization combined escalation, institutionalization, defection, disillusion, and repression.

Do not mistake our message: These were very different contentious phenomena. Elites responded very differently to the occupation of a church in Lyons, the cycle of student and worker protests in Italy, rural insurgencies in Guatemala and El Salvador, and the tide of contention in the Middle East and North Africa. The nature of the claims people were making varied enormously, from the demand to be left alone by Lyons sex workers, to the much broader but still negotiable claims of most students and workers in Italy, to the demand for land and regime change in Central America, to the call for the overthrow of authoritarian regimes in North Africa and the Middle East. There were also great differences in the degree and nature of repression, from the simple ejection of a group of women from a church in Lyons to the selective repression of extemist groups in

Italy, to the wholesale repression of the movement sector in El Salvador, to the genocidal campaign of the Syrian regime of Bashar al-Assad in Syria.

In all four cases, however, people perceived and seized opportunities, identified and framed claims, mobilized consensus, formed coalitions, and adopted new and innovative forms of collective action. In all four, elites responded with different combinations of repression and facilitation. If these episodes ended differently—failure for the Lyonnais prostitutes, reintegration for Italian students and workers, civil wars in Central America, and the collapse of the regimes of Egypt, Libya, and Tunisia and the civil wars in Syria, Libya, and Yemen—that was because their claims-making interacted with very different regimes.

Note the implications of our discovery. It means that regularities in trajectories lie elsewhere than in standard sequences, whether scripted episodes, protest cycles, or otherwise. Regularities lie in the mechanisms that bring in new actors, eliminate old ones, transform alliances, and shift the strategies of critical actors. By identifying which mechanisms and processes put an episode of contention in motion and where they take it, we can better understand why some episodes are brief, while others are protracted and lead to the implosion of some regimes and the creation of new ones.

A key combination of mechanisms in our cases was the process we called *upward scale shift*. It largely determined the relative capacity of the actors to create broader social movements out of initial episodes of contention. Even simple episodes sometimes spread widely. Recall how prostitutes in other French cities soon copied the occupation of the Saint-Nizier church; how, in Italy, contention diffused from a few major universities and large factories to provincial universities and high schools as well as to smaller firms throughout the economy; how it spread in El Salvador from land claims and moderate urban sector reforms in a few areas to a national insurgency; how it shifted from an isolated self-immolation in Tunisia to the overthrow of entire regimes and the changing configuration of power in the entire Middle East.

Not all contentious episodes give rise to such sequences of mechanisms, and few of those that do so endure beyond the end of the cycle. The ones that are most likely to survive draw on preexisting social networks or create self-sustaining organizations. Those networks and organizations sustain their claims and recruit new supporters. When these claims involve sustained campaigns, concerted displays of identity, and such means as demonstrations and public meetings, they become powerful social movements. Chapter 7 looks closely and directly at two such movements: Polish Solidarity and the American women's movement.

NOTES

1. The use of the figure of 1,000 battle deaths is entirely arbitrary, but since it has been adopted by the majority of scholars of civil war, we adopt it conventionally.
2. Note that the record of organized violence that Brockett traced cuts off in 1980, because the conditions of civil war in that decade made it impossible to collect even approximate data for that period.

PART FOUR

Movement and Lethal Politics

During the great strike led by Solidarity at the Lenin Shipyard in Gdánsk, Poland (August 1980), a priest blesses one of the strikers. (Photo by Keystone/Getty Images).

CHAPTER 7
Social Movements

Not all episodes of contention constitute social movements, and not all movements endure. Remember the definition of the *social movement* from chapter 1: a sustained campaign of claim making, using repeated performances that advertise the claim, based on organizations, networks, traditions, and solidarities that sustain these activities. The first episode we examine in this chapter—Poland in 1956—shows that contention can be widespread and threatening to its regime but fail to survive repression and disorganization. The second episode—Poland's Solidarity in 1980—provides a key by introducing the crucial distinction between social movement bases and social movement campaigns. The shape of institutions and regimes always affects movements. Our third episode shows how the American women's movement interacted with American institutions. We close the chapter with observations on what happens to social movements after their major campaigns end.

POLAND'S 1956

The year 1956 was a bad one for the Soviet empire that had run East-Central Europe since the end of World War II. In 1953, Soviet leader Josef Stalin died. The disappearance of the longtime dictator of the USSR left a void that was filled by an unstable "troika" of Communist Party bosses. Nikita Khrushchev was one of them. When Khrushchev emerged at the top of the heap, he tried to consolidate his power by attacking Stalinism. In a dramatic "secret speech" to the delegates of the Twentieth Communist Party Congress, Khrushchev enumerated Stalin's crimes. To underscore how different his own rule would be, Khrushchev called for more plural-ism within the party and the Soviet bloc.

Announcing Stalin's crimes at a meeting attended by non-Soviet Com-munist elites was actually a strategy of upward scale shift. If it percolated through the international Communist movement, it would be harder for Khrushchev's Stalinist enemies in the USSR to suppress. Member parties' reactions ranged widely. They ran from rejection in China and uneasy quiet in France, to the embrace of pluralism in Italy, and to an outright revolt in Hungary. More than that, the speech divided many Communist parties internally. That helped to open new and wider opportunities for dissent among the weak and divided oppositions in East-Central Europe, just as it threatened the authoritarian traditions of the ruling parties of these countries.

This combination of opportunity and threat promoted explosions of contentious episodes across the Soviet bloc's restive populations. The tragic Hungarian revolution of 1956 attracted the most attention in the West. Hungary was the most "liberal" Communist state in Eastern Europe, and its reform Communists used Khrushchev's secret speech as an oppor-tunity to move gingerly toward a more pluralistic system of government. Even this action was too much for the Soviet Union, which brought tanks into the center of Budapest and smothered the sparks of reform.

Khrushchev's secret speech exacerbated existing internal conflicts between reformers and Stalinists in the Polish Communist Party, the PZPR. Disunity deepened when the relatively liberal Warsaw Party Committee circulated the speech both in Poland and in the West (Osa 2003b: 29). With Stalinists in the leadership thrown off balance, re-formers seized the advantage to increase the powers of parliament, re-place Stalinist officials, and rehabilitate reform Communist Wladislaw Gomulka. Gomulka soon emerged as party secretary. Divisions within the Bloc and the PZPR led to an opening for dissident groups—a classi-cal case of the opening of political opportunities. "In short," concludes Maryjane Osa (2003b), "de-Stalinization in Poland created an opening for political mobilization" (29–30).

Contention broke out locally in June. A group of workers from the Cygielski factory in Poznan sent a delegation to Warsaw to complain about their working conditions. When the delegation received a runaround in Warsaw and police detained them on their return, angry coworkers organ-ized a march to Poznan's city center. As other workers, students, and local citizens joined them, clashes with authorities ensued. When some of the demonstrators stole arms and stormed party headquarters, the party re-sponded by sending in the troops. But Poland's protest episode in 1956 had no more success than Hungary's revolt. Faced by repression and lacking a solid basis in society, it rose and fell rapidly. Though it raised the hopes of opponents of Communism in Poland and beyond, it lacked the bases for a sustained social movement.

Osa's study of oppositional networks in Poland supports this conclusion. In the period just before 1956, she could identify only three organizations with a significant presence in what she calls "the oppositional domain" (2003b: 45–47). Encouraged by Khrushchev's call for pluralism and by the divisions in the PZPR, Catholics, intellectuals, radical youth, and secular left-wing reformers in 1956 began to organize. The events of 1956–1957 expanded the domain of independent Polish groups fivefold, both increasing the number of active organizations and creating new links among them. But in the conditions of Cold War Poland, such a dense network of organizations couldn't endure, and demobilization soon set in.

In response to the flowering of oppositional groups in 1956–1957, Communist authorities employed a combination of repression and reform: repression of the Poznan workers and reform inside the party (Osa 2003b: 38–39). By 1960, Poles had returned to the state of surly but largely silent dissent characteristic of the pre-1956 period (Osa 2003b: 55). As one wit put it, "We pretend to work and they pretend to pay us." By the late 1950s, most of the organizations created in the wake of the 1956 events had disappeared from Osa's network maps. No sustained social movement formed in response to the events of 1956.

SOCIAL MOVEMENT BASES AND SOCIAL MOVEMENT CAMPAIGNS

Why begin a chapter on social movements by recalling a protest wave that failed to create a sustained movement? The story of Poland's response to Khrushchev's "secret speech" tells us a number of things.

First, it shows that in authoritarian regimes, social movements are hard to construct, even when contention is widespread. This would change as the regime weakened and new bases for contention appeared.

It also shows how, even in authoritarian regimes, political opportunities grow out of the interaction between contentious and institutional politics. Conflicts and reforms within the ruling party triggered both contention and new forms of organization, which in turn led to grudging reform within the regime and repression against its enemies.

Third, despite its particular properties, Poland in 1956 demonstrates many of the mechanisms of mobilization and demobilization we saw working in chapter 5: response to the opening of opportunities, innovation with different performances, radicalization in the course of the mobilization, and the repression of challengers. But this combination of mechanisms was not sufficient to produce a social movement.

Why not? In this chapter, we return to a distinction introduced in chapter 1 that will help us to understand the dynamics of social movements both in Poland and wherever they occur: the distinction between a social movement base and a social movement campaign.

- A *social movement base* consists of movement organizations, networks, participants, and the accumulated cultural artifacts, memories, and traditions that contribute to social movement campaigns.
- A *social movement campaign* is a sustained challenge to power holders, in the name of a population living under the jurisdiction of those power holders, by means of concerted public displays of worthiness, unity, numbers, and commitment, using such means as public meetings, demonstrations, petitions, and press releases.
- Poland in 1956 revealed a courageous campaign against state socialism, but there was very little basis on which to construct an enduring social movement.

Some scholars use the term *social movement* to cover most or all of the overlap between contention and collective action, whether it happens in politics or some other arena. In popular usage, it often describes all major changes in society and culture, including scientific, intellectual, and cultural movements (Frickel and Gross 2005). But for purposes of explanation, expansion of the term *social movements* to embrace most or all of contentious politics has three serious drawbacks.

First, such broad definitions make systematic comparison across types of contention difficult. In order to describe and explain contentious politics adequately, we need to identify the special properties of revolutions, military coups, peasant revolts, industrial conflict, and social movements before discovering what they have in common.

Second, so broad a definition makes it difficult to examine transitions between different forms of contention. The conditions that lead an isolated protest to become a social movement are impossible to determine if we raise the umbrella label "social movement" over both. Conversely, we can only understand the failure of contentious episodes like the prostitutes' protest we saw in the last chapter or the failure of the 1956 events in Poland to generate a sustained movement if we begin with clear boundaries around the concept of movements.

Third, such a broad definition obscures the difference between the bases on which contentious politics builds and the campaigns that launch those politics. While there is a general correlation between the existence of social movement bases and the strength and duration of a campaign, the transition from bases to campaigns is not automatic. It requires the triggering of the sorts of mechanisms and processes we have been presenting in this book.

Remember the British antislavery campaign with which the book began? That campaign built on bases ranging from reformist religious groups—especially the Quakers—to the local newspapers that popularized the cause, to manufacturing towns like Manchester, to influential elites and members of Parliament. But the abolitionists' campaign depended on Clarkson's writing an essay on slavery, deciding to commit his life to its demise, and forging ties with the Quakers. It also depended on interactions among campaigners, their targets, and influential third parties.

While movement bases tell us when a social movement is possible, a movement campaign is claim making *in motion*. Our distinction between social movement bases and social movement campaigns helps us to sort out the organizations, networks, participants, and traditions that make up a social movement and constitute a movement campaign. It helps to understand why Poland's struggles of 1980, unlike those of 1956, produced a successful social movement.

FROM POZNAN TO SOLIDARITY

In the summer of 1980, a strike broke out at the Lenin shipyard in the Baltic port of Gdansk. Like previous outbreaks, it began over largely economic issues. Like other episodes, it escalated to a conflict over the right of the workers to form an independent union (Laba 1991). It also triggered the familiar combination of repression and compromise that Polish authorities had used successfully since 1956 to stalemate, divide, and repress the workers. But, unlike these largely local events, it spread across the country rapidly, paralyzed the government temporarily, led to the recognition of a free trade union, and, ultimately, brought an end to state socialism in East-Central Europe.

The Solidarity strike of 1980 differed from previous Polish episodes of contention in four main ways. First, it enjoyed the certification of the country's most authoritative institution, the Catholic Church. The strike's leaders built an explicit linkage between Poland's national/Catholic heritage and the material demands of workers. Not only had the Polish pope, John Paul II, recently visited the country, but the organizers self-consciously merged Catholic symbols with claims for workers' rights (Kubik 1994).

Second, rapid diffusion moved claim making outward from Gdansk, and a shift in scale upward to the national level occurred. The strike at the Lenin shipyard spread not only to other factories along the Baltic coast but also to industrial centers around the country and into Poland's vast peasant population. In fact, when the shipyard workers voted to accept a management proposal, delegates on the interfactory committee from outside the factory convinced them to hold fast. The rapidity of diffusion and the organization of a solidarity base around the strike center in Gdansk rapidly lifted the scale of the conflict into a national struggle.

Third, repression was more contained in 1980 than in 1956. Polish authorities offered the usual compromises and employed standard divide-and-conquer tactics. But, much to the frustration of Poland's "fraternal" allies in the Soviet Union, their Polish allies applied only limited repression. This happened in part because the strike paralyzed many different parts of Polish society at once—including parts of the state apparatus—but also because of Poland's growing ties with Western bankers. The government feared that sending tanks in to suppress the strikers would lead to the government's loss of credits from the West.

Fourth, more than anything, Solidarity's success resulted from expansion of the oppositional domain—its social movement base—in the years after 1956. Since that episode, the oppositional domain had become denser, more diverse, and more centralized—with a few key "nodes" at the heart of a broader map of independent groups. These groups did not start the Gdansk strike or spread the strike to other industrial centers. Many of them, under the rubric of "building civil society," explicitly denied the desire to attack the state (Ost 1990), which helped to protect them from repression. But in 1980, they were ready to swing into action in response to the strike, diffusing it, certifying it, and raising its scale to the national level. Figure 7.1, which reproduces Osa's (2003a) findings, maps the extensive oppositional bases in Poland at the time of the Solidarity strike in 1980.

Do not attempt to memorize the groups in figure 7.1. Use the figure to see how dense the number of Polish oppositional groups and their connections had become by 1980, even in the stifling atmosphere of an authoritarian polity. Osa's corresponding map from 1956, not shown here, displays much less density with many fewer connections. Her 1980 map reveals that when Solidarity emerged on the scene in 1980, it could connect to a dense *social base* of groups and organizations.

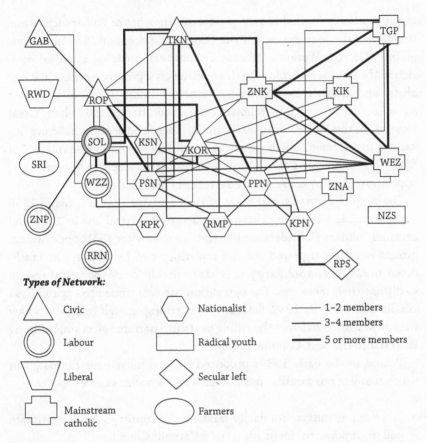

Types of Network:

△ Civic	⬡ Nationalist	—— 1–2 members
◎ Labour	▢ Radical youth	—— 3–4 members
⏢ Liberal	◇ Secular left	▬▬ 5 or more members
✚ Mainstream catholic	⬭ Farmers	

Figure 7.1:
Oppositional Networks in Poland, 1980
Source: Osa (2003a: 99).

Since the 1970s, many social scientists have recognized the importance of social networks in triggering collective action (Diani 1995, 2015; Diani and McAdam 2003). In settings as diverse as the 1848 revolution in Paris (Gould 1995), Republican and Communist China (Perry 1993; Zhao 1998), the Italian environmental movement (Diani 1995), post-1960s America (McAdam 1988, 1999), and the transnational climate change network (Hadden 2015: 201), networks have been shown to be the crucial building blocks of social movements. If the Solidarity strike in Gdansk triggered a national movement in 1980 and not in 1956, it was largely because, in the intervening years, a broad base of oppositional groups provided its leaders with a social movement base on which to build.

Note three specific factors that Osa's figure reveals. First, by 1980, workers' and farmers' groups belonged to the oppositional base. This gave the opposition a foothold in the productive trenches of Polish society and threatened the mainsprings of the Communist economy. Second, a civic group, KOR (the Worker's Defense Committee), occupied a central position in the base, with brokerage ties to other civic groups, workers, nationalists, and mainstream Catholics (Bernhard 1993). Third, in the years since 1956, and especially following the celebration of the Polish "Great Novena" in the 1960s (Osa 2003b: ch. 2), a dense base of Catholic organizations had formed, which we see in the cluster on the right-hand side of figure 7.1. In heavily Catholic Poland, these groups helped to certify the opposition in many conservative sectors of Polish society.

The deep and broad social bases of the campaign that erupted in 1980 became visible when the government declared martial law in 1981 and arrested Solidarity's leaders. Unlike the situation after 1956, oppositional groups went underground but did not disappear. Even after the crackdown, underground Solidarity activists were able to use the postal system to diffuse their messages. The opposition base continued to expand (Osa 2003b: 163–165). By 1989, Solidarity was strong enough to mount a new wave of strikes and defeat the ruling party in a national election, bringing Poland into the post-Communist age.

Poland in the early 1980s produced a social movement campaign in which many of our familiar mechanisms and processes came together:

- *Social appropriation*: Solidarity built on the country's most legitimate and most powerful institution—the Catholic Church.
- The organizers *certified* their campaign through identification with Catholic symbols and with the memory of the "martyrdom" of victims of past episodes of contention.
- Their movement *diffused and shifted upward in scale* as other organizations that had grown up after the 1956–1957 defeat took up a local conflict on the Baltic coast.

But these mechanisms appeared in many episodes of contention examined earlier that did not qualify as social movements. What made Polish Solidarity's a *social movement campaign*? Let us see how such campaigns work. The social movement is a particular historical form of contentious politics. As it developed in the West after about 1750, movements emerged from an innovative, consequential synthesis of three elements: campaigns, forms of association and action, and public self-representations. Before we turn to an important contemporary exemplar of that form— the new American women's movement—let us specify what these terms mean and illustrate them from the case of Polish Solidarity.

MOVEMENT CAMPAIGNS

A *campaign* is a sustained, organized public effort making collective claims on targeted authorities. Unlike a one-time petition, declaration, or mass meeting, a *campaign* extends beyond any single event—although social movements often include petitions, declarations, and mass meetings. A campaign always links at least three parties: a group of self-designated claimants, some object(s) of claims, and a public of some kind. The claims may target governmental officials, but the "authorities" in question can also include owners of property, religious functionaries, and others whose actions (or failures to act) significantly affect the welfare of many people.

Even if a few zealots commit themselves to the movement night and day, furthermore, the bulk of participants move back and forth between public claim making and other activities, including the day-to-day organizing that sustains a campaign. The attempt on the part of Solidarity to gain the right to an independent union for Polish workers was a campaign, one that centered on the strike committee in Gdansk but coordinated with strikes throughout the country, attempted to influence public opinion on the part of KOR and other groups, and employed the vast cultural force of the Catholic Church. We call that process *social appropriation*.

PUBLIC SELF-REPRESENTATION

Movement participants make concerted public representations of their worthiness, unity, numbers, and commitment on the part of themselves and/or their constituencies. For example:

- *Worthiness*: sober demeanor; neat clothing; presence of clergy, dignitaries, mothers with children or, alternatively, signs of militancy such as wearing army uniforms or carrying the tools of a trade
- *Unity*: matching badges, headbands, banners, or costumes; marching in ranks; singing and chanting; symbols of solidarity such as a signature color
- *Numbers*: head counts, signatures on petitions, messages from constituents, filling the streets
- *Commitment*: braving bad weather; visible participation by the old and people with disabilities; resistance to repression; ostentatious sacrifice, subscription, and/or benefaction

The most dramatic element in the self-representation of the Solidarity strikers was their identification with the "martyred workers" of previous suppressed strikes. The very symbol of Solidarity—a silhouetted group of people supporting one another and carrying a banner—reflected workers' unitary commitment and their ties to the general population. Certification by association with Catholic faith was also a key factor. No sooner had the occupation of the factory begun than the local bishop negotiated an agreement with the local party secretary: Priests could say mass outside the factory gate and symbols of Christian faith went on display where the media could record them.

ASSOCIATIONAL AND ACTION REPERTOIRES

Movements employ combinations from among the following forms of political action: creation of special-purpose associations and coalitions; public meetings; solemn processions; vigils; rallies; demonstrations; petition drives; statements to and in public media; pamphleteering. We call the variable ensemble of performances the *social movement repertoire*.

The social movement repertoire draws from the general repertoire of contention. But it differs from most forms of collective action we encountered earlier in the *modularity* of its performances: employment of similar forms of collective action by a wide variety of social actors around very different goals against similar actors. As movements developed around a wide range of claims, they elaborated forms of action that could be adopted and adapted in a variety of settings against a wide range of objects: the strike against any kind of employer; the petition on behalf of a wide variety of claims; the street march and demonstration (Favre 1990; Fillieule 1997; Tartakowsky 1998).

Solidarity activists employed traditional tools of working-class insurgency such as strikes and factory occupations. But they also mounted marches, demonstrations, religious processions, and a host of supportive activities such as the handing of food into the factory by family members and friends. The strike committee's meetings with party officials and management around a round table in the Lenin works accomplished two things: It achieved certification of the union and symbolized the equal status of union, management, and state actors. Though separated by eight years, the talks of 1980 prefigured the politically important "round table" negotiations of 1988–1989, which brought Solidarity into power. The form of the round table then spread across East-Central

Europe. One by one, Communist parties negotiated the end of their regimes in 1989 using the modular form of the round table employed by the Polish workers nine years earlier.

From Movements to Parties

Campaigns, public self-representations, and associational and action repertoires vary enormously from one movement to another, but movements connect those properties in logical ways. Consider the American antislavery movement. Beginning in the 1830s abolitionists launched a long and varied campaign against both slaveholders and public authorities. They used forms of association and public action that drew heavily on the evangelical revival of the previous decade, presenting their movement as righteous, unified, numerous, and stalwart (Young 2006). That movement interacted by fits and starts with institutional politics. By the 1850s, many with abolitionist leanings had joined the mainstream parties and were present in Congress. Then one branch converged with the "free soil" movement. Together with opportunity-seeking politicians from the old Whig Party and breakaway Democrats, that branch formed the Republican Party. The party elected a little-known reformer, Abraham Lincoln, as president in 1860.

We see a similar transformation of a movement into a party in Poland. As martial law wore on in the course of the 1980s, Solidarity leaders (many of them still in prison) began to reshape their roles from the representatives of industrial workers into political party leaders. When, in 1989, the regime was forced to call meaningful elections, Solidarity emerged with a solid majority in both houses of parliament. That transformation brought the movement into intimate connections with institutions.

Poland's Solidarity was a social movement that produced a change from an authoritarian regime to a democratizing one. The regime change would ultimately have disintegrating effects on the movement, dividing its activists among trade unionists and politicians. Within the latter group, furthermore, it drove a wedge between economic liberals and Catholic populists. New movements would eventually take their place, illustrating the symbiotic relationship between democracy and the form of the social movement. The next section turns to the "new" American women's movement, to examine interactions among social movement bases, political institutions, and contentious politics in a democratic regime.

THE NEW AMERICAN WOMEN'S MOVEMENT

Many changes took place in the role of women in American society in the half-century after World War II, but not all were part of "the women's movement" as we have defined it. For example:

- Changes in employment brought more women into the workforce.
- Public attitudes regarding the status of women evolved.
- Legislatures passed laws favorable to women—in part because members of Congress wanted women's votes.
- Philosophies and schools of feminism developed that became part of the base of that movement.
- A base of women's social movement organizations developed around new publications, new forms of friendship relations—for example, "consciousness-raising" groups—and institutional innovations like women's studies programs in colleges and universities.

Our concept of social movements recognizes these changes and their relevance to the formation of the new women's movement. But, as in the Polish case we have just examined, we must distinguish changes in the bases of women's political action from the important movement campaigns that developed in the late 1960s and beyond. While an early women's movement had emerged in the fight for women's rights (Banaszak 1996), it remained largely dormant during most of the interwar and early postwar years (Rupp and Taylor 1987). The 1960s added a new base to women's resources and opportunities. That base came in part through "spillover" of activists from the civil rights movement (Evans 1980; McAdam 1988; Meyer and Whittier 1994) and in part from autonomous social and political sources. Of course, the new movement drew on both liberal and radical feminist ideas, on the increased presence of women in the workforce, and on opportunities in American political institutions. These were part of its movement base. But it went into motion through a series of campaigns that placed it in contentious interaction with other groups, with the government, and against a countermovement that it actually helped to trigger—the antiabortion movement.

The new American women's movement produced innovative solutions to all three aspects of our sketch of social movements: campaigns, public representations, and claim-making repertoires. It consisted of campaigns such as the Equal Rights Amendment (ERA) campaign, which occupied the energies of vast numbers of women activists during the 1970s and early 1980s (Costain 1992: ch. 4; Mansbridge 1986). Parts of the movement sought a new self-representation through changes in women's dress, language, manners, and collective activities. Although only representative of one branch of the movement, consciousness-raising was a creative tool for the development of a new representation of women. Such grassroots activities fostered "sisterhood," women who had previously been demure and retiring learned to speak up for themselves, and new frames of meaning emerged.

In both its associational and action repertoire, the movement innovated equally. Although national groups such as the National Organization for Women (NOW) adopted the increasingly common form of the public interest group, groups such as the Women's International Terrorist Conspiracy from Hell (WITCH) expanded women's action repertoire into theatrical actions, while feminists within professions such as the church and the military quietly organized to advance the status of women within their institutions (Katzenstein 1998). Not all of these innovations lasted into the new century. Some merged with general changes in the repertoire that arose in the protest cycle of the 1960s and declined with the end of that cycle. Others (e.g., the caricatured image of "bra-burning" feminists) never gained acceptance. In fact, they were appropriated by an antifeminist countermovement to roll back feminist gains (Meyer and Staggenborg 1996).

One of the movement's bitter ironies was that its gains helped to crystallize a religious countermovement holding a traditionalist view of women's role. This contributed to the defeat of the ERA, to a powerful grassroots movement against abortion (McCarthy 1987), and to the triumph of a raw form of conservatism in the Reagan and George W. Bush administrations (McAdam and Kloos 2014). Ultimately, these countermoves led to a retrenchment of state programs favoring women, children, and the poor. They rolled back many of the movement's gains (Banaszak, Beckwith, and Rucht 2003).

Like Polish Solidarity, the rise of the new American women's movement offers a prime example of a sustained challenge to power holders in the name of a population living under the jurisdiction of those power holders by means of concerted public displays of that population's worthiness, unity, numbers, and commitment, a social movement. But unlike Polish Solidarity—which had to struggle against instituted power for most of its early history—the new American women's movement developed through an intimate interaction with institutions.

MOVEMENTS AND INSTITUTIONS

Remember from chapter 3 what we mean by *institutions*: Within any particular regime, they are established, organized, widely recognized routines, connections, and forms of organization employed repeatedly in producing collective action. Some (e.g., the armed forces) are fairly insulated from contentious politics; others (e.g., political parties and elections) are highly sensitive to such politics; while still others (e.g., legislatures, courts, and executives) are both contention-shaping and contention-responding institutions.

Our way of thinking about social movements denies any rigid boundary between institutionalized and noninstitutionalized politics (Tarrow 2012). We see contentious politics embracing both institutions and social movements. Social movement bases develop both within and outside institutions. Movement campaigns act within, against, and outside institutions. They can contribute to the rise of new institutions—for example, the American women's movement fostered the rise of a new kind of women's magazine—and can bolster the role of institutions sympathetic to the movement's claims—like the growing legitimation of the "liberal" Warren Supreme Court among African Americans after the *Brown* decision. What is more, different institutions harbor, oppose, or stimulate the formation of social movement campaigns.

Boundaries between institutionalized and noninstitutionalized politics are hard to draw with precision. Take the movement coalition that formed around defeating President Reagan's nuclear arms policy in the 1980s. It bridged the space between institutional groups and protesters outside institutions. Newly formed movement organizations such as the Nuclear Weapons Freeze Clearinghouse (NWFC) combined with established peace organizations, on the one hand, and with congressional Democrats, on the other, to form a coalition that persuaded the government to preempt the movement by starting an arms control process (Meyer 1990). Only by looking at both sides of the formal boundary between institutional and noninstitutional politics and at their interactions can we understand the dynamics of episodes of contentious politics.

Of course, much of the work that political institutions do lies outside the boundaries of contentious politics. Executives sign laws, preside at openings, greet foreign dignitaries, and turn on the Christmas tree lights on the lawn of the White House. Legislators declare days of commemoration, make speeches aimed only at pleasing local constituents, and greet visiting Boy Scout troops. Much of what they do is uncontentious and routine.

Social movement activists engage in contentious activities only part of the time. To build their bases, and before any action mobilization begins, movement organizations often engage in "consensus mobilization" (Klandermans 1988). To please their members, they organize

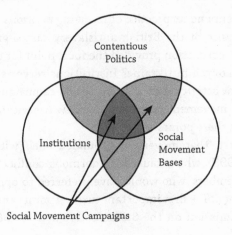

Figure 7.2:
Contentious Politics, Social Movement Campaigns, Social Movement Bases, and Institutions

festivals and ceremonials. To gain a broader following, they engage in educational activities. To broadcast who they are and the nature of their claims, they cultivate the media. Figure 7.2 portrays graphically the intersection of social movement campaigns, social movement bases, institutions, and contentious politics.

Do not regard figure 7.2 as the vehicle of our arguments about the dynamics of contention. See it instead as a road map to the interactions among our key terms. Any such vehicle would have to put these concepts into motion, asking questions such as these:

- When and how do social movement bases produce movement campaigns, what kinds of institutional frameworks offer them opportunities to do so, and which ones suppress their emergence?
- When and under what conditions do institutional actors produce or assist social movement campaigns, by reaction, transmutation, or fractionation?
- When and under what conditions do movement campaigns ignite broader forms of contentious politics, such as civil wars, nationalist episodes, or revolutions, that threaten institutions?
- When and under what conditions do movement campaigns create new institutions and new social movement bases?

From the beginning of social movement politics, political institutions provided opportunities for movement development, found ways to repress them, but also processed movement claims. Remember how the

British Parliament and its practice of receiving petitions served as a vehicle for the advance of the British antislavery campaign? And how the struggle against corruption provided the focal point for the overthrow of President Yanukovych in Ukraine? Institutions serve as an umbrella for social movement activity, a focal point for its campaigns, and the major source of social movement outcomes. The new American women's movement illustrates these points.

From the first, that movement grounded itself within institutions (Katzenstein 1998), which caused it enormous conflict from among its more radical members, who would have preferred to oppose institutions dominated by men. The first important turning point came with President Kennedy's Commission on the Status of Women in 1961 and with the

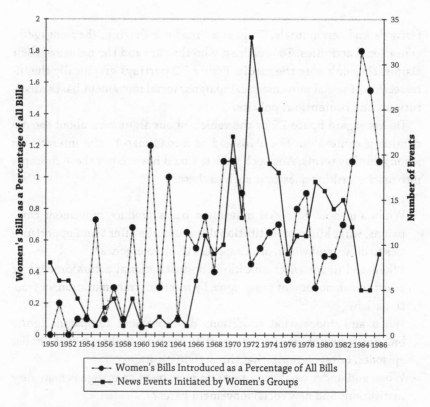

Figure 7.3:
News Events Initiated by Women's Groups and Women's Bills as Percentage of All Bills Introduced in the US Congress, 1950–1985
Source: Costain (1992: 108, 113).

inclusion of women's rights in the Civil Rights Act of 1964 (Beckwith 2003: 193). Then came executive orders that assigned the task of monitoring wage equality and discrimination in hiring to government agencies and a burst of legislative activity favoring women in the 1970s (Katzenstein 2003: 205–207). Figure 7.3 plots Anne Costain's (1992) time line of legislative enactments in her book *Inviting Women's Rebellion* alongside the activities of major women's organizations such as NOW. It illustrates the general co-occurrence of the new women's movement with congressional activity on behalf of women.

One reading of figure 7.3 would see in it evidence that Congress was responding to the pressures of the movement—a direct policy effect of a movement's campaigns. Two other readings are also possible: first, that Congress, or its majority, was responding with electoral motivations to changes in public opinion that were, in large part, independent of the women's movement; second, that members of Congress were ideologically but independently committed to the policy goals they advanced. We cannot, on the basis of the time lines in figure 7.3, decide among these three different readings. But the only partial parallels between NOW's efforts and Congress's legislation suggest that the movement's policy impact was at least indirect and at best partial.

MOVEMENT IMPACTS

Movement impacts never end with policy change alone. We can distinguish roughly among three kinds of impacts, all of them visible in American women's movements: (1) direct impacts of social movement campaigns on public policies, (2) effects of participation in claim-making campaigns on the lives of activists—and thus on culture, and (3) beyond individual campaigns, effects of involvement in the social movement base on political contention in general:

On Public Policy

As Costain's analysis suggests, the first category—direct effects of campaigns—is difficult to assess. Most scholars now believe that policy impacts are, at best, mediated by political contexts (Meyer, Jenness, and Ingram 2005), while others are even more cautious. Piven and Cloward (1977), focusing on four episodes of contentious politics in the 1930s and the 1960s, conclude that movements seldom succeed, and when they do, success is often followed by failure. Other movement scholars, including Paul Burstein and his collaborators, are even more pessimistic. Referring to a variety of evidence from the United States, they find that collective action on the part of social movement organizations is most often ineffective in influencing public policy (Burstein and Linton 2002; Burstein and Sausner 2005). Policy changes have a great impact on movements (Amenta 2006). For example, simple changes in the tax laws can deprive a movement group of its tax-exempt status. More broadly, the retrenchment of the American welfare state since the 1990s has created a more constrained opportunity structure for women (Banaszak et al. 2003). That in turn has created the need for women to rethink the mechanisms of worthiness, unity, numbers, and commitment that produced their gains in an earlier generation.

On the Lives of Activists

With respect to the second category—the effect of participation on the lives of activists—the impact of the women's movement appears to have been more certain. Nancy Whittier's study of radical women activists in Columbus, Ohio, shows that well outside public claim-making activity, involved women supported each other and kept each other committed. During the campaign lull of the Reagan years, one woman Whittier (1995) interviewed declared:

> Some of these people, I've known them for so long now that we can refer back to a certain event or series of events with just a word or two. It's that kind of communication you can have with someone you've known for a long time, so that we don't really discuss it, we know what we mean. And we get that kind of good feeling that you have with people that you've been through a lot with and you've known for so long. (112)

For her and for women like her, involvement in the movement base had become a defining feature of day-to-day life.

On Future Contentious Politics

With respect to the third category—movements' effects on future patterns of political contention—the balance sheet for the American women's movement is truly mixed. On the one hand, women's movement support was critical in producing a distinguished cadre of women political leaders such as Senator Hillary Rodham Clinton, Senator Barbara Boxer, and Nancy Pelosi, leader of the Democratic Party in the House of Representatives between 2012 and 2014. On the other hand, the successes of such "threatening" women as Clinton and the support of the women's movement for such controversial issues as abortion have helped to polarize American politics and create a countermovement. We still occasionally read journalists commenting on how Hillary Clinton looks in a pantsuit and how "shrill" Nancy Pelosi sounds. This countermovement first grouped around the opposition to the ERA, which was defeated in the 1980s (Mansbridge 1986), and it continues to attack the Supreme Court's legalization of abortion in the case of *Roe v. Wade*. From the time when that decision came down, antiabortion forces have mustered a powerful coalition that has used the state legislatures to whittle away a woman's right to choose.

AFTER MOBILIZATION

What happens to movement bases after movement campaigns subside? Building on his research on "new" social movements such as the American women's movement (Kriesi et al. 1995), Hanspeter Kriesi has constructed a typology of movement dynamics that can help us to answer this question. Figure 7.4 reproduces his typology. All four of the groups that Kriesi and his collaborators studied emerged from the 1968 period; all relied on loose bases of activists rather than on solid bureaucratic bases; all focused their activities around precise claims rather than on general ideologies. All followed a cyclical trajectory like the one we traced in Italy in chapter 5 (Koopmans 2004; Kriesi et al. 1995). Yet despite their similarities in origins, structure, issue focus, and trajectory, these social movement organizations (SMOs) ended their active period of contention in very different ways.

Starting out from the ideal type of SMO—a formal organization that mobilizes its constituency for collective action with a political goal (Kriesi 1996: 153)—Kriesi deduces four processes of transformation.

First, he sees as one possibility the *institutionalization* of a movement organization, a process we encountered in Italy after the protest cycle of the 1960s (see chapter 5). This process combines formalization of an SMO's internal structure, moderation of its goals, adoption of a more conventional action repertoire, and integration into established systems of government. Figure 7.4 argues that institutionalization involves a shift from the direct participation of a movement's constituency to delegation to professional organizers. This resembles the familiar idea of the "iron

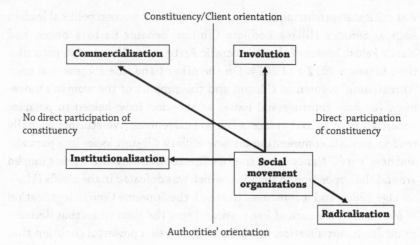

Figure 7.4:
Typology of Transformations in Goal Orientations and Action Repertoires of Social Movement Organizations
Source: Kriesi (1996: 157).

law of oligarchy" detected a century ago by Robert Michels (1962) and after the last cycle of American protest by Theodore Lowi (1971).

Second, Kriesi sees the possibility of *commercialization*, the transformation of a movement organization in the direction of a service organization. This pattern was typical of the autonomous firms and cooperatives that developed out of the new social movements of the 1970s in Europe, and it can also be seen in the United States in what happened to the consumer group Consumer's Research as it went from consumer advocacy to becoming a product-testing and product-endorsing firm (Rao 1998).

Third, Kriesi sees the possibility of *involution*: a path that leads to exclusive emphasis on social incentives. SMOs that experience involution become self-help groups, voluntary associations, or clubs. Many of the communes that developed out of the American 1960s experienced a process of involution from active participation in politics to the cultivation of personal and religious development (Kitts 2000).

Kriesi's fourth variant, *radicalization*, or "reinvigorated mobilization," we also saw in the escalation of collective violence in Italy after 1968, in the transformation of America's Students for a Democratic Society into the Weathermen and the splintering of the Weathermen afterwards into a more moderate and a more violent branch.

Kriesi's typology can serve as a rough guide to the changes in the American women's movement's base after the height of its campaigns in the 1960s and 1970s. In this largely "liberal" family of movement groups, institutionalization was the dominant process coming out of its phase of mobilization. Its major expression was the large number of public interest groups that grew out of the 1960s (Schlozman et al. 2010). Most of these, such as NOW and what started out as the National Association for the Repeal of Abortion Laws (now NARAL Pro-Choice America), became active in lobbying and educational work in Washington, leading to the formation of an array of public interest lobbies. Though their dedication to the women's movement remained strong, their tactics and interactions with others resembled those of conventional business and professional lobbies.

Commercialization occurred in American women's groups in the founding of new women's magazines like *Ms*. Some of them kept their feminist stands after the 1960s, while others—depending on ads from makeup and clothing companies—drifted into lifestyle preoccupations. Women's bookstores developed for a time but soon disappeared within the general expansion of book megastores. Services for women's health, such as Planned Parenthood, inherited some veterans of the new women's movement but could hardly be called "commercial."

We find evidence for involution in the development of women's self-help groups—for example, in the groups formed to counsel women on abortion and to help women who have been raped and those diagnosed with breast cancer. The breast cancer coalition in particular embodied both the new conception of gender that grew out of the new women's movement and an unwillingness to delegate authority to the (mainly male) medical hierarchy (Parthasarathy 2003).

Radicalization shook the movement in the internal struggles that developed between competing philosophies of feminism. Conflict over the admission of lesbians to the ranks of the "straight" feminist community compounded the initial cleavage between liberal and Marxist feminists. Another axis of competition differentiated groups of women of color from mainstream white feminism (Roth 2004). But since the most radical groups were in the universities—where they had little effect on the lives of ordinary women—this development had less impact on the movement than its overwhelming institutionalization.

Scholars have sometimes seen movements inexorably turning into interest groups or disappearing into institutions. Kriesi's typology shows how periods of high mobilization give rise to a variety of forms of exit that keep a movement base alive during periods when campaigns are in abatement (Rupp and Taylor 1987). By joining self-help groups, working for women's service organizations, and paying dues to public interest groups, women activists from the 1960s and 1970s kept up their contacts with old

comrades, remained available for mobilization at times of stress or opportunity (e.g., when two new Supreme Court appointments threatened the
legal protection of a woman's right to choose an abortion in 2005), and
kept the flame of activism alive to fight another day. That day seemed to
be coming, as an increasingly conservative Republican Party, which gained
control of a majority of statehouses and states legislatures in 2010, worked
to narrow the scope of the Supreme Court's abortion decisions.

CONCLUSION

This chapter's main arguments summarize easily. First, we argued that
not all episodes of contentious politics are powered by social movements.
The 1956 events in Poland were contentious, at times violent, and, like
many of the episodes we have examined, responded to changes in political
opportunities. But they did not constitute a social movement, either in
our sense of the term or in comparison to what occurred in that country
in 1980.

In contrast, Solidarity, like many social movements, emerged from a
local episode of contention and, like many of the episodes we have examined in our book, grew through a process of brokerage, certification, diffusion, and scale shift. It qualifies as a social movement campaign because it
mobilized an until-then passive social movement base that had grown up
after 1956, drew on the certification of the Catholic church, and because it
developed the properties of worthiness, unity, numbers and commitment
that made it a powerful social and political force.

Similarly, in 1960s America, many changes of great interest to women
occurred: changes in labor force participation, presence of many more
women in colleges and universities, and increasing participation of women
in politics. Not all these changes belonged to or resulted from social movement campaigns. Changes in public opinion, vote-seeking members of
Congress, judges favoring equal rights, as well as determined women legislators, all affected American public politics. The distinction matters:
Only by singling out social movement campaigns can we detect relations
between them and other sources of change. Without the distinction, we
cannot easily examine transitions between movements and other forms
of contention or their responsibility for policy or cultural change.

Third, movements frequently challenge institutions. Both Solidarity
and the American women's movement did challenge their countries' institutions. But movements also work within institutions. They often dovetail
with parallel changes in institutional politics, as the women's movement

did in the 1970s and 1980s. Movements sometimes become institutional actors, as did Solidarity in 1989, when it forced the Polish regime to hold competitive elections, in which it triumphed. Their very success sometimes defeats them, as institutional logic takes over from the logic of contentious politics.

Movements frequently trigger the formation of countermovements. The American women's movement did so in the failed campaign for the ERA and in the struggle over abortion rights. So did the movement for same-sex marriage (Dorf and Tarrow 2013). The give and take of institutional politics often reflects a more civilized version of the struggle for supremacy between movements for change and countermovements that attempt to return to a more traditional society. That is why a symbiotic relationship exists between and social movements and democratic or democratizing politics: Democracy gives scope to the conventional and disruptive activities of social movements and their characteristic properties—broad, alliance-building and consensus-building—expand the range of democratic politics.

If social movements twin with democratic and democratizing politics, what about other forms of contention and other kinds of polities? If a symbiotic relationship prevails between democratic politics and social movements, do similarly symbiotic relations appear between these other forms and other types of polities? The next chapter turns to more violent forms of contentious politics and their relationship to the dynamics of undemocracy.

A young demonstrator is silhouetted against a burning building in Ferguson, Missouri after a grand jury has absolved the policeman who shot an unarmed teenager. (Photo by Jim Young/Reuters).

CHAPTER 8
Lethal Conflicts

Large-scale lethal conflicts occur most often in regimes with intermediate and low levels of governmental capacity, including the unstable intermediate cases that James Fearon and David Laitin (2003) call "anocracies" and that we have called "hybrid regimes." In this chapter, we move from chapter 7's relatively nonviolent world of social movements into regimes where government agents, popular challengers, and other competitors for political power regularly use armed force to back up their contentious claims. Three forms of lethal conflict provide our primary examples: *violent ethnic or religious conflicts*, which we will examine in the case of the collapse of Yugoslavia; *civil wars*, which we will turn to briefly in Sudan; and *revolutions*, which we will look at in the case of the Nicaraguan revolution.

WHAT IS AND ISN'T SPECIAL ABOUT LARGE-SCALE LETHAL CONFLICTS

In one sense, violence changes everything. Think of the effects of police shootings of young African American men in the United States in 2014 and in 2015; they triggered a widespread movement against police brutality in both the black community and among its allies. But the killing of two police officers in Brooklyn by a deranged man who claimed to be representing the interests of African Americans reversed the tide of public opinion and stilled the voices beginning to call for police reform. Both the violence by police and violence against the police were turning points in the relations among the police, the public, and the African American community. Violence clearly matters as a turning point in contentious politics.

And not only in contention itself, but also in its outcomes: When three French jihadists murdered seventeen people in Paris, the immediate result was a wave of largely peaceful demonstrations on behalf of free speech and against anti-Semitism. But within a few days of the massacres, the French state was tightening controls on the country's borders, arresting people for spoken support of the jihadists, and increasing surveillance in the minority North African community. Not only that: within weeks, the government and the European Commission were reconsidering previously rejected surveillance powers that resemble the practices of the American National Security Agency and the British GCHQ.[1]

But those incidents of violence were rare in patterns of contention that are largely peaceful, if often contentious, in the high-capacity constitutional democracies of North America and Western Europe. In this chapter, we enter a realm in which both governments and other political actors regularly use organized armed force as part of their claims making. Organized armed force ranges from local gangs to disciplined national armies, passing through militias, paramilitaries, private armies, and mercenaries. Sometimes organized armed force remains very one-sided, as when military units attack demonstrators or paramilitaries hunt down labor organizers. But it becomes especially lethal when at least two armed organizations battle each other.

Three features in particular make a difference: the high stakes of claim making, the problem of sustaining armed force, and the problem of what happens to fighters after they are initiated into armed conflict:

> *High stakes*: Killing, wounding, and damaging property affect the survival and the continuing conflict of participants well after the immediate struggle has ended. They break up families and communities, destroy available labor power, and eliminate means of production. With such high stakes, potential participants in violent encounters often flee or defect, unless they are likely to prevail or to get away unscathed. (Remember how quickly Ukrainian President Yanukovych's security detail fled as soon as it became clear that he might be defeated.) But once committed, they exit less easily so long as their organizations remain intact.
>
> *Sustaining armed groups*: Large-scale lethal conflicts include interstate wars, civil wars, revolutions, and genocides as well as a significant subset of struggles across religious, ethnic, linguistic, and regional boundaries. Unlike recruiting people for demonstrations or public meetings, creating and maintaining armed force requires extensive resources (Weinstein 2006). Some

military organizations (e.g., the militias formed by Guatemala's peasants) live on their own land, drawing support from their own communities. But they also need weapons, ammunition, information, means of communication, and personnel to replace those they lose (Viterna 2013). This is why civil strife continues longest in places where substantial deposits of oil, diamonds, or other minerals fuel their continuing conflicts.

Fighters who keep fighting after the battle: We saw in chapter 6 how veterans of the 1960s movements in Italy either moved into institutional politics or into clandestine armed groups. The problem is much greater after civil strife in undemocratic regimes because there is so little opportunity for fighters to move into institutional politics. Think of the separatist insurgency in Ukraine that we looked at in chapter 1: if the eastern region ever rejoins Ukraine, few Ukrainians will welcome them into political life. This is why so many of the participants who take up arms— even in a defensive mode—retain them and why postconflict countries experience repeated bouts of civil strife after the battle ends.

Occasionally mass killing occurs without much use of high-powered weapons. In the huge Rwandan genocide of 1994, for example, most killers slaughtered their victims with clubs, machetes, and other everyday tools. Even in that extreme case, however, the killing began with a well-trained presidential guard and militias organized by the ruling party (Dallaire 2003; Des Forges et al. 1999; Mamdani 2001). Reproducing a disciplined military organization depends on extensive brokerage and internal coordination. Religion and religious affiliations often serve to solder this internal coordination.

Those are the differences. Yet we will soon recognize familiar mechanisms and processes within large-scale lethal conflicts. To see them, we must avoid two fallacies that commonly blur people's understanding of such conflict. We can call them the motivational fallacy and the general law fallacy.

The *motivational fallacy* assumes that we would know the true, fundamental cause of large-scale violence if we could only read the perpetrators' minds: What do they want and feel? Are they animated by "greed"? By "grievances"? By threats? Or by Opportunities (Collier and Hoeffler 2003)? Even if we could read their minds, in fact, we would soon discover that participants in large-scale violence want and feel a great many different things at different times; that whether and how large-scale violence occurs depends on such nonmotivational matters as whether weapons, victims, and previous connections among perpetrators are available; and—most important—that large-scale violence is not a solo act but a complex interactive process.

The *general law fallacy* assumes that each type of large-scale lethal conflict has its own distinctive character and therefore follows its own general laws. Genocides, civil wars, revolutions, lethal ethnic or religious conflict, and violent nationalism, in this view, differ dramatically from each other, and each have their own distinctive necessary and sufficient conditions. On the contrary, as we will soon see, these various forms of contention overlap, mutate into each other, and result from and evolve through similar mechanisms and processes in different combinations, sequences, and initial conditions. Mechanisms and processes do, indeed, conform to general laws; brokerage, for example, operates in essentially the same way across a wide variety of political circumstances. But the laws do not cover whole classes of episodes such as revolutions or civil wars.

As we look at large-scale lethal contention, we revisit the political opportunity structures we met in chapter 3. Just as in the contained episodes of contention we saw in that chapter, in the former Yugoslavia, purveyors of ethnic violence responded to the institutional opportunities offered in their crumbling state. In lethal conflict as in contained contention, we will discover that existing political opportunity structure regularly interacts with established repertoires to shape what sorts and degrees of large-scale violence can occur within a given regime. We will also see the identity mechanisms and processes we found in chapter 5. We will find political actors declaring themselves to be revolutionaries, defenders of the true religion, or members of suppressed nations, through combinations of mobilization, brokerage, diffusion, certification, and boundary activation. We will recognize again that the overall character of a political regime (especially the capacity of its central government and its degree of democracy) strongly affects the location and the sheer possibility of large-scale lethal conflict.

Central states ordinarily control the largest single concentrations of coercive means within a given regime. Concentrated coercive means identify an organization as a state or something like a state. Because of that fact, large-scale lethal conflict inevitably involves states in one or both of two ways: as direct participants in the conflict and/or as third parties whose own power the conflict threatens. As we saw in chapter 3, high-capacity states reduce the threat by making it difficult for anyone to create rival concentrations of coercive means within their territories. That chapter also showed that low-capacity states face precisely the threat that some rival actor will build up a major concentration of coercive means and use it to topple existing rulers.

Struggles for control of concentrated coercive resources grew up with the emergence of centralized states thousands of years ago. But they only started to involve religious, ethnic, racial, and cultural identities more directly with the growth of nationalism in the era of the French Revolution. During the later eighteenth century, American revolutionaries overthrew British rule in the name of an American nation. French revolutionaries upended their old regime in the name of the French nation and then went out to conquer other people in the name of national liberation. The revolutionary era established top-down and bottom-up nationalism. From the top down, rulers say, "We run the state; therefore, we have the right to define the ethnicity, religion, race, and culture of our nation." From the bottom up, people who occupy distinctive religious, ethnic, racial, and cultural niches reply, "We are a separate nation; therefore, we have the right to a separate state." A great deal of the world's large-scale lethal conflict within regimes pits the two principles against each other.

In large-scale lethal conflict, two dramatic possibilities loom larger than in social movement campaigns: *regime split* and *transfer of power*. The first is that the entire regime will implode, so that at least two different clusters of political actors, including agents of government, have broken their alliances and routine interactions with the others. At the extreme, two rival governments or segments of government can contend with each other, as when a rebel army establishes control over a region far from a national capital and acts like a government within that region. This is, of course, a matter of degree. In the United States, for example, antitax rebels, libertarian militias, and Indian tribes sometimes declare their independence from the national government and draw a local following without much shaking the national regime. But the Civil War really did split the entire American polity along the lines of regional identities.

Small transfers of power occur all the time in every regime. One political actor gains greater access to government, another loses access, and a third forms a new alliance with the rising actor. Competitive elections always involve some possibility of a greater realignment. But fundamental transfers of power more often occur in the company of large-scale violence of the kinds this chapter analyzes. Again we are dealing with a matter of degree: from minor, incremental shifts in power to major, rapid overturns of the existing power structure. Figure 8.1 sketches the range of possibilities.

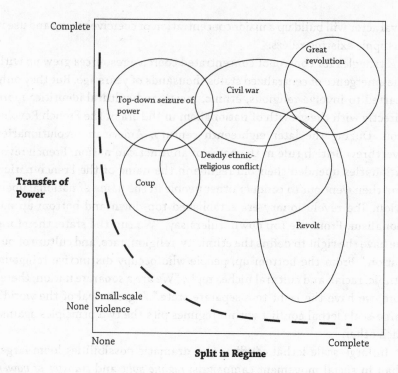

Figure 8.1:
Forms of Lethal Conflict

Figure 8.1 makes two valuable points. First, coups, top-down seizures of power, revolts, civil wars, lethal ethnic-religious conflicts, and great revolutions are all cousins; they combine varying extents of split and transfer. The diagram's overlapping circles stress that point. Second, a great revolution is simply the extreme case—a very extensive split followed by a major transfer of power. In fact, as the diagram suggests, a civil war or revolt can become a great revolution if it produces a fundamental transfer of power. Looking back at the "Arab Spring" and its violent aftermath, we can see all of these forms of lethal politics, sometimes in series and at other times combined.

We have already encountered violent conflicts in the disintegrating Soviet Union, as well as in certain phases of Italian contention and in the "Troubles" in Northern Ireland. We have also seen sustained lethal conflict in Charles Brockett's (2005) analysis of Guatemalan politics and in Paul Almeida's historical reconstructions in El Salvador (2003, 2007, 2008). In both countries, we saw both low-capacity undemocratic regimes and outright civil wars. Summing up his study of El Salvador and Guatemala and putting it in comparative perspective, Brockett comments that levels and sites of collective violence result from the interaction between popular mobilization and state repression:

> Repression generally succeeds in smothering contention if the prior level of mobilization was low. However, if state violence is increased after a protest cycle . . . is well underway, this repression is more likely to provoke even higher levels of challenge, both nonviolent and violent, rather than deter contention. This provocation is especially likely if state violence is inconsistent. But revolutionary toppling of thrones such as Nicaragua in 1979 are rare events. El Salvador and Guatemala are extreme examples of the more usual outcome: When regimes are willing to repress as necessary and have the capacity to do so, they usually succeed in eliminating popular contention as a threat to their regime and often to their own rule as well. (327)

DEADLY ETHNIC AND RELIGIOUS CONFLICT

Large-scale deadly ethnic and religious conflict usually concentrates in lower-capacity undemocratic regimes. It concentrates in those regimes for many of the same reasons: because whoever runs the relatively weak governments commonly distribute whatever benefits they gain from ruling to members of their own ethnic and religious networks, because the same governments cannot prevent excluded parties from amassing their own military means, and because informal systems of rule often build on existing relationships of kinship and religion. When violent contention arises in such regimes, it is not generally diffused at the national level but in enclaves in which minorities live who are excluded from the political process or from the benefits enjoyed by the majority (Cederman et al. 2013).

Large-scale ethnic and religious conflicts tend to endure—or repeat themselves—in such systems. It used to be thought that class cleavages were the most deep-seated and enduring sources of conflict. But the economic "pie" over when such conflicts are fought are capable of compromise—or at least of shifts in the balance of benefits. Not so ethnic or religious conflicts which are often seen by participants as a "zero-sum game." Think of the conflict between Armenians and Ajerbaijanis in Nagorny-Karabakh that we examined in chapter 5. Once triggered by the end of the Soviet regime in 1991, it has endured for more than two decades because each group sees the claims of the other as fundamentally illegitimate.

Ethnic and religious divisions create hybrid states in which even minor tensions escalate into conflicts between broad segments of society (see chapter 4). India, the world's largest democracy and a relatively high-capacity democracy at that, recurrently produces deadly confrontations between Hindus and Muslims. During the 1860s, the United States fought one of history's bloodiest civil wars over the place of African Americans in its polity, economy, and everyday social life. The days of regular white-on-black lynchings only disappeared during the later twentieth century. On invading Afghanistan and Iraq, furthermore, the United States found itself stirring up large-scale, deadly ethnic and religious conflict.

But if deadly ethnic and religious conflict concentrates in low-capacity undemocratic regimes, it is not because ethnic and religious divisions are absent from high-capacity states. High-capacity states simply manage to reduce the scale and armament of their domestic ethnic and religious conflicts. Democracies and near-democracies do so by channeling them into mainly nonviolent forms of contention, thus reducing the levels of death, damage, and destruction that result directly from contention. Their political opportunity structure and prevailing repertoires move them in the direction of social movements. Authoritarian and near-authoritarian states reduce the threat of contention between ethnic fractions by repression and the threat of repression, which makes the outbreak of ethnic or religious conflict all the more explosive when the hard hand of the state is relaxed. It is when high-capacity authoritarian states break apart that the "primary frameworks" of ethnic or religious identities come to the fore, displacing the more instrumental frameworks that are disappearing, as we see in the case of the breakup of Yugoslavia in the early 1990s (Johnston and Alimi 2012).

The Breakup of Yugoslavia

Most of the civil strife in the 1990s was the result of the collapse of the Soviet system early in the decade. Especially violent was the breakup of the former state of Yugoslavia and the wars that it triggered (Glenny 1994). This was only in part because of violence directed from the center—what Statis Kalyvas calls "Schmittian violence," quoting the German legal theorist Carl Schmitt—of which there was plenty; but also from violence from below, which he calls "Hobbesian violence," named after the great English political theorist, Thomas Hobbes (Kalyvas 2003; 2006). One reason violent politics becomes so lethal in the breakup of ethnically-divided states is because mass publics take advantage of divisive policies from the top and interact with them to produce violent conflicts even where there has been no conflict before. In other words, a process of "downward scale shift" diffuses violence into the relations of everyday life.

During the later 1990s, despite such sore spots as Chechnya and Kosovo, most postsocialist regimes settled into more stable, less violent forms of rule. But not in Yugoslavia. Why this difference? Journalistic accounts soon fastened on the "ancestral hatreds" among Muslims, Orthodox Christians, and Roman Catholics on the Balkan peninsula (Kaplan 1993). Of ancestral hatreds there were indeed plenty, in a region that had been fought over and colonized by Slavs, Austrians, and Ottoman Turks for centuries. But we know better than to try to account for changes in contention with reference to constant factors that lie deep in a nation's past. The real question is why such identities, and the conflicts they engendered, exploded in the 1990s, and this requires a more fine-grained account of the mechanisms and processes in play.

The way the Yugoslav Communist state was formed at the end of World War II was the structural cause of these conflicts. Like his Soviet former mentors, Communist guerilla leader, Josip Broz Tito, adopted a particular form of federal state at war's end which provided each of the constituent Yugoslav republics with their own Communist parties, their own array of regionally- based and regionally-controlled social and cultural institutions, and their own schools, academies of sciences, and their own mass media (Bunce 1999: 46). In theory, these institutions were supposed to produce national integration under the banner of socialism, but in practice, according to Valerie Bunce, they *"redistributed political power and economic resources from the center to the regions"* (48).

The second problem was that there was no one-to-one correlation between particular ethnic groups and individual republics: While each republic was populated by a majority ethnic group—as in the Soviet Union—most of them contained significant minority populations with ties to majorities elsewhere in the Federation. Not only that: within Serbia there were two areas—Vojvodina and Kosovo—with distinct ethnic minorities, the first with several non-Serbian minorities and the second with an Albanian majority—that had autonomous provincial status. The largest group—the Serbs—dominated both the largest republic and had significant disasporas in both Croatia and Bosnia-Herzegovina, where their "fate" under the disintegrating federal state became the justification for Serbian aggression against these two republics. Figure 8.2 demonstrates the overlapping between ethnic group memberships and republic lines within Yugoslavia at the sunset of the state's unified existence.

Figure 8.2
Ethnic Groups and Republic Boundaries in Yugoslavia, 1989
Source: Central Intelligence Agency, "Ethnic Groups in Yugoslavia," Making the History of 1989, Item #170, http://chnm.gmu.edu/1989/items/show/170

As long as the Communist party remained in the saddle and Tito was alive to manage the complicated relations among the six republics and the two autonomous provinces, the federal constitution functioned reasonably well to keep ethnic identities in check. But with Tito's passing in 1980, and with the passage of constitutional revisions that loosened the control of the center still further, republic elites began to exploit the opportunities for enhanced power and prestige that the federal system afforded them. This was particularly true for the leader of Serbia, Slobodan Milošević, who built up his popularity by defending the "threatened" interests of Serbs in the emerging states of Croatia and Bosnia-Herzegovina. Even before the collapse of the Soviet Union, the end result, concludes

Valerie Bunce there was "an optimal environment for the republicanization of sovereignty and for the rise within the republics of "ethnopolitical
machines" (Bunce 1999: 51).

While Yugoslavia was distinct for its *degree* of ethno-religious diversity,
it was not unique in this regard. After all, both Czechoslovakia after 1968,
and the Soviet Union, from the beginning, had federal constitutions to
manage ethnic diversity. What was distinct in Yugoslavia was the degree
to which "republicanization" was enhanced by the "market socialism" that
the Yugoslavs practiced, the presence of substantial ethno-national minorities across republican lines, and the tendency of republican elites to
embrace nationalism as an alternative to the stale ideology of the dying
Yugoslav state (Bunce 1999: 107). While the leaders of the other two federal systems in the region—Václav Klaus of the Czech Republic and Boris
Yeltsin of Russia—embraced reform and accepted the end of the national
state, Milošević "rejected reform and made noises about defending the
state, while preparing at the same time to expand his republic's borders in
the event of dismemberment" (107). That involved both transforming Serbian identities into a political identity, and constructing a boundary between the Serbs and the Croat and Muslim groups where there were substantial Serbian minorities.

But the will to exploit opportunities for political gain is never sufficient
to achieve political success. In other high-capacity states like the Soviet
Union, there was ethnic strife aplenty, as we saw in chapter 5. But during
the cycle of nationalist mobilization in that country, the Red Army remained largely neutral, serving as the instrument of central rule until it
became evident that the Union was in danger. Even then, only part of the
military supported the attempted coup against Secretary Gorbachev, and
they did so in the name of national unity—not separatism.

Not so in Yugoslavia, where the Yugoslav National Army (JNA) had
close historical connections with the Serbian Republic, and where there
were territorially-based militias under the control of the various republics. This proved to be crucial, for as the federation began to come apart,
these militias defended the majority ethnic groups in their Republics and
"leaked" weaponry to their populations (Bunce 1999: 118–119). When the
JNA lined up on the side of Serbia and the republic militias took the side
of the other republics, the process of state dismemberment became lethal,
and once violence was used against one ethnic group in one area, members
of that group in other areas mobilized to defend themselves and politics
itself became deadly.

We will turn to the dynamics of civil war in the next section. What is important to emphasize here is that the conflicts among the ethnic fractions of

the disintegrating Yugoslavia took different forms in different parts of the federation, some more lethal than others. While the Slovenian Republic's establishment as an independent state was peaceful, and Macedonia escaped major violence, the multi-ethnic composition of Bosnia-Herzegovina, and the presence of a sizeable Serbian minority linked to Serbia led to a civil war and to a spiral of genocide.

Observe what we have been saying: While the "motivational fallacy" would trace the violence in the breakup of Yugoslavia to "ancestral hatreds," and the "general law fallacy" would classify it into distinct forms—ethnic violence, civil wars, revolutions, etc.—what we see in the dismemberment of Yugoslavia is that power-seeking elites, aided by a divided military, used the opportunity structure provided by Yugoslav federal institutions to transform existing identities into political ones. Whether what emerged was moderate nationalism, ethnic separatism, or outright genocide was the result of the interaction between these mechanisms and the social and political context of each republic.

CIVIL WAR

Civil war occurs when two or more distinct military organizations, at least one of them attached to the previously existing government, battle each other for control of major governmental means within a single regime (Collier and Hoeffler 2003; Fearon and Laitin 2003. We have already considered civil strife that raged in Yugoslavia as the federation imploded. As part of their effort to analyze and organize peaceful conflict resolution, Scandinavian scholars have made a specialty of cataloguing violent conflicts across the world. One group of them does annual tallies of major conflicts, counting as civil wars those armed conflicts between governments and other actors in which at least twenty-five people die during the year.

In 2003 alone, Scandinavia's professional conflict spotters identified civil wars above their twenty-five-death threshold in Afghanistan, Algeria, Burma/Myanmar, Burundi, Chechnya, Colombia, Iraq, Israel/Palestine, Kashmir, Liberia, Nepal, the Philippines, Sri Lanka, Sudan, Turkey/Kurdistan, and Uganda (Eriksson and Wallensteen 2004: 632–635). These cases range from regimes in which the major parties were fighting for control of a single national government (e.g., Nepal) to others in which at least one major party was seeking to escape entirely from a central government's jurisdiction (e.g., the Philippines).

Over the years since World War II, a remarkable change in the world's armed conflicts, including civil wars, has occurred. For two centuries up to the end of that war, most large-scale lethal conflicts had pitted independent states against each other. Colonial conquests and anticolonial resistance constitute the main exceptions to that rule. During the immediate postwar period, European colonial powers faced resistance and insurrection in many of their colonies. Colonial wars surged before subsiding during the 1970s. As the Cold War prevailed between the 1960s and 1980s, great powers—especially the United States, the USSR, and the former colonial masters—frequently intervened in postcolonial civil wars such as those that ravaged Angola between 1975 and 2003 (Dunér 1985). But increasingly, civil wars without direct military intervention by third parties became the main sites of large-scale lethal conflict (Kaldor 2006; Tilly 2003: ch. 3).

American researchers working in the framework of the "Correlates of War" (COW) project divide armed conflicts since World War II into these categories:

- *Extrastate*, which occurs between a state and a nonstate group outside its own territory, the most typical cases being colonial wars
- *Interstate*, between two or more states
- *Civil Wars* between the government of a state and internal opposition groups without intervention from other states

Table 8.1, drawn from the work of the "COW" scholars, shows trends in the three categories of conflict. The table shows extra-state wars declining after 1929; interstate wars fluctuating but never disappearing; and civil wars reaching their maximum from the 1970s through the 1990s, then declining after 2000. Soviet and Yugoslav disintegration contributed to the surge in the number of civil wars and the deaths they caused in the 1990s (Beissinger 2002; Kaldor 1999).

Over the longer period since World War II, civil wars have concentrated in two kinds of regimes: (1) relatively high-capacity regimes, however democratic or undemocratic, containing significant zones that escape central control (of recent cases, Israel/Palestine, the India-controlled part of Kashmir, Peru, Chechnya, the Philippines, Turkey, and Colombia); (2) low-capacity undemocratic regimes (the rest). In both sorts of regimes, armed opponents of central governments range from defenders of regional turfs to activists seeking the overthrow of central governments. They range from warlords and beleaguered peasants, at one end, to outright secessionists or revolutionaries, at the

Table 8.1 NUMBER OF WARS OF DIFFERENT TYPES INVOLVING AT LEAST
A THOUSAND DEATHS, BY DECADE, 1900–2007, AND NUMBER
AND PERCENTAGE OF TOTAL KILLED IN CIVIL WARS

Decade	Extra-State Wars	Inter-State Wars	Civil Wars	Deaths in Civil Wars (N) %	
1900–1909	16	18	11	45,330	18.7
1910–1919	9	43	25	963,460	9.7
1920–1929	9	4	22	175,100	68.2
1930–1939	4	25	12	992,335	14.4
1940–1949	6	31	13	1,393,357	10.2
1950–1959	6	29	12	63,351	6.2
1960–1969	2	22	35	189,265	15.0
1970–1979	7	30	53	350,428	70.4
1980–1989	2	10	40	280,334	17.4
1990–1999	2	33	71	150,628	44.4
2000–2007	18	10	26	42,115	58.8
Total	81	255	320	4,645,703	13.0

Data Source: COW Wars v4.0, 1816–2007; available at http://www.correlatesofwar.org/COW2%20
Data/WarData_NEW/WarList_NEW.html. Also see Meredith Sarkees and Frank Wayman, *Resort to War, 1816-2007* (2010)

other. All along that continuum, however, they face the dual problems of high stakes and sustaining armed force.

In both types of regimes, furthermore, warlords and revolutionaries alike have the incentives and the means to create their own armed forces and mark out their own zones of territorial control. Arms are widely available on a worldwide clandestine market fed especially by distributors in the United States and the former Soviet bloc (Boutwell, Klare, and Reed 1995). Access to outside support (e.g., of Middle Eastern Islamic activists in Chechnya and of Congo-based militias in Burundi) and availability of high-value contraband (e.g., diamonds in Liberia and heroin in Afghanistan) makes arming all the easier. Civil wars, then, illustrate dramatically how the form of a regime generates a political opportunity structure, which in turn interacts with established claim-making repertoires to shape the character of contentious politics. Sudan's civil war and its aftermath illustrate these arguments and also how difficult it is to end violence after civil wars have ended.

Civil War in Sudan

The independent state of Sudan, due south of Egypt, long lived under Egyptian domination. It occupies the largest territory of any African state.

Toward the Egyptian border on the north and the Red Sea coast on the northeast, the Sudanese population is increasingly Muslim in religion and Arab in self-identification. Toward the south and the west, higher and higher proportions speak sub-Saharan African languages, identify with black African tribes, and practice either Christianity or African regional religions. The central government, based in mainly Muslim and Arabic-speaking Khartoum, exercises tight control over the Khartoum metropolitan area and the northeast, but it had an uncertain grip on the rest of the country. Few roads penetrate the poor and mainly agricultural southern and western regions.

Sudan's politically troubled neighbors include not only Egypt but also the Central African Republic, Chad, the Democratic Republic of the Congo, Eritrea, Ethiopia, Kenya, Libya, and Uganda. From independence in 1956 to the strife-torn year of 2005, Sudan had suffered active civil wars during forty of its fifty postcolonial years. Many of those civil wars spilled over its boundaries into adjacent countries or sprang from conflicts already going on in those countries. During most of that half-century, military officers ran the regime but could not extend their control over the country's entire territory.

Periodically, Sudan's rulers called their regime Muslim and have tried to install Islamic principles as national law. They also monopolized substantial revenues from oil exports and Red Sea commercial zones. Southerners and westerners repeatedly resisted both moves by armed force. With varying degrees of unity, warlord-led armies often effectively ran the south since independence. Under pressure from neighboring states and international organizations, the central state seesawed between granting the south extensive autonomy and attempting to annihilate or co-opt its rebels.

After years of internal territorial and ethnic strife, fueled by the substantial oil deposits in disputed parts of the country, South Sudan voted to become a state in 2011 in a referendum with 98.3 percent voting for independence. The new state was quickly legitimated by the United Nations, joined the African Union, and signed the Geneva Conventions. But after gaining independence, violence continued in South Sudan, between the President and a former aide, which expanded into inter-ethnic fighting between the two main tribal groups, the Dinka and the Nuer, with Ugandan troops fighting on the side of the government. Since 2013, an estimated 1,700.000 people have been displaced by the fighting, which had not ceased as this book went to press.

Though it is also an ethnically and regionally divided country, Sudan differs from the Irish case we dealt with earlier, first because of the lure of oil within its soil, and second, because it is a low-capacity state in which the contained forms of contention that led to a solution of the Northern Irish "Troubles" do not exist. This takes us to the broader phenomenon of revolutions, which are also more likely to occur in low-capacity regimes.

REVOLUTIONS

Revolutions, as we will soon see, share some properties with civil wars. But they also have their own distinctive dynamics. Let us define a *revolution* as a forcible transfer of power over a state in the course of which at least two distinct blocs of contenders make incompatible claims to control the state, and some significant portion of the population subject to the state's jurisdiction acquiesces in the claims of each bloc.

A full revolution combines a revolutionary situation with a revolutionary outcome. A *revolutionary situation* involves a broad split in the regime, with each party controlling some substantial territory and/or instruments of government. Clearly, we are talking about a matter of degree, about a continuum from no split at all to a split that completely divides the regime. A *revolutionary outcome* is different: an extensive transfer of power over the government, such that few of those who controlled it before now hold power. Once again we are dealing with a matter of degree, from no transfer to an utterly complete transfer. Figure 8.1 made that point by placing great revolutions in its upper right-hand corner: extensive split in the regime followed by a large transfer of power within the regime.

With those insights in mind, let us look more closely at revolutionary situations and revolutionary outcomes. Here are the components of a revolutionary situation:

- Contenders or coalitions of contenders advancing exclusive competing claims to control of the state or some segment of it. This component results from mobilization, which in turn often involves brokerage and boundary activation; it constitutes a revolutionary coalition.
- Commitment to those claims by a significant segment of the citizenry. Again, we regularly see mobilization at work, often accompanied by diffusion, boundary activation, and external certification.
- Incapacity or unwillingness of rulers to suppress the alternative coalition and/or commitment to its claims. This component involves ruler-subject interaction, often with alliances forming between challengers and previous members of the regime. If all three elements occur together, this means that a significant split has emerged within a previously integrated regime.

A revolutionary outcome has four components:

- *Defections of regime members*: Although sometimes members simply flee from the threat of destruction, often they form new coalitions with segments of the revolutionary coalition.
- *Acquisition of armed force by revolutionary coalitions*: Such coalitions can occur through external support, incorporation of previously separate dissident units, purchase, or mobilization of arms already under control of coalition participants.
- *Neutralization or defection of the regime's armed force*: At times the rank and file melt away as they see a superior force rising and their leaders dividing, but more often military leaders themselves take their units into neutrality or opposition.
- *Control of the state apparatus by members of revolutionary coalition*: Rarely does this happen without some collaboration, however temporary, between revolutionaries and previously loyal agents of the threatened regime.

If all four elements occur together, a major transfer of power has transformed the regime.

Across history, far more revolutionary situations—political splits that cut across whole regimes—have occurred than revolutionary outcomes. Nevertheless, revolutionary outcomes continue to occur in the contemporary world. Dealing only with cases that he considers to qualify as major social revolutions since World War II, for example, Jeff Goodwin (2001: 4) mentions Vietnam, China, Bolivia, Cuba, Algeria, Ethiopia, Angola, Mozambique, Cambodia, South Vietnam, Iran, Nicaragua, and Grenada. But if we extend the concept of revolution to include what many would consider "political" revolutions, the number and extent of of the phenomenon increases enormously (Tilly 1993).

Revolution in Nicaragua

Nicaragua from 1961 to 1990 shows us the opening of a deep revolutionary situation, creation of a revolutionary outcome, prolonged civil war with uneven external support for both sides, and a settlement that reversed a significant portion of the revolution's earlier power transfer. Whether we count Nicaragua's experience as a "great revolution" therefore depends on the points in time we consider. Certainly the transformations of 1979–1980 undid much of the preceding Somoza regime's corruption and made significant moves toward socializing the national economy. At their height, the Sandinistas, who overthrew the Somozas, provided a model for revolutionaries across Latin America.

Let us apply the two checklists of revolutionary elements to Nicaragua. The checkoff for a revolutionary situation looks something like this:

> *Contenders advancing exclusive competing claims to control of the state*: Formation of the Sandinista National Liberation Front (1961) identifies this element; it resulted from polarization, brokerage, and mobilization.
>
> *Commitment to those claims by a significant segment of the citizenry*: Between the popular reaction to the government's mishandling of the Managua earthquake (1972) and the assassination of Pedro Chamorro (1978), this process was clearly under way. More polarization accelerated this process, with diffusion, brokerage, attribution of similarity, and a resulting scale shift powerfully promoting it.
>
> *Incapacity or unwillingness of rulers to suppress the alternative coalition and/or commitment to its claims*: President Jimmy Carter's 1977 decertification of the regime signaled the limits to previously enthusiastic US support for the Somoza regime, but the following disintegration of the National Guard as it failed to suppress the government's growing opposition capped that decertification. Failed repression, signaling spirals concerning the government's vulnerability, and diffusion all contributed to this third element of a revolutionary situation.

Although the three elements of the revolutionary situation reinforced each other as they took shape, somewhat different sets of mechanisms and processes shaped each one of them.

What of the revolutionary outcome, considering the situation in 1979–1980 as the maximum transfer of power from old regime to new? Here is the review:

> *Defection of regime members*: Although a "group of twelve" prominent Nicaraguans early repudiated the regime (1977) and soon fled into exile, after Chamorro's assassination in 1978, we see massive defections by previous collaborators (however reluctant) with Somoza, many of whom moved actively into coalition with the Sandinistas. Defections accelerated as the National Guard vainly tried to restore its control with massive force. In this

regard, polarization and failed repression played major parts in producing one element of a revolutionary outcome.

Acquisition of armed force by revolutionary coalitions: After a disastrous defeat of their attempt to produce a mountain uprising in 1967, the Sandinistas concentrated heavily on creating a clandestine national military organization. They acquired some arms from outside with the help of their international supporters, bought or stole some from the National Guard, and assembled weapons already held by individual households, but created much of their insurrectionary military organization from scratch, inspired by models already known elsewhere in Latin America. Mobilization and coordination were the dominant processes.

Neutralization or defection of the regime's armed force: The Somoza regime provides a spectacular example of this element, as a once fearsome National Guard melted away. Failed repression and (now domestic) decertification figured importantly in the regime's loss of effective armed force.

Control of the state apparatus by members of the revolutionary coalition: In 1979, Anastasio Somoza's flight on the collapse of his army and the defection of his erstwhile allies produced a double movement, in which Sandinistas and their collaborators moved quickly into the principal centers of power and existing officials quickly transferred their allegiance to a revolutionary coalition now enlarged by the presence of non-Sandinista reformers. Domestic decertification of the old regime and international certification of the new one accelerated the turnover, but top-down coordination within the revolutionary coalition played the central part.

Notice what we have been doing. The three elements of a revolutionary situation and the four elements of a revolutionary outcome are true by definition. When all are fulfilled, they simply tell us that a revolutionary situation has given way to a revolutionary outcome. Struggle has produced a significant transfer of power over the government, and a deep split within the regime has first opened and then closed. But distinguishing the seven elements greatly clarifies the work of explaining revolutions. It emphasizes that although the appearance of one element affects the appearance of the others, each element springs from a somewhat different set of causes—of mechanisms and processes.

The distinction also makes clear why revolutionary situations occur so much more frequently than revolutionary outcomes. Actually taking over an existing government depends on even more demanding activities than opening a split within a regime. Among other things, the people who already run the government generally resist being thrown out; even Nicaragua's hapless Somoza regime, after all, held on eighteen years after the Sandinistas' launching and seven years after the disastrous Managua earthquake of 1972. Defections of regime members, acquisition of armed force, neutralization of a regime's armed force, and control of a state apparatus all involve momentous organizational activity, far surpassing the establishment of power at a regional base.

CONCLUSION

The ethnic-religious conflicts, civil wars, and revolutions examined in this chapter look like quite separate phenomena, a world apart from the politics of the social movements we encountered in chapter 7. Massacres and demonstrations have little in common, even if troops occasionally shoot down demonstrators. Social movement campaigns arise disproportionately in open regimes, such as the United States, or in less open regimes in which cracks are appearing, such Poland in the 1980s. In contrast, the large-scale lethal conflicts analyzed in this chapter took place disproportionately in regimes that did not feature social movements, especially in low-capacity undemocratic regimes. Yet the chapter's look at deadly ethnic-religious conflict, civil wars, and revolutions revealed great affinities among them and substantial connections with less violent forms of contention.

The secret is no secret: Once we take the analysis to the level of mechanisms and processes, we discover that similar causes and effects operate across the whole range of contentious politics, from viciously violent to pristinely peaceful. Much like the main subjects of chapter 7—Solidarity in Poland and the new women's movement in the United States—Nicaragua's Sandinista movement took hold through combinations of mobilization, brokerage, diffusion, certification, and boundary activation.

Of course, differences existed, but they were not idiosyncratic or unpredictable. In all these cases, existing political opportunity structure interacted with established repertoires to shape what sorts and degrees of contention occurred within a given regime. In all these cases, the overall character of the regime (especially the capacity of its central government and its degree of democracy) strongly affected the location and the sheer possibility of contention.

That summarizes the two main messages of our book so far: (1) similar mechanisms and processes operate across the whole range of contentious politics, and (2) existing opportunity structures and established repertoires shape the forms and degrees of contention. In mainly democratic regimes, the repertoire of contention leans toward peaceful forms of contention that intersect regularly with representative institutions and produce social movement campaigns; in mainly authoritarian regimes, the repertoire leans toward lethal conflicts and tends to produce religious and ethnic strife, civil wars, and revolutions.

Two additional factors complicate the picture we have drawn. First, contention in national states does not operate in airtight boxes, if it ever did. Absent the opportunity of the breakup of the Soviet empire, Yugoslavia might have hobbled along for decades with its semi-market economy and federal socialist system. Second, globalization and internationalization have created interdependencies between states and peoples. Like the Ukrainian events with which we began this book, the Yugoslav conundrum eventually led to the intervention of foreign states and international institutions. It is logical to ask how these interdependencies and interventions affect contentious politics. Chapter 9 takes us up to the present with an examination of the growing linkages between the global and the local in today's contentious world.

NOTE

1. For the French legislation, see "French Lawmakers Vote for Sweeping Power to Spy on Citizens" at http://www.dw.de/french-lawmakers-vote-for-sweeping-powers-to-spy-on-citizens/a-18430523. For the EU counter-terrorism plan, see Alan Travis, "European counter-terror plan involves blanket collection of passengers' data," *The Guardian Online*, January 28, 2015. http://www.theguardian.com/uk-news/2015/jan/28/european-commission-blanket-collection-passenger-data.

PART FIVE

Expanding Contention

So the happy individual is he whom Allah (swt) has taken as a 'Shaheed' (martyr)

A video shows Osama bin Laden speaking, thus proving that he had survived the United States' attack on his Afghanistan headquarters after September 11, 2001. (Copyright @ Reuters/CORBIS).

CHAPTER 9
Transnational Contention

Not long after the fall of Muammar Gaddafi, the Libyan dictator (see chapter 6), a group of rebels, journalists, and Human Rights Watch activists stormed the offices of Gaddafi's former intelligence chief, Moussa Koussa. There they found a trove of documents, including a fax in which he was congratulated by Sir Mark Allen, then Britain's foreign intelligence director, on the "safe arrival" of Libyan rebel Abel Hakim Belhadj in Libya in 2004. Belhadj and another Gaddafi opponent, Sami al-Saadi, were Libyan rebels who had fled from Gaddafi's police in the 1990s to Britain, Gaddafi's sworn enemy since the Lockerbie plane crash in 1988 over Scotland. From there, the two dissidents moved to Asia with their families, where they continued to agitate against the Libyan regime. They were arrested in Thailand and Hong Kong, together with Belhadj's pregnant wife and Saadi's wife and four children.[1] After several weeks, Belhadj and his wife were put on a plane in restraints by US agents and transferred to Tripoli, where he was taken to the notorious Tajoura prison and tortured for about four years, before he was released and made his way back to the United Kingdom. Belhadj's and al-Saadi's torture was carried out by Gaddafi's police but they were also questioned by British agents and asked a series of questions intended to help the British root out jihadis in the United Kingdom. MI6 at one point thanked the Libyan intelligence agents for "kindly agreeing" to pass the questions along to their "interview team."[2] This was a truly transnational operation.

Belhadj's rendition was not very different than the kidnapping and transfer of other suspects in the War on Terror to countries where they could, with impunity, be tortured. But the Libyans' rendition was also the result of a shift in policy toward the Libyan regime. When, after

September 11, 2001, Gaddafi decided that his future would be protected if his stormy relations with Britain and America were healed, British security agencies cracked down on Libyan dissidents who had taken refuge in the UK. The rendition of Belhadj and al-Saadi to Gaddafi's torture chambers was the result of this change in policy. When Belhadj and his wife arrived in Tripoli, Allen glowed that the rendition, "demonstrates the remarkable relationship we have built over recent years."[3]

Based on the documents that came to light when Koussa's office was raided after Gaddafi's fall, Belhadj and al-Saadi sued former British foreign minister Jack Straw, Allen, and other British officials, alleging false imprisonment and a host of other charges. Al-Saadi was eventually awarded 2.2 million pounds in compensation by the British government, while Belhadj's case is still under consideration. But on December 19, 2013, High Court Justice Sir Peregrine Simon ruled that Belhadj and his wife could not sue either MI6 or Straw "because to do so would damage Britain's relations with the US." Simon said he was ruling against Belhadj "because American, as well as British officials were involved in the operation." The judge admitted that "the conduct of US officials acting outside the US was unlawful" and that there was "what appears to be a potentially well-founded claim that UK authorities were directly implicated in the extraordinary rendition."[4]

But the story did not end there. The arrest, prosecution, and abuse of these two Libyan dissidents with the intervention of British and American agents led to a change in the strategy of their organization, the Libyan Islamic Fighting Group (LIFG). Prior to their arrest, the group's goal had been the overthrow of the Gaddafi regime. In an assessment made eleven months after the rendition, MI5 concluded that their capture had cast the group into disarray, leading it to be susceptible to "outside influences"—the transnational terrorist group, al Qaeda. "In particular," the British spy agency warned, "reporting indicates that members . . . may be pushing the group toward a more pan-Islamic agenda inspired by AQ [al-Qaeda]." Two years after this assessment, the group's new leader announced that his group had formally joined forces with bin Laden's group, and he became a leading member of the organization that carried out a series of suicide attacks in Afghanistan.[5] The transnational rendition helped to strengthen the most powerful transnational Islamist group at the time.

Why begin a chapter on transnational contention with this admittedly extreme story of anti-Gaddafi rebellion and exile, kidnapping and rendition to Gaddafi's regime, the fall of the dictator, the involvement of British and American agents in rendition and torture, and the affiliation of a domestic Islamic group with transnational terrorism?

First, the story tells us that transnational terrorists are not born as such—as the "motivational fallacy" would suggest (see chapter 8), nor can they be easily pigeonholed in the neat divisions of the "general law fallacy": the LIFG evolved from domestic insurgency to affiliation with al Qaeda through contentious interactions—both domestic and international.

Second, this evolution did not occur within the "field" of transnational contention alone: involved was the repressive government of Libyan dictator Gaddafi, the American agents who rendered the two suspects to his police, the British government that questioned them, and only then the group's affiliation to al Qaeda.

Third, the mechanisms and processes we find in this story are the same as what we have found in many *non*-lethal, *non*-transnational episodes of contention. We see mobilization, scale shift, repression, identity shift, and—in the form of al Qaeda brokerage of a global network of jihadists.

In concentrating so centrally on political regimes, repertoires, and opportunities, we may have given the impression that the arenas of contentious politics are purely national and local. Thinking back, many of the episodes in our book were linked to other parts of the world, either through militants' transnational ties or through the impersonal diffusion of their claims:

- Slavery was a transnational industry, and the British antislavery movement diffused rapidly to Western Europe and the Americas.
- The Irish Fenian movement that gave rise to the IRA was born among Irish immigrants to the United States, received support from Irish American groups, and the Northern Irish "Troubles" were only resolved in the 1990s with foreign intervention.
- The Ukrainian Maidan protests were triggered by the strained links between the Ukrainian President and the European Union and the separatist rebellions in Crimea and the east of the country were supported by the Russian Federation.
- Although Polish Solidarity was a national movement, it depended on support from the Vatican and its success inspired dissidents throughout Eastern Europe.
- The "shantytowns" that American college students built in the 1980s were part of an international movement against apartheid.
- Many of the religious Zionists who settled in the Gaza strip were Americans, and Hamas, which took over the strip after Prime Minister Sharon evacuated the settlers in 2005, is part of the transnational Shi'a movement sponsored by Iran.

These conflicts were all to some extent transnationally embedded, but in today's contentious politics, transnational links have taken on a qualitatively new character due to two large processes that are transforming the contemporary world: globalization and internationalization.

Globalization is the increasing volume and speed of flows of capital and goods, information and ideas, people, and forces that connect actors between countries (Keohane 2002: 194). Scholars including Jackie Smith and Hank Johnston (2002) have argued vigorously that globalization sets the stage for transnational contention. Others have derived from this process the idea that something called a "global social movement" is resulting (Evans 2005; McMichael 2005). These writings have an empirical counterpart in the hundreds of thousands of young activists who have flocked to the World Social Forum each year since 2000—most recently in Tunisia, linking the movement to what remains of the "Arab Spring." Many thousands of others have participated in regional forums in Western Europe, Latin America, and elsewhere (Pianta 2001; Pianta and Silva 2003) and taken part in solidarity movements with the insurgent Zapatista movement in Chiapas, Mexico (see chapter 5).

Globalization takes many forms that affect the mounting and transmission of contentious politics. Here are some of them:

- The growing linkages between the economies of North and South put southern workers at the mercy of market forces controlled by producers, investors, and consumers from the North.
- The same trends have a converse effect in the North: the loss of industrial jobs by workers whose firms move to countries where labor is cheap and trade unions are repressed.
- Improvements in travel and communication make it possible for activists from different parts of the world to travel to the sites of contention, meet others like themselves, and form transnational coalitions. A special vehicle of this convergence is the Internet, which plays a role similar to that of newspapers and television in earlier eras (Bennett 2005; Bennett and Segerberg 2013).
- Cultural and institutional standardization makes it easier for activists to frame issues in similar ways and for modular forms of contention to be understood and aropted in a wide variety of places (Boli and Thomas 1999).

In *internationalization*, you will find a parallel to our concept of political opportunity structure. Political opportunity structure was introduced in chapter 3 and has appeared at the local, regional, and national levels throughout our book. Internationalization influences contentious politics through three components: (1) increasing the horizontal density of relations among states, governmental officials, and nonstate actors and (2) increasing vertical ties between these and international institutions or organizations; (3) offering a kind of "coral reef" around which nonstate actors—NGOs, social movements, unions, and business associations—form transnational networks (Tarrow 2005: ch. 2).

An important component of internationalization is legalization. As international agreements become more complex and involve larger numbers of actors, they acquire a legal structure, which in turn requires the creation of international panels and agencies (Goldstein et al. 2001). This development in turn creates focal points, incentives, and threats that lead to the creation and cooperation of transnational networks of activists. When the latter discover one another and identify their mutual interests, transnational coalitions and movements result.

Think of the transnational network that formed around the United Nations Framework Convention on Climate Change (UNFCCC) which organized a climate change summit in Copenhagan, Denmark in 2009. Previous summits—in Rio de Janeiro, Kyoto, and Poznan had attracted a group of "mild-mannered, scientifically sophisticated nongovernmental organizations."

But by 2009, especially in Europe, there was growing alarm that the climate was becoming increasingly overheated and that states and international organizations were not moving fast enough to deal with the problem. As the Copenhagen summit approached, the UN security team realized that more than 10,000 activists, some of whom had made explicit threats of radical action, would have access to a venue housing world leaders (Hadden 2015). Figure 9.1, drawn from Jennifer Hadden's work, shows how many NGOs had been registered to the UNFCCC by 2009, and how the number of these groups continued to grow after the failure of the Copenhagen summit. The UN climate change process is an archetypical example of how international institutions serve as a focal point for the formation and networking of a stratum of transnational collective action.

When the Copenhagen summit began, many of the traditional climate change groups assembled decorously in the conference chamber. But many others, associated with a new and more assertive "climate justice" network, congregated in the streets and squares and inside the conference hall itself. Hadden's data show a marked increase in the number of contentious events around the Copenhagen summit, from only ten in 2008 to almost eighty in 2009 (Hadden 2015: 146). Hadden's work also shows that the character of contentious protest became more aggressive

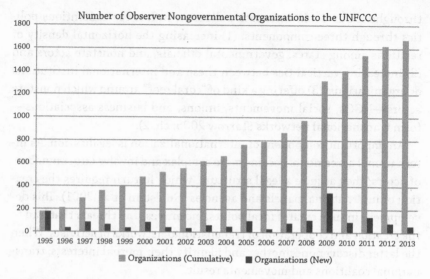

Figure 9.1:
Number of Observer Nongovernmental Organizations to the UNFCCC
Source: Courtesy of Jennifer Hadden

in Copenhagen. "Before 2009," she writes, "most of the (limited) protest that occurred around the UNFCCC was of a nonthreatening character ... but Copenhagen marked the emergence of a more confrontational and transgressive repertoire of climate change activism, which had previously been rare" (147). Not only that: contentious protest was "catching": in contact with the climate justice network, many of the more moderate, groups at Copenhagen shifted from the "contained" forms of contention they had used in the past to the more transgressive forms that emerged in Copenhagen (155). But after the failure of the summit, transnational climate change action sagged. Why was this?

THE DIFFICULTIES OF TRANSNATIONAL MOBILIZATION

In the 1990s and early 2000s, many scholars became convinced that national boundaries were giving way to a "Global Commons" and that domestic movements were on their way to creating a "global civil society." Key events like the protests against the Seattle Summit of the World Trade Organization, and international conferences, like the World Social Forum lent enthusiasm to this hypothesis. But in the move to study and embrace global justice movements, there was perhaps more enthusiasm than detached analysis.

First, although not all domestic contention targets governments directly, governments structure domestic contention, respond to it, repress actors who go beyond the bounds of tolerated forms, and offer potential allies to those willing to interact with institutions. Although transnational actors find focal points in individual governments, international institutions, or transnational corporations, in world politics there is no stable focal point like a government around which to organize contention.

Second, building transnational social movements is immensely more difficult than carrying out the same task in domestic politics. Think of our concept of social movement bases: As difficult as these are to build and mobilize in domestic politics, they are immensely harder to assemble across borders. As a result, transnational social movement campaigns are generally fleeting and inconsistent, often leading to failure.

Third—this follows from the second factor—activists who seek to build transnational movements find they have to federate small cadres of cosmopolitans at the international level with domestic groups in different countries. These face a host of different threats and opportunities, and their claims may only partially coincide with the transnational activists who attempt to coordinate their collective action.

The world-historical change initiated on September 11, 2001 reinforced these difficulties. Between the post-Cold War world in which international treaties and institutions expanded until the post-9/11 world in which national interests and state hegemony grew, there was a fundamental change in the environment for transnational organizing. Yet the mechanisms that triggered transnational contention in the 1990s remain alive, and have even been reinforced by innovations in digital communication, as we will see in the next chapter.

MECHANISMS AND PROCESSES OF TRANSNATIONALIZATION

Transnationalization triggers a whole array of mechanisms and processes (Imig and Tarrow, eds. 2001):

- *Internalization* of international controversies manifests as domestic contention.
- *Diffusion* of a domestic controversy spreads into the politics of other countries.
- *Brokerage* of transnational alliances is conducted by transnational agents.

- *Boundary activation* and *scale shift* of contention occur from the domestic to the international level.
- *Mobilization* unfolds as transnational protest events, such as the mobilization around the Copenhagen UNFCCC summit.
- To the extent that transnational movements displace domestic contention, they will *deactivate the boundaries* between states and *activate new boundaries* across broader constellations of states.

Three broad processes mark the current phase of transnational activism from past epochs of contention: transnational activism, the formation of transnational coalitions, and rapid transnational diffusion.

In *transnational activism*, a new stratum of activists supports the claims of others beyond their own borders in a wide variety of sectors of activity (Keck and Sikkink 1998; della Porta and Tarrow 2005; Smith 2008; Tarrow 2005). When Clarkson went to France to convince that country's revolutionaries that slavery was an affront to the Rights of Man, his effort was almost unique. But today's transnational activists can be in Syria or Iraq in a matter of days with help for insurgents or for victims of aggression. These "rooted cosmopolitans" are as comfortable in the halls of international institutions or in foreign fields of conflict as they are in their own countries (Tarrow 2005: ch. 3).

Second, *transnational coalitions* are far more common than they were in the past. These have been encouraged by the growth of international institutions like the World Bank, the International Monetary Fund, the United Nations, and the European Union, which act as institutional "coral reefs" around which activists, advocates, and those simply seeking their own advancement form *transnational coalitions* (O'Brien et al. 2000).

Finally, regarding *international diffusion of contention*, local contention often has profound effects on contentious politics in other countries. Of course, this was also true in the past. The 1848 revolution spread across Europe like an inkblot (Weyland 2009). But advances in communication and transportation and the links among peoples and groups across borders today hasten and intensify both diffusion and scale shift. Here the role of the Internet and social media are important, but so are cheap and rapid international travel, and the diffusion of similar norms and cultural symbols to many parts of the world (Boli and Thomas 1999). All three of these processes—transnational activism, transnational coalition formation, and rapid international diffusion—can be seen in both the "good" movements that gained the attention of scholars in the 1990s and in the "bad" movements that preoccupied experts after 2001.

"GOOD" AND "BAD" TRANSNATIONALISM

When scholars first began to study transnational social movements in the 1990s, they tended to focus on "good" movements—movements like the international ecology, human rights, and women's movements (Keck and Sikkink 1998)—which expanded at the end of the Cold War. As international treaties and international organizations moved into new areas—banning torture and land mines, protecting women and children, fighting for peace and against climate change—thousands of young people from across the Global North took time out from their careers to work for the welfare of others around the world. They are what we might call the "rooted cosmopolitans" of transnational activism (Tarrow 2005: ch. 2).

But alongside these mainly liberal, largely western groups, a very different family of transnational movements developed: religious groups using both antiwestern propaganda and violence and linked to diaspora populations in the global North. Especially in the wake of 9/11, much government-sponsored research has developed to study, and to attempt to combat these groups. In the process, as in the study of other types of contentious phenomena, a "terrorism industry" has been formed (della Porta 2013). There is nothing wrong with specialization, but in the process, many terrorism specialists ignored the progress that social movement scholars have made in understanding transnational contention in general. An archtypical "good" movement has been the movement for transitional justice against military leaders of the authoritarian regimes of the 1970s and 1980s; the most notorious "bad" one is the transnational Islamist movement that gave rise to both al Qaeda in the 1990s and the Islamic State more recently.

EL CONDOR NO PASA

"General Augusto Pinochet, former military dictator of Chile, really wanted to travel," writes Naomi Roht-Arriaza (2006: 1) of his life after his repressive regime was defeated in a referendum. His problem, among others, was that he was internationally suspected of human rights violations and that thousands of other Chileans had been forced to leave their native land for fear of death or torture during the years when his ruthless regime had ruled Chile. These diaspora Chileans formed the core of a social movement to try Pinochet for crimes against humanity when he was arrested in England in 1998.

As one Chilean exile told the story:

> During the dictatorship years, we had created a fabulous support network
> throughout Europe, including artists, unions, politicians and the like. We had
> been organizers in Chile, so we knew how to organize . . . We knew each other
> all over Europe because we had either been prisoners together or knew some-
> one who had. So as we learned English, got jobs, and developed good contacts
> in British society, we kept in touch with others throughout Europe. (quoted in
> Roht-Arriaza 2006: 38)

Those contacts turned out to be crucial when, in October, 1998, Pinochet traveled to London for surgery. It was members of the Chilean diaspora network that spread the word to compatriots all over Europe,
tipped off the Spanish magistrates who were investigating torture in
Chile and Argentina, sat in on and demonstrated outside court hearings
in London, took notes on the proceedings, and sent them around the
world (Roht-Arriaza 2006: 39). These exiles fulfilled a classical *brokerage*
function in the sense we have used that mechanism in our book. They
helped to put Chilean human rights lawyers in touch with British civil
liberties lawyers and formed "a key part of the coalition of legal and
human rights groups that eventually formed to press . . . for [Pinochet's]
extradition" (38).

Spanish magistrate Balthazar Garzón was investigating human rights
abuse in Argentina when word came through that Pinochet was in
London. The link that Garzón established from Argentina to Chile was
the secret military intelligence pact between the two countries and four
other Latin American dictatorships. Called "Operation Condor," this
transgovernmental conspiracy took its name from the giant raptor that
traverses the Andes. The pact allowed the "rendition" of captured militants from any one of these countries to their home country, where many
were tortured and killed. Garzón's case against Pinochet was based on
the ex-dictator's role in coordinating Operation Condor (Roht-Arriaza
2006: 29–31). It was the transgovernmental conspiracy headed by Pinochet that gave Garzón the legal leverage to seek his extradition from Britain to Spain.

Operation Condor was only one of the ways in which internationalization affected the Pinochet case. In seeking to extradite the ex-dictator,
Garzón employed a radically new theory in international law—universal
jurisdiction. Traditionally, international law only operates for what are
generally recognized as international crimes, such as piracy. It only allows
for the extradition of a suspected criminal to his or her own country, not

to a third country. But increasingly, magistrates in countries such as Belgium and Spain have been applying the theory of universal jurisdiction to try people for a wide variety of crimes, from genocide to crimes against humanity to war crimes. Garzón based his case on the theory that Pinochet's actions against Spanish and other victims rose to the level of such international crimes. International law was becoming part of the opportunity structure that could enable a Spanish magistrate to seek the extradition of a former Chilean head of state from the United Kingdom.

Although Home Secretary Jack Straw of Britain ultimately allowed Pinochet to return home, the events in Madrid and London produced what Ellen Lutz and Kathryn Sikkink (2001) call "a justice cascade." It led, in Argentina, to an infamous torturer, Carlos Guillermo Suarez Mason, being arrested for the theft of children of Argentina's disappeared (Keck and Sikkink 1998: 20–21); in Mexico, to the arrest of retired Argentine navy torturer Miguel Cavallo as the plane on which he was traveling stopped in Cancun; and in Italy, to a criminal case that had been languishing for years against seven Argentine military officers for the murder of eight Argentines of Italian descent. The cascade came full circle when, in the Chile of 2004, Pinochet came under indictment and a government commission called for reparations for the survivors of his reign of terror.

In the Pinochet case, we see all three transnational processes we stipulated earlier. First, a group of transnational activists triggered the sequence of events in London. Second, a transnational coalition formed around the issue. Third, rapid diffusion of contention occurred across national boundaries. (There was even a whiff of scale shift, as the case contributed to the drive for the creation of the International Criminal Court.) In 2005, Pinochet was indicted in Chile for both human rights abuses and international money laundering.

POLITICAL ISLAMISM GOES TRANSNATIONAL

As transnational NGOs were organizing around the world on behalf of "good" western values in the 1990s, a new family of actors was mobilizing support for more lethal forms of action, as we indicated in the introduction to this chapter. Organizing first against the rulers of Arab countries, and then spreading to both other Muslim-majority countries and to western Europe, where many Muslim immigrants live, these groups became transnational through the use of the Internet, cheap airline travel, and in response to what they saw as the West's domination and repression of Muslims. Beginning with the Iranian revolution of 1979, and the Soviet invasion of Afghanistan, this transnational network grew after 9/11 and the American invasion of Iraq and Afghanistan and its abuse of Muslims, both imagined and real (Wiktorowicz 2004).

In his study of the modern Islamist movement, Gilles Kepel traced its origins to three main countries: Egypt, Iran, and Pakistan (Kepel 2002: ch. 1). In Egypt, Sayyid Qutb made a signal contribution to the movement, according to Kepel, along with Ruholla Khomenei of Iran and Mawlana Mawdudi of Pakistan. Despite their differences, and the differences in their three countries, "All three men shared a vision of Islam as a political movement, and they all called for the establishment of an Islamic state" (23 ff.).

But note that like the Libyan group with which we began this chapter, the movements they founded were all national; they did not automatically become the transnational Islamist movement of today. Qutb, who was hanged in Egypt 1966, attracted a cross-section of Muslim youth to a movement against the secular nationalist regime of Gamal Nasser. He stigmatized secular nationalism with an Arab word from the Koran, *jahiliyya*, which describes the state of ignorance or barbarism in which the Arabs are supposed to have lived before the revelation of Islam to the Prophet Mohammed (Kepel 2002: 25). The Muslim Brotherhood, which predated Qutb by several decades but which he helped to revive in the 1960s and 1970s, spread his ideas to Saudi Arabia and Jordan through his writings. But it was in Egypt, with the resounding defeat of Arab nationalism in the Six Day War, that the movement was able to gain a hearing (32).

Political Islamism has its core in the Arab world, but Arabs are less than a fifth of the world's Muslims, and modern Islamism also took root in South Asia. Islamic texts originally written in Urdu were translated into Arabic and English and had a major influence on the movement throughout the twentieth century. The major figure in South Asia was Mawlana Mawdudi, who attacked the "irreligious" independent states that had emerged after World War II. For him, "all nationalism was impiety, more especially as its conception of the state was European-inspired." For Mawdudi, Islam had to be political, but he favored "Islamization from above," founding, in pre-independence India, Jamaat-e-Islam, which he saw as a vanguard of the Islamic revolution (Kepel 2002: 34). This was the program of action that Qutb eventually adopted, laying the groundwork for the future linkage between Arab and South Asian Islamism (36).

As political Islamism developed in these various sites, its adherents experimented with a wide repertoire of action. From outright attacks on the rulers of their countries and on foreigners, as in Egypt, to electoral competition and then civil war, as in Algeria, to providing social services in the densely-populated slums of Middle Eastern cities and organizing madrasa schools in Pakistan and elsewhere, Islamist activists adapted to the variety of structures of opportunity and constraint they found around them in the Muslim world.

In recent years, a new strand of political Islamism has emerged in the slums and ghettoes of European cities, where millions of South Asian and North African Muslims gathered during the "boom years" of European economic development. While the first generation of these immigrant groups worked hard to establish themselves in their new homes, second and third generation young men—and even women—resentful at their rejection in Christian societies, began to gravitate towards the message of *jihad* emanating from the Middle East. Beginning in the breakup of partly-Muslim Yugoslavia and spreading to France, Germany, and Britain, this conversion experience led many hundreds of "birds of passage" to join violent jihadist groups in the Middle East and in Europe (Tarrow 2005). It was from among these groups that the bombers of the World Trade Center and the Pentagon in September, 2001, emerged.

But none of these strands of what became a global movement would have spread very far without the successful example of the Iranian revolution in 1977–1979. Ruhollah Khomeini, who emerged as its leader, represented the clerical strand of Iranian radicalism; but another important strand was a reinterpretation and politicization of Shiite doctrine. "The Ayatolla's genius lay in appropriating the aspirations of the young militants" and including in his audience "the educated middle class who otherwise would have remained aloof from a personality perceived as preposterously traditional and reactionary" (Kepel 2002: 37).

In its stated or implied goal of reinstating the Caliphate that had been destroyed with the collapse of the Ottoman Empire, political Islamism was always implicitly transnational. It began, however, with critiques of local regimes, which were accused of having betrayed the values of the Koran and fallen into a state of *jahiliyya*. It was Khomeni who first raised the scale of political Islam when, in 1964, he condemned the presence of American "advisers" to the Shah (Kepel 2002: 40). This led to his exile, first to Iraq, then to France and, indirectly, to his contacts with other elements in the Iranian opposition and to the shift in scale of the movement's message.

A twenty-year period elapsed between the Iranian revolution of 1979 and the formation of a broader transnational Islamist movement. First, because Iran was a Shia state, the majority of Sunni Muslims looked upon it with suspicion. Second, for much of its first decade, the new Islamic Republic was bogged down in a savage and costly war with Iraq, leaving few resources for proselytizing abroad. Finally, Khomeini and his followers did not share a common culture with the urban masses in Cairo, Jedda, or Algiers. It would take a broader international conflict, involving the superpowers, to lay the groundwork for a truly transnational Islamist movement.

WAR AND TRANSNATIONAL MOVEMENTS

Ironically, it was the Soviet occupation of Afghanistan and the war against it, financed and organized by the United States and its Saudi and Pakistani proxies, that produced the first major opportunity for the shift in the scale of political Islamism. It offered thousands of Islamic militants the chance to travel outside their own countries, meet others like themselves, and theorize the concept of *jihad* from the varieties of forms of action familiar from their home countries to a model for transnational military struggle. In this process of scale shift, the United States was an unconscious broker of alliances among different Islamic groups and ideologies because its anti-Soviet policy led it to finance—along with Saudi Arabia—the formation of *mujahaddin* fighting groups in Afghanistan (Eickelman 1997).

From the beginning, there were ties across the Muslim world. Eickelman traces them among three main sources of the movement:

> Many older members of Egypt's Muslim Brotherhood have strong ties with Saudi Arabia and the Gulf states. . . . Likewise, Bangladesh's Jama`at-I-Islami . . . retains close ties with the movement's world headquarters in Punjab and appears to accept . . major donations from individuals and institutions in Saudi Arabia and elsewhere in the Gulf for its campaign for Islamicization. In Europe and North America, first- and (to a lesser extent) second-generation immigrant communities offer better bases for the exchange of ideas and information than those available in countries of origin (Eickelman 1997: 31).

Both relational and non-relational paths broadened the reach of political Islamism. Early developments in electronic technology helped to spread the message. Audiocassettes, which had been important instruments in the Iranian revolution, became transnational means of communication in the 1980s. They were "less a sign of direct intergroup cooperation than the popularity of topics and speakers who have developed a following large enough to allow modest profits to the informal network of kiosk vendors who distribute them" (Eickelman 1997: 32). There were also direct connections fostered by religious figures and scholars. Unlike Catholicism, Islam has no central hierarchy that can certify or decertify religious teachers or mosques. This made it easy for self-styled imams to establish mosques throughout the Muslim world and in the centers of immigration in Europe. Mosques became sites for social appropriation in which "Muslim activists are likely to borrow from one another through face-to-face encounters and collect the literature of like-minded groups" (32).

But scale shift is more than a horizontal process of diffusion: a series of bridging relationships spread the movement beyond Afghanistan and shifted it vertically to a higher level. As the most dynamic society in the Middle East, Egypt was for years at the core of the movement. Not only was its Muslim Brotherhood the most prominent of the national Islamist movements; academics from across the Islamic world who studied in Cairo made contact there with adepts of the Brotherhood, returning to their home countries to help found youth movements—for example, like the movement that was founded at Kabul University in the late 1960s (Eickelman 1997: 33).

Once connected to one another, "Afghan Arabs" who had fought in Afghanistan became a restless transnational force and many of their camps became training grounds for militants who moved elsewhere to coordinate new insurgencies. One camp in Paktya province trained Kashmiri militants, Philippine Moros, and Palestinian Islamists, many of whom offered their services and their military expertise to other Islamist movements in the Middle East (Eickelman 1997: 37–38). This was the main source of the transnational movement we know today as al Qaeda, which coordinates and finances insurgencies around the globe. It has narrowed its repertoire of contention from the wide range of collective claims making that characterized Islamism in domestic politics to an almost unique focus on causing death and destruction.

The South Asian, Egyptian, and Iranian activists who were the intellectual sources of the early Islamist groups probably had no inkling of the global range of the movement that would grow out of their writings. Indeed, without exception, their targets were the secular nationalist regimes of their own countries. But determined repression in some countries and calculated co-optation and support from others led these national movements to pose broader claims against more distant targets like Israeli occupation of Jerusalem, American troop presence in Saudi Arabia, and the secular regime in Algeria. Ultimately, they shifted the scale of their claims from the implementation the law of the Koran in the Muslim world to defeating "the conspiracy of the Jews, the Americans, and their Muslim puppets" wherever they could be found. This was scale shift with a vengeance!

Events in the Middle East following the attacks of September 11 expanded the range and the ferocity of the struggle between the West and transnational Islam. War is the most extreme form of contention. It is often triggered by social movements—as was the "War on Terror" initiated by the attacks of al Qaeda on 9/11; it is often fought by movements—as was the case in both the Iraq and Afghanistan wars, when the American-led coalition faced a spreading network of militant Islamist groups there and elsewhere; and it often creates new movements, as when the Iraq war and the Syrian civil war after 2011 gave rise to the group calling itself "The Islamic State" (Tarrow 2015).

EUROPEAN CONTENTION, INSIDE AND OUTSIDE THE EU

Both the progress and the difficulties of transnational contention can be seen in the most highly developed international regime in the world today—the European Union (Hooghe and Marks 2002; Imig and Tarrow 2001; Balme and Chabanet 2008). As the EU gained competence in more and more areas of policy after the turn of the century, contentious action began to focus on Brussels, where a host of transnational NGOs cluster and transnational protest events are mounted. But domestic actors, including French farmers, Belgian workers, Italian pensioners, and British environmentalists, have repeatedly protested against their own governments, attempting to prod them to take action against such EU policies as reductions of farm subsidies, plant closures, the cutting of pension plans, and the importation of genetically modified seeds. Transnational NGOs from time to time succeed in coordinating collective action among these different national constituencies, but the differences among the institutions of the European Union and the opportunities and threats faced by activists in (now) twenty-eight different countries make the task of coordination daunting.

In the last decade, the EU has not only become the focus and the target of collective action by citizens' groups; a new generation of transnational movements has organized on its territory against broader issues, using more contentious means of action. Consider the response to the European economic crisis touched off by the American financial breakdown in 2008; as the EU—led by the German government—cracked down on public spending in its weaker (mainly southern) members, in country after country, worker, students, consumers, pensioners and the unemployed rose up in what Donatella della Porta and Alice Mattoni call "movements of the crisis" (2014).

First in Iceland, Ireland, and Greece, then in Italy, Spain, and Portugal, masses of citizens mobilized against the austerity policies forced on their governments by the EU. While protesters in each country had their own grievances, and while each government responded differently to their challenges, there was a common structural incentive for their protests and a considerable degree of transnational learning across the territory of the EU. Future scholarship will need to examine the degree of actual diffusion among these protests, but the existence of common targets—the European Commission and the European Central Bank—provided protesters with a target for their grievances.

The most interesting sign that transnational diffusion was at work in the wake of the European financial crisis was common symbolism of "indignation" that was provided the protesters by the publication and the almost-instant translation of Stéphane Hessel's book *Time for Outrage: Indignez-vous!* (2011). First published in France and soon republished across the continent in the wake of the financial crisis, the book provided a justification and a label—*los indignados*—for protesters across the continent.

These new "movements of the crisis" (della Porta and Mattoni, eds., 2014), soon influenced the party systems of various European countries: in Greece and Spain through the formation of new leftwing political parties, *Syriza* and *Podemos;* in Italy with the formation of the populist Five Star Movement led by comedian Beppe Grillo; and in France, in the renewed growth of the rightwing National Front of Marine Le Pen. Even in the stable United Kingdom, the crisis appears to have influenced voters in the dramatic Scottish referendum of 2014, which almost succeeded in detaching Scotland from its 300-year alliance with England.

But Europe is not isolated from the rest of the world. In this age of instant electronic communication, rapid and cheap international transportation, the financial crisis that swept across the world's integrated stock markets, Europe's "crisis movement" was joined by other waves of contention. We have seen one such wave in the United States in the form of the "Occupy Wall Street" and another in the "Arab Spring" that began in the same year. In turn, the latter movement connected to another, darker cycle of contention: the political Islamist movement that began in the last century and has led to the weakening of the Arab states and to the attacks of the so-called "Islamic State" in Iraq and Syria in 2014.

CONCLUSION

These very different movements—from the international climate change movement, to the demand for transitional justice in Latin America, to the radical Islamist movement, to European NGOs and social justice movements—show that transnational activism is as multi-faceted as the internationalism from which it has emerged. Although globalization and global neoliberalism are frames around which many activists mobilize, the protests and organizations we have seen in this chapter are not the product of a global imaginary but of domestically-rooted activists who are affected by global trends to target dictatorship, human rights abuse, HIV/AIDS, militarism and its side-products, or emerge from within religious denominations or their surrogates.

Nor are the forms of activism limited to what you may have seen in the press or on the Internet. From Greenpeace activists in slickers opposing oil platforms at sea to well-dressed human rights campaigners in New York and Geneva; from Doctors Without Borders ministering to Ebola victims in Africa to the militants of the Islamic State in Iraq or Syria; from quiet supporters of the "good" NGOs supporting peace, the environment, or human rights to the noisy protesters of Seattle or Genoa: transnational activism is a many-sided phenomenon. Its activists are the connective tissue between the global and the local, working as activators, brokers, and advocates for claims both domestic and international.

The end of the Cold War opened the gates to the expansion of the "bright side" of transnational activism. But the events surrounding September 11, 2001 revealed that transnational activism has a "dark side." As anti-globalization protesters were gathering in Seattle to shut down the meeting of the World Trade Organization in that city in 1999, the adherents of political Islamism were preparing to attack the Pentagon and the World Trade Center. Although there is little in common between the liberal and progressive groups that planned the Seattle demonstration and the militant adepts of political Islamism who attacked the World Trade Center, both reflect the tangled skein of transnational ties that weave our world together.

Notice that we did not claim that the processes of transnational contention we have described are breaking down the walls of the state system altogether. Internationalism takes a number of forms that impinge on, but do not destroy the power of states. The "multilevel governance" that Liesbet Hooghe and Gary Marks uncovered in their study of the European Union (2002); the "complex multilateralism" described by Robert O'Brien and his collaborators for the big international financial institutions (2000);

the weaker mechanisms of NAFTA, the International Landmines Convention, and the Kyoto climate change process: these are not going to destroy the power of states. Internationalization is not an inexorable force working against the state but a loose framework of institutions, regimes, practices, and processes that include state actors and penetrate domestic politics. The lesson of the episodes described in this chapter is that internationalism is partial, many-faceted, and intersects with the determined powers of states and international institutions.

The nationalistic reaction of the American government to the massacres of 9/11 reveal the reversible nature of internationalization. From a sleeping giant that seemed unable to defend itself against the terrorist attacks of the 1990s, the United States responded to the September 11 outrages like a wounded tiger, transmuting itself into an aggressive military power abroad and a semi-praetorian state at home (Margulies 2013; Tarrow 2015). That dynamic profoundly affected the global justice movement too; in response to September 11 and the war fever that it triggered, many American activists retreated from the broad terrain of global neoliberalism to the more immediate ground of electoral politics (Heaney and Rojas 2015). Were they turning permanently inward? It is still too soon to tell.

Both domestic and transnational movements depend on threats and opportunities; but these are more volatile in international politics, where institutional routines are less established, allies and enemies change their strategies at will, and there is no public authority to either challenge or cling to. We saw an example of this volatility and indeterminacy in how the Maidan movement in Kiev—empowered by the desire to associate Ukraine with the European Union—led to the Russian takeover of Crimea and the sparking of a separatist movement in the east of the country. Domestic contention was sparked by internationalization but led to a separatist reaction and an internationalized civil war like those we saw in chapter 8. If we define internationalism as a triangular opportunity space made up of states, international institutions, and nonstate actors, we are bound to see states—especially powerful ones—asserting themselves periodically within this framework and movements struggling to reshape themselves around these changes, as we did in the United States after September 2001.

What is our basic message? Although we see a lot more global framing of contentious issues than in the past and a faster rate of diffusion of contention across national boundaries, domestic contention is still mainly organized at the grassroots, and is alive and well, as we will see in the conclusion to this book.

NOTES

1. These facts, and the remainder of this narrative, come from Belhadj and his wife's Letter of Claim for Damages to the British High Court of Justice of October 8, 2012. These documents were kindly provided by Reprieve, the British non-profit group that supported their claims. I am grateful to Cori Chider, Katherine Craig, and Clive Stafford-Smith for their help in investigating this case, which remains open as of this writing.

2. Ian Cobain, "MI5 Says Rendition of Libyan Opposition Leaders Strengthened al-Qaeda," *The Guardian Online*, January 29, 2014 at www.theguardian.com.

3. See Reprieve, "Gaddafi Opponents Sue Ex-MI6 Counter-Terror Chief Sir Mark Allen over Libya Torture Complicity," press release, www.reprieve.org.uk/press/2011_01_31_allen_lawsuit.

4. Richard Norton Taylor, "Libyan Told He Cannot Pursue Rendition Claim in Case It Harms UK Interests," *The Guardian*, December 20, 2013, www.theguardian.com/world/2013/dec/20/libyan-rendition-claim-uk-interests.

5. Cobain, *The Guardian Online*, January 29, 2014 at www.theguardian.com. Libi was eventually killed by an American drone attack.

A same-sex marriage in San Francisco. (Photo by Justin Sullivan/Getty Images).

CHAPTER 10

Contention Today and Tomorrow

We began our journey through contentious politics with an incident that occurred two centuries ago when future antislavery activist Thomas Clarkson sat down by the side of the road on his way to London. That apparently insignificant event triggered a movement to end slavery that began in Britain, diffused to Western Europe and across the Atlantic, and eventually produced the Civil War and led to the civil rights movement we examined in chapter 2. We will end our book with two equally localized episodes from the second decade of the twenty-first century— the movement against economic inequality that was triggered by the financial crisis of 2008, and the movement for marriage equality in the United States. We will use the former to reflect on the role of digital mobilization in the movements of the new century and the latter to recapitulate the lessons of our book. Both will help us to raise some of the questions we have so far only hinted at. We will conclude with some advice to students who want to use the lessons of this book.

MOVEMENTS OF THE CRISIS

Until the 1960s, students of social movements were more concerned with what we can call the "structural" sources of contentious politics than with its actual mechanisms and processes. For these scholars, the key actors producing contentious politics were social classes, and, in particular, the working class—the hero of Marxist and even many non-Marxist histories of modern societies. Class remained an important category of analysis for some theorists—for example, adherents to the "world systems" approach (Arrighi 1990, 1994; Silver 2003; Wallerstein 1974).

But the 1960s, which brought a combination of ethnic, racial, student, urban, and women's movements, questioned the predominance of class in the study of contentious politics and placed a greater emphasis on the political process of contention. The present authors shared in this shift from a focus on the structural causes, to the political processes producing contentious politics (Tilly 2000; Tarrow 2006).

From the 1970s through the 1990s, most students of movements focused on the organization of movements, the beliefs and actions of activists, and their relationship to the political process. With the coming of a "cultural turn" in movement studies, the subjects of contentious politics, instead of being classified as part of a "class," were defined as they defined themselves—as African Americans, Hispanics, women, gay and lesbian people, ecologists, animal rights advocates, and so forth. As for the working class, with the triumph of neoliberalism in the world economy, workers' capacity for collective action was rendered weaker and weaker (Tilly 1995). "Labor markets," writes Lowell Turner, "have reached new levels of fragmentation, stagnant in the middle, with expanding low-wage workforces not benefiting from any kind of collective representation" (Turner 2014: 3). Some authors even relegated the workers to the status of "old" social movements, as the organizations that historically represented them—the trade unions—lost ground and became more institutionalized (Offe 1985; Touraine 1971).

The new century was not kind to workers either, but with the financial crisis of 2008, the entire northern economy went into crisis. Housing bubbles, low-quality mortgages, mortgage-backed securities, overexpansion of the financial sector and the loss of industrial jobs to the low-wage economies of Asia and Latin America were symptoms of an underlying economic disease: what Lowell Turner calls the result of "global liberalization driven by unsustainable economic policies" (2014: 3; Piketty 2014). Across the developed economies of the North, financial panic spread, financial firms crashed, jobs dried up, and governments made the situation worse by adopting stringent policies of austerity. Figure 10.1 portrays the declining situation of ordinary people in Western Europe and the United States graphically by measuring the changes in the Gini coefficient—the measure economists use to assess economic inequality.

As you would expect, there were soon major consequences for contentious politics. In both Europe and the United States, the crimes of the financial sector, the bumbling responses of governments and international institutions, and the deepening deprivation of major sectors of the populations led to the wave of movements that Donatella della Porta and Alice Mattoni have called "movements of the crisis" (2014). In these

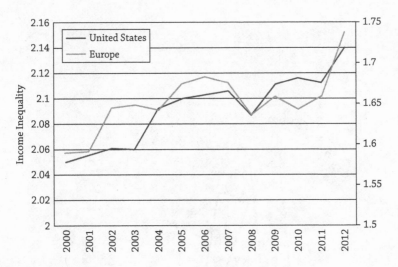

Figure 10.1:
Income Inequality in the United States and Europe: 2000–2012
Note: Income inequality is measured as the decile ratio of earnings between the 5th decile and the 1st decile. The numbers reflect the distance between high-income and low- or middle-income earners.
Source: OECD.Stat http://www.oecd-ilibrary.org/employment/earnings-and-wages/indicator-group/english_4ead40c7-en;jsessionid=760vh0aptrutu.x-oecd-live-03 (2014)

upswellings of popular outrage, trade unions, radicals of left and right, and left-wing intellectuals played important roles; but what was most striking about them on both continents was that they did not call upon the class imagery of the past, but on a broader populist imagery. They focused on the mood of outrage among the protesters (*los indignados*); on the breadth of the public they claimed to represent ("the 99 percent"), and on the forms of contention they employed—mainly the occupation of public space (Graeber 2011). Even new right-wing movements like the American tea party and the Italian "Five Star" party employed a similar populist imagery.

These performances were not simply forms of encampment, familiar from the long history of contentious politics. They produced an entire repertoire of actions, based on an underlying theory of direct democracy and participation. From the beginning, David Graeber writes of the Occupy movement:

> organisers made the audacious decision to operate not only by direct democracy, without leaders, but by consensus. The first decision ensured that there would be no formal leadership structure that could be co-opted or coerced; the second, that no majority could bend a minority to its will, but that all crucial decisions had to be made by general consent (Graeber 2011).

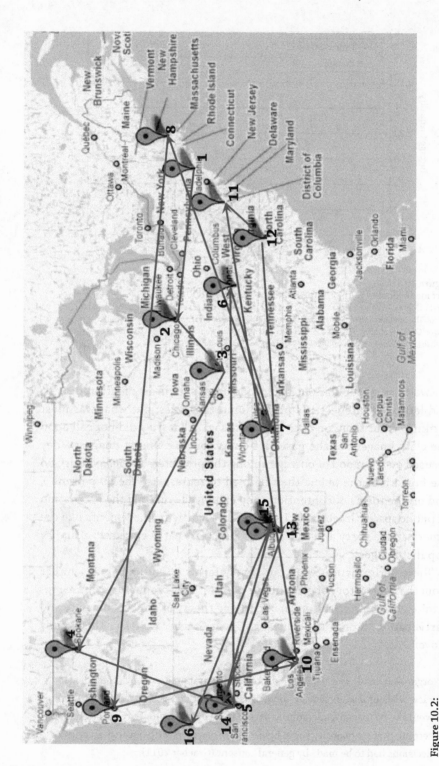

Figure 10.2:
The Spread of "Occupy Wall Street," September 17, October 1, 2011

Source: The dates of occupation are retrieved from the Occupy Together website (www.occupytogether.org).

The movements diffused rapidly: in Europe, from Ireland and Iceland to Portugal and Greece, Italy and Spain; in the United States from New York City to hundreds of sites across the country with amazing rapidity. Figure 10.2 charts the spread of the Occupy Wall Street (OWS) movement in the United States during the first two weeks after the appearance of the first encampment in Zuccotti Park in downtown Manhattan on September 17, 2011.

Was this a purely western phenomenon, or was it part of the global outrage against inequality reflected, in one form, in the Arab Spring, and, in another, in the "Indignant" movements in Western Europe? While the connections between the relatively peaceful occupations in Zuccotti Park and the far more turbulent encampments in Tahrir Square are difficult to establish, there were certainly interactions—if only symbolic ones—between the American and European movements against inequality. Table 10.1, which draws on the "Mission statements" of European and American occupy sites, records the presence of words found only in the American occupy sites; those found only in "indignant" sites outside the United states; and works that were found in the mission statements of both families of movements. The data in Table 10.1 suggest a high degree of mutual learning across the globe was going on.

Table 10.1. "OCCUPY" AND "INDIGNANT" LANGUAGE IN THE MISSION STATEMENTS OF PROTESTERS IN EUROPE AND THE UNITED STATES

Words found in the "Occupy" Movement only	Words found in the "Indignant" Movement only	Words found in both movements
Canada, Columbia, Ecuador, Estonia, Mexico, Nicaragua, Peru, Puerto Rico, Turkey, United States	Greece, Ireland, Montenegro, Serbia	Argentina, Austria, Belgium, Bosnia, Bulgaria, Croatia, Czech Republic, Brazil, Chile, Costa Rica, Denmark, Finland, France, Germany, Hungary, Ireland, Italy, The Netherlands, Norway, Poland, Portugal, Romania, Slovenia, Spain, Sweden, Switzerland, United Kingdom

Source: The table contains information gathered by Chan Suh and Lisook Lim from the Guardian's data (www.guardian.co.uk/news/datablog/2011/oct/17/occupy-protests-world-list-map), various movement-related Facebook accounts, and the movement's own websites.

How did these movements of the crisis spread so far and so fast? One of the messages of this book is that structural factors—like social class or economic inequality—do not in themselves explain contentious politics. It takes a combination of mechanisms like brokerage, identity shift, and coordination and processes like mobilization, scale shift, and polarization to turn the structural potential for contention into confrontations with authorities and elites. There were many mechanisms underlying the European and American occupy and indignation movements; but one set of mechanisms in particular—electronic mobilization empowered by the recent innovations in digital technology—appear to have played a key role in the rapidity and the extent of this episode of contention.

It would be easy to exaggerate the importance of digital communication in contemporary contention. For some observers, for example, the Arab Spring has been called the "Twitter revolution." Advocates of this view point to how rapidly websites were put up in Cairo and elsewhere to communicate what was happening in Tahrir Square to other Egyptians and around the Arab World. But we should not exaggerate: for example, after the Mubarak government shut down the Internet in early 2012, the uprising still spread through the lower-class neighborhoods of Cairo—probably through friendship and family networks (Hassanpour 2014). Besides, every step in the evolution of contentious politics has been marked by advances in the technology of communication, from the penny press in nineteenth century England, to the role of TV in the civil rights movement, to the importance of the transistor radio in the Iranian revolution of 1979, to the use of the cellphone by Philippine protesters at the turn of the new century, to the use of websites and social media today.

Yet it is striking how closely the beginning of actual Occupy sites was matched by the creation of Occupy-linked websites. The websites were used not only to communicate the sites' mission statements to occupiers, but to communicate with supporters in the surrounding communities and to urge the diffusion of the movement further afield. Figure 10.3 charts the co-occurrence of "online" and "offline" occupy activity in the first weeks after the Occupy encampment in New York City. Analyses of Twitter and Facebook activity by Bogdan Vasi and Chan Suh, from whose work Figure 10.3 is drawn, show a significant correlation between the diffusion of Occupy sites and online activity (Vasi and Suh 2014).

The movements of the crisis of 2010–2012 eventually petered out, for the same reason that all cycles of contention eventually end: a combination of fatigue, dispersion into other activities, police repression, and

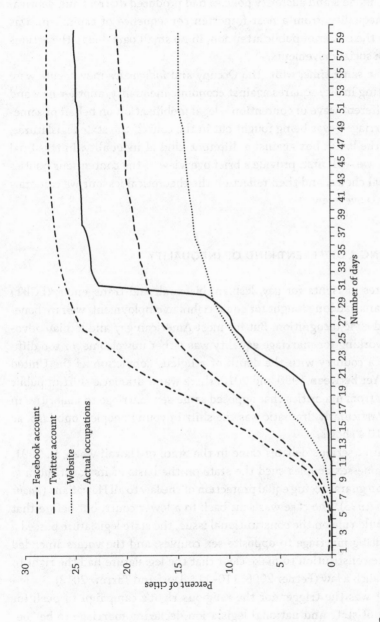

Figure 10.3:
Cities that Experienced On-Line and Off-Line Protests in the Occupy Movement
Sources: Vasi and Suh (2012).

institutionalization (see Chapter 7). But before it ended, the cycle of contention these movements mobilized helped to change the discourse of both American and European politics and to recognize that neoliberal economic models and austerity policies had produced distress and deprivation. Inequality, from a near-forgotten consequence of capitalism, was back in the center of public attention, in no small part due to the actions of these social movements.

At the same time, while the Occupy and *Indignados* movements were mobilizing in city squares against economic inequality, another new and very different wave of contention—legal mobilization on behalf of same-sex marriage—was being fought out in the courts, the state legislatures, and at the ballot box against a different kind of inequality. In this final section, we will, first, provide a brief overview of the contentious politics of sexual choice, and then reflect on the theoretical lessons we can draw from this overview.

FIGHTING A DIFFERENT KIND OF INEQUALITY

Advocates of rights for gay, lesbian, bisexual, and transgender (LGBT) Americans had long fought for equal rights in employment, welfare benefits, and civic recognition. But for most American gay and lesbian advocates, working for marriage equality was either unwelcome, or too difficult, in a country with the depth of religious conviction as the United States. Yet between 1990 and 2010, there was a dramatic shift in public opinion from majorities that opposed same-sex marriage to majorities in favor. Particularly dramatic was the shift in young peoples' opinions, as Figure 10.4 shows.

The first serious debates came in the State of Hawaii when, in 1991, three same-sex couples sued the state on the basis of its constitutional provision guaranteeing equal protection of the law to all Hawaiians (*Baehr v. Lewin* 1993). The case was sent back to a lower court, but before that court could rule on the constitutional issue, the state legislature passed a law limiting marriage to opposite-sex couples, and the voters amended the state constitution to make clear that the legislature had the right to impose such a law (Fetner 2008: 110–111; Dorf and Tarrow 2013).

Baehr was the trigger for the religious right's campaign to push for passage of state and national legislation declaring marriage to be "between one man and one woman." It was mainly in response to this strategy that the United States Congress, in 1996, passed the Defense of Marriage Act (DOMA). The national DOMA was followed by the passage of

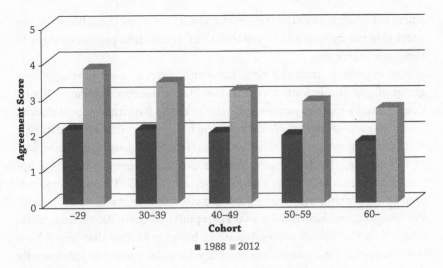

Figure 10.4:
Americans' Attitudes to Same-Sex Marriage, 1988 and 2012, by Age Cohort
Note: The question asks as follows: "Do you agree or disagree with the following statement: Homosexual couples have the right to marry one another."
Source: General Social Survey data provided by the National Opinion Research Center at the University of Chicago (available at: http://www3.norc.org/GSS+Website/Download/)

fifteen state-level DOMAs in 1995 and 1996. These statewide laws were successful, not only in freezing progress in the LGBT right to marriage, but in rallying conservatives and dividing liberal legislators from their gay constituents (Stone 2012: 31). To this point, the initiative mainly seemed to lie with the countermovement, while the LGBT movement seemed unable to adapt to the right's strategy of using popular referenda to advance its goals.

To be sure, same-sex marriage advocates scored a victory in 1999, when the Vermont Supreme Court invalidated that state's opposite-sex-marriage-only law (*Baker v. State*). But the remedy was only partial: the Vermont legislature was given the choice of legalizing same-sex marriage or civil unions. (Eskridge 2002). And after legislators opted for the lesser status of civil unions, they faced a backlash from voters who thought that even this went too far (Klarman 2012: 77–83). The LGBT rights movement was once again thrown on the defensive.

The initiative shifted with a key decision of the US Supreme Court in 2003 about rights other than marriage. In *Lawrence v. Texas*, the court invalidated a Texas criminal statute that forbade sodomy (but only when performed by people of the same sex). Justice Anthony Kennedy's majority opinion did not say that same-sex intimacy was a fundamental right akin to freedom of speech or even contraception, but he left little doubt where his sympathies (and the court's) lay. At the same time, however, the court was not quite ready to say that the Constitution protects a right to same-sex marriage.

Not everybody took the hint. Later that year, in a case brought by a group of gay and lesbian activists, the Massachusetts Supreme Judicial Court found a right to same-sex marriage in the Bay State's Constitution. (*Goodridge v. Dep't of Pub. Health*). For the first time in American history, a state law gave recognition to same-sex marriage. Beginning in the middle of the decade, the debate over civil unions and same-sex marriage appeared to galvanize activist groups, especially the LGBT community. Referenda supporting marriage equality passed in the states of Maryland, Washington, and Maine (where voters repudiated their 2009 ballot initiative), while Minnesota voters defeated a ballot initiative that would have written opposition to same-sex marriage into the state's constitution. By 2015, same-sex marriage had been declared legal in thirty-six states, and in Washington, DC.

The result was that civil unions were largely left behind as the refuge of fence-straddling politicians. Although the early innings in the struggle for same-sex marriage had taken the form of state referenda—which were mainly won by anti-gay marriage activists (Stone 2012)—as in many other areas of law and culture in the United States, the debate over marriage equality ended up in the Supreme Court. In a key case in 2013, and in the refusal to override lower court decisions in October 2014, the court overruled California's refusal to abide by a lower court's ruling, leaving the district court's ruling in place. (*Hollingsworth v. Perry* 2013). The same day, the court ruled that the section of DOMA that defined marriage as opposite-sex marriage for federal purposes was invalid (*United States v. Windsor* 2013).

As public opinion began to shift, the opportunity structure opened for popularity-seeking politicians like Barack Obama to trim their sails to adjust to the changing national mood. In 2004, as a candidate for the United States Senate, Obama had declared that marriage was "between a man and a woman"; in the 2008 campaign, his position had moved to support for civil unions; and in May 2012, he made his first clear expression of support at a campaign stop in Seattle, where he included "the freedom to love" along with tried and true elements of the American Creed:

> We came together because we believed that in America, your success shouldn't be determined by the circumstances of your birth. If you're willing to work hard, you should be able to find a good job. If you're meeting your responsibilities, you should be able to own a home, maybe start a business. You should be

able to give your kids the chance to do even better than you—no matter who you are, no matter where you come from, no matter what you look like, no matter what your last name, *no matter who you love* [italics added] (http:// projects.washingtonpost.com/obama-speeches/speech/1056/).

In roughly two decades, same-sex marriage went from being a fringe cause to very mainstream. The question is "why?" Our voyage through contentious politics should help us to answer this question.

WHAT HAVE WE LEARNED?

The marriage equality movement triumphed through a complex process of movement-countermovement interaction, as chapter 5 would have predicted (Dorf and Tarrow 2013). It was after the Hawaiian case—hardly a social movement—that religious conservatives passed DOMA in Congress and a number of state-level DOMAs, and took the issue of same-sex marriage to the electorate in many states. In fact, as these authors argue, the counter-mobilization arose while the LGBT movement was still cautious about placing marriage equality on the agenda, fearing a reaction. Faced by forceful opposition from religious conservatives and nudged forward by grassroots activists, LGBT advocates took on the cause of marriage equality.

The marriage equality movement also profited from the kind of scale shift we saw in chapter 6: as long as the conflict was lodged at the level of state legislatures and local politicians, the LGBT movement had no hope of winning; it was only as the focus shifted to the courts—and especially to the federal court system—that a shift in scale helped the movement to gain advantages from the doctrine of equal protection of the laws. The movement was also able to shift what it means to be gay or lesbian, focusing its public campaigns on the love between gay couples and on their desire to bring up their children in a normal family.

The gay marriage campaign resembled the two social movement campaigns that chapter 7 reviewed. All three took advantage of political opportunities offered by their respective regimes and worked their ways through a roughly similar set of mechanisms and processes. All three built on social movement bases. All three used different combinations of repertoire choices to mobilize supporters, expand the public's support for their causes, and have an effect on public policy. All of these had profound effects.

If the title of our book had been *Social Movements*, readers could have relaxed after reading chapter 7. But unlike many fine texts focusing on movements, our aim has been much broader. Comparing the two cases in chapter 7 with the ones examined in chapters 8–9, you can see that social movements are only one of a wide array of forms of contentious politics. While all the episodes we have studied make claims on authorities, use public performances to do so, draw on inherited repertoires of collective action, forge alliances with influential members of their respective polities, and take advantage of existing regime opportunities while making new ones, the degree to which they use institutional routines to advance their claims varies sharply.

Think back to the list of concepts presented in chapter 1. Each of them offers you an orienting point for describing and analyzing the story we have just sketched. In the same-sex marriage campaign, gay couples constituted themselves as *political actors* and assumed the *political identities* of people unwilling to accept the subaltern status assigned to those with their sexual preferences. As they demonstrated, fought referenda campaigns, and went to court, their actions became a political *performance*, one with a pedigree in the *repertoire of contention*, but one that they innovated on like jazz musicians improvising on a theme. As they did so, they engaged with public *institutions*—the press, the local and state governments, and, ultimately, the Supreme Court. They also involved themselves in the broader conflict brewing between the state and federal governments in the American political *regime*. They mounted a classic social movement campaign that succeeded in changing policies of most states and the federal government toward marriage.

But we cannot leap directly to policy outcomes from the actions of the activists. We first need to search the *episode* for the *mechanisms* and *processes* that produced significant changes—in particular, the key mechanism of diffusion. The marriage equality movement spread from the geographic perimeter in the state of Hawaii to three relatively liberal coastal states—Massachusetts, Vermont, and California—and then to heartland states like Iowa, before ending up in the courts. But as we have seen throughout our book, diffusion seldom operates on its own. The same-sex marriage movement spread through the mechanism of *brokerage*, which coordinated the actions of gay couples across the country; through *certification*, as they sought recognition as legitimate actors to the legislators, judges, and institutions that took up their claim; and through *boundary activation*, as their actions insisted that gay couples had the same right to marry as heterosexuals.

Chapter 3's lessons take us one step beyond the struggle for marriage equality. Like the cases we examined there, the movement responded to relations among regimes, repertoires, and opportunities. Remember how electoral contests produced the political opportunities of the Otpor and other movements in post-Socialist countries in chapter 3. And how contentious politics shifted in close connection with shifts of political power in the unstable history of Venezuela in chapter 4? Those connections operated both in authoritarian systems and in the regimes we have called "hybrid states."

In contrast to authoritarian regimes, in which repertoires are rigid, American politics has always left open opportunities for innovation in the repertoire of contention. This is particularly true during periods of rapid political change. In the history of civil rights, the sit-ins marked a significant shift in the challengers' repertoire, one to which political elites had to struggle to catch up (McAdam 1983). Remember how important Congressional action was in the success of the women's movement in chapter 6? In the marriage equality movement, it was largely in the courts—but also in the electorate and the state legislatures—that contention proceeded.

Chapter 3 also explained that the causal interaction between regime characteristics and repertoire change runs in both directions. Not only does the character of a regime shape contention, but changes in contention lead to changes in regimes. The broad wave of contention of the 1960s led, first, to the "normalization" of many forms of contention that had previously been considered illegitimate (Piven and Cloward 1992). It also included the spread of contentious politics to new sectors of the population—women, Hispanics, gays, and lesbians (Meyer and Tarrow 1998). It contributed to the most significant democratization of American politics since the passage of women's suffrage after World War I. The same-sex marriage movement built on that foundation and drew much of its narrative from the movement for black and other minority rights.

The change did not happen at random. As in many of the episodes we have examined, the gay couples were taking advantage of a changing *political opportunity structure*. Chapter 3 pointed out that we can trace political change in any regime through reactions of political actors to six dimensions of opportunity: (1) the multiplicity of independent centers of power within the regime, (2) its openness to new actors, (3) the instability of current political alignments, (4) the availability of influential allies or supporters for challengers, (5) the extent to which the regime represses or facilitates collective claim making, and (6) decisive changes in any and all of these regards. Gay marriage protesters took advantage of all of these dimensions of opportunity.

The multiplicity of independent centers of power in the American regime played to the advantage of the movement. Although Vermont and Massachusetts are by no means "typical" of the American states (which states are?), the fact that they legitimated same-sex relationships with no evident adverse outcomes convinced many ordinary Americans that what had been portrayed as a threat to the family was really only a way to mainstream their gay compatriots. Gay marriage became an instrument in the institutionalization of gay and lesbian couples, a process that we saw in Italy in chapter 6.

We cannot judge the outcomes of an episode simply through the programs or policies it produces (Giugni, 1998, 1999; Meyer et al. 2005). Chapter 5 explained that challengers make claims along three broad dimensions: identity, standing, and program. *Identity claims* declare that an actor exists. They constitute an answer to the questions "Who am I?" and "How do I relate to you?" *Standing claims* say that the actor belongs to an established category within the regime and therefore deserves the rights and respect that members of that category receive; for that reason, standing claims often imply answers to a further question: "How would I like this relationship to change?" *Program claims* call for the objects of claims to act in a certain way: to do something, to stop doing something, to make someone else do something, and so on.

Although the LGBT rights movement certainly offered a program for fundamental change in the behavior of American governments, merchants, and citizens at large, it did not simply seek programmatic changes. Its claims fundamentally concerned identity, which had become a central issue in the black community during the 1960s. The entire gay rights movement forwarded a process of identity reassessment (Burns 1997: 244). After the landmark Supreme Court cases, refusing to enforced marriage inequality, gay Americans who had been in the closet for most of their lives began to expand the boundaries of legitimacy even in conservative states.[1]

Gay and lesbian Americans were also demanding recognition of their *standing* as citizens with equal rights. Through a variety of boundary-challenging actions, they sought certification from courts, legislatures, committees, and organizations. They also sought changes in the relations between themselves and other Americans through the boundary activation mechanisms examined in chapter 5. Those boundaries expanded: in response to the gains being made by gays and lesbians, transgender and bisexual Americans overcame their timidity and demanded equal rights as well. The language Americans use reflect this broadening of boundaries: instead of speaking of "gays and lesbians," Americans were learning to use the expression "LGBT rights" (Tarrow 2013).

Big changes in politics connect with broad political processes. Remember our key process of *scale shift*, which chapter 5 introduced? It is a composite process including the mechanisms of *diffusion, attribution of similarity, brokerage,* and *emulation.* The same-sex marriage movement began as far from Washington, DC, as one could get and still be in the United States, but its state-by-state diffusion and its capacity to adapt its repertoire to different state settings eventually led to a national turning point in the Supreme Court decisions of 2013–2014.

Chapter 6 introduced the broadest processes surveyed in this book: *mobilization* and *demobilization.* We saw them operating briefly in Lyons, longer in the Italian cycle of contention, and more dramatically in Central America, and the Arab Spring. But if we think about it, we realize that we also saw these processes in British antislavery, the Ukrainian conflicts, Central and South American contention, the Zapatista rising, nationalism in the former Soviet Union, and the climate change movement. In all these cases, the interactive mechanisms we identified with mobilization included our old friends *diffusion, brokerage,* and *boundary activation.*

But mobilization is not a one-way process. All cycles of contention eventually decline; what is interesting is their different outcomes. In chapter 6, we saw a number of mechanisms combining to produce demobilization. But the outcomes were very different: In Italy a minority of the activists who rose up in 1968 ended up in the terrorist Red Brigades, while a much larger number entered the party system and the political institutions. In the Muslim Middle East, secular autocracies, like the Iraqi and Syrian ones, hid the region's underlying religious and ethnic divisions, which exploded when the democratization movement of 2011 opened the gates for their expression. The same mechanisms took the American civil rights movement from its emergence in the late 1950s to its radicalization in the early 1960s and to its decline in the late 1960s and after. The sexual equality movement has yet to demobilize, but it very early followed a route that many movements took decades to accomplish: *institutionalization.* Americans are no longer surprised to find gay comedians, gay politicians, and even gay athletes announcing their sexuality and suffering no sanctions, as they would have in even the recent past.

Chapter 7 first distinguished between episodes of collective action that fail to crystallize into sustained movements (e.g., Poland's response to Khrushchev's "secret speech") and those that do so (e.g., the Polish Solidarity movement of 1980). The contrast between the short-lived strike wave of 1956 and the long-lasting Solidarity movement pinpointed that difference and its relationship to changes in the Polish regime and the Soviet bloc more generally. That chapter also introduced the fundamental distinction between social movement bases and social movement campaigns.

By the 2000s the broader gay rights movement had a thick organizational infrastructure and a cultural legitimacy resulting from past struggles that the same-sex marriage campaign could draw upon. The campaign for marriage equality was the most visible part of the gay rights movement after the turn of the century, but it was far from the only one. LGBT Americans began to organize unobtrusively from the 1960s onward—in gay bars, in theatres, in universities and law offices, and ultimately in the public sphere. Not all gay activists supported marriage; indeed, an articulate minority condemned it as an institution; but by 2014, the campaign could draw upon a movement's social movement base that was both deep and wide (Dorf and Tarrow 2013).

Gay marriage did not trigger violent contention of the kind we examined in chapter 8. But it did trigger a vitriolic and dangerous reaction on the Internet and in social media sites. there was—and remains today—hostility to gay Americans in many sectors of the population. As more young people declared their sexuality to be different from the norm, bullying of self-declared LGBT youngsters increased in schools across the country. Protecting their rights is probably the next frontier in the fight for equality. Despite the gains in equality since the 1960s, America is still a country that is "deeply divided," where cultural and political cleavages have actually increased in reaction to those gains (McAdam and Kloos 2014).

CONCLUSION

We began our book by comparing the British antislavery mobilization of the 1780s with the Ukrainian conflicts of 2013–2014. We ended with the movement for equality in Europe and with the same-sex marriage movement in the United States. Between the two, we examined a great range of popular contention in Europe, Africa, the Middle East, and the Americas. But much more remains to be done:

- Except for brief narrative on the Hong Kong electoral protest in chapter 4, we have neglected Asia, because we prefer to write about regions on which we have done research and some of whose languages we know.
- We have had little to say about the social psychology of contention, a well-studied field in which many specialists know much more than we do (Klandermans 1997).
- Apart from the marriage equality movement discussed above, we have largely ignored the spread of contentious forms of politics to new sectors of the population and whether this has turned once-transgressive and

forbidden means of contention into contained and tolerated ones (Meyer and Tarrow 1998).

- Nor have we attempted to systematically demonstrate our explanations for any of the episodes we have examined. That undertaking would have required another book or expanded this one exponentially.

By now, you can draw your own conclusions about the tools the book has laid out and about the dynamics of contentious politics in general. As a reminder, nevertheless, here are some generalizations and some practical conclusions to take away from your reading.

As generalizations, let us drum away at these:

- Although they generally occur in different sorts of regimes, revolutions, civil wars, lethal ethnic conflicts, social movements, and other forms of contentious politics result from similar causes in different combinations, sequences, and initial conditions.
- We can usefully break those causes into recurrent mechanisms and processes. Explaining contention means identifying the mechanisms and processes that lie behind it.
- In all sorts of regimes, from low capacity to high capacity, from undemocratic to democratic, and in both types of hybrid regimes, routine interactions between governments and political actors produce political opportunity structures that channel what forms of contention different potential makers of claim can actually initiate.
- At the same time, governmental action and popular contention interact to form repertoires of contention—limited arrays of known, feasible ways to make collective claims—that also limit possible forms of contention in any regime.
- Nevertheless, all parties to contention are constantly innovating and negotiating, often attempting to persuade, block, defeat, punish, or collaborate with each other. That incessant give and take makes contentious politics a dynamic drama rather than a stale reenactment of old scenarios.

These general features of contention lead directly to some practical conclusions for students of contentious politics:

- Before you try to decide whether some contentious episode is a revolution, a social movement, or something else, describe the episode and its setting carefully. The appendix sums up advice this book has given for the work of describing contentious episodes and their settings.

- Early in the process, sort your description into the elements this book has taught you: governments, political actors, political identities, contentious performances, institutions, and more. Trace how each of them changes, if at all, over the course of the episode.
- When you have made clear what you must explain, turn to the book's explanatory concepts: not only the regimes, political opportunity structures, repertoires, mechanisms, and processes mentioned earlier, but also sites, conditions, streams, and outcomes of contention. Again, the appendices can help you to set up your explanations.
- Instead of trying to explain everything about a contentious episode, close in on its most surprising, interesting, or consequential features— for example, how sit-ins changed the political connections and public image of the US civil rights movement or how the movement for marriage equality helped to move public opinion toward its acceptance.
- Use comparisons—including comparisons with episodes studied in this book—to single out similarities and differences between your episodes and others in the same general categories. Some of our comparisons would take you far afield—for example, our comparison between British antislavery and the Ukrainian conflicts of 2013–2014.
- Armed with a number of mechanisms and processes, do not be afraid to make broad comparisons, but more proximate ones work just as well— for example, Soule's Cornell-based comparison between American campuses that produced shantytown protests and those that did not. The differences—and the similarities—will be just as revealing.

Even if you don't undertake major investigations of your own, you can still use this book's lessons to better equip you as a citizen to evaluate the news of political contention that bombards you every day. Almost every daily newspaper and blog post carries reports on contentious politics across the world. By now, you should have a clearer idea of what reporters are talking about when they tell you that French people demonstrate, civil wars ravage Africa, and Iraqi insurgents set off bombs under American humvees. Here are three lessons to apply in judging what they say.

First, beware of the catchall terms that journalists and politicians habitually use to describe contention. Not all displays of violence are "riots," and not all lethal conflict is touched off by rioters. In fact, history teaches that in democracies and semi-democracies, while ordinary people are the sources of most damage to property, the greatest source of violence against persons is the police. Before deciding that a particular performance is a riot, ask yourself who is telling the story—a participant, an onlooker, or an opponent of the claim makers.

Second, use the comparative method in judging the news. If a television broadcaster assures you that masses of Iraqi citizens pulled down the statue of Saddam Hussein following the American-led invasion, ask yourself who was present at that scene. You may be surprised to discover that its organizers were American troops propping up the few Iraqis in attendance. Compare that picture to the exhilarated crowds in Eastern Europe in 1989 that toppled statues of Lenin and Stalin without official assistance.

Third, don't stop with analyzing actually occurring contention. In Arthur Conan Doyle's mystery "Silver Blaze," Sherlock Holmes solves the case because of a dog that didn't bark. In 2003, Americans were falsely assured that their sons and daughters were sent off to Iraq to find and destroy Saddam Hussein's weapons of mass destruction. When word crept out that these weapons were nonexistent and that the intelligence that justified the invasion had been faked, why did they not rebel? When residents of New Orleans who were washed out of their homes by Hurricane Katrina went without government assistance for days and weeks, why did they not demand better than that from their rulers? And when unarmed black men were shot down in cold blood by police officers, why were so few white citizens present in the protests that followed?

As our theories and narratives have taught, modern politics contains recurring streams of contention, but it also includes oceans of apathy. We now know a lot about why citizens of authoritarian regimes are normally compliant, rising in resistance only when dramatic windows of opportunity open up. But why do citizens of democratic regimes fail to "bark"? Why do they so often sit on their hands when they have the right to resist? And when democracy depends on their active participation? That might well be the next stage in the study of contentious politics. We invite you to take it.

NOTE

1. *New York Times*, October 8, 2014. www.nytimes.com/2014/10/08/us/politics/same-sex-marriage-gay-rights-supreme-court.html.

APPENDIX A

Concepts and Methods

Box A.1 identifies the book's main descriptive concepts: governments, political actors, political identities, contentious performances, and more. The concepts in box A.1 supply the major terms we use when describing different varieties of contention. Our comparison of British antislavery with Ukraine's 2014 anti-Presidential uprising and separatist movement in chapter 1 made it obvious that political actors, political identities, performances, and other aspects of contention vary dramatically from one time and place to another. The concepts specify what sorts of variation and change we have to explain.

As chapters 6 and 7 and 8 show, for example, social movements occur mainly in very different circumstances from lethal ethnic and religious conflicts, civil wars, and revolutions. That sets our explanatory problem: What sorts of circumstances favor social movements rather than large-scale lethal conflicts, how, and why? What causes connect contentious episodes with the settings in which they occur? In order to answer that sort of question, we must go on from descriptive to explanatory concepts.

Box A.2 identifies the main explanatory concepts the book employs: sites, conditions, streams of contention, and so on. We use these terms to identify causal connections among the descriptive elements—for example, by showing which mechanisms bring political actors into social movements. As they differentiate between social movements and large-scale lethal conflicts, chapters 7 and 8 lay out how very different regimes and political opportunity structures underlie the two broad classes of contention. Let us review our major explanatory concepts one by one.

Sites of contention include all human settings that serve as originators, objects, and/or arenas of collective claims. Sites may be human individuals, but they also include informal networks, organizations, neighborhoods, professions, trades, and other settings of social life. Each kind of

Box A.1: MAJOR DESCRIPTIVE CONCEPTS IN THE STUDY OF CONTENTIOUS POLITICS

- *Government*: within a given territory, an organization controlling the principal concentrated means of coercion and exercising priority over all other organizations within the same territory in some regards. In England of 1785, the organization included a king, ministers, civil servants, Parliament, and a network of appointed agents throughout the country.
- *Political actors*: recognizable sets of people who carry on collective action in which governments are directly or indirectly involved, making and/or receiving contentious claims. In Ukraine, supporters of outgoing president Kuchma, backers of presidential candidate Yushchenko, Interior Ministry troops, and external sponsors on both sides all figured as weighty political actors.
- *Political identities*: as applied to political actors, organized answers to the questions "Who are you?," "Who are they?," and "Who are we?" In late eighteenth-century England, some of those answers included abolitionists, slaveholders, and Parliament.
- *Contentious politics*: interactions in which actors make claims that bear on someone else's interests, leading to coordinating efforts on behalf of shared interests or programs, in which governments are as targets, the objects of claims, or third parties.
- *Contentious performances*: relatively familiar and standardized ways in which one set of political actors makes collective claims on some other set of political actors. Among other performances, participants in Ukraine's Orange Revolution used mass demonstrations as visible, effective performances.
- *Contentious repertoires*: arrays of contentious performances that are currently known and available within some set of political actors. England's antislavery activists helped to invent the demonstration as a political performance, but they also drew on petitions, lobbying, press releases, public meetings, and a number of other performances.
- *Contained* contention takes place within a regime's prescribed and tolerated forms of claim making, even if it pushes the limits, as when participants in a public meeting start shouting seditious slogans.
- *Transgressive* contention crosses institutional boundaries into forbidden or unknown territory.

- *Institutions*: within any particular regime, established, organized, widely recognized routines, connections, and forms of organization employed repeatedly in producing collective action. Eighteenth-century antislavery activists could work with such available institutions as religious congregations, parliamentary hearings, and the press.
- *Social movements*: sustained campaigns of claim making, using repeated performances that advertise that claim, based on organizations, networks, traditions, and solidarities that sustain these activities.

These divide into the following:

- *Social movement campaigns*: sustained challenges to power holders in the name of a population living under the jurisdiction of those power holders by means of public displays of that population's worthiness, unity, numbers, and commitment.
- *Social movement bases*: the social background, organizational resources, and cultural framework of contention and collective action.

Box A.2: MAJOR EXPLANATORY CONCEPTS IN CONTENTIOUS POLITICS

- *Sites of contention*: human settings that serve as originators, objects, and/or arenas of contentious politics. Example: Armies often play all three parts in contention.
- *Conditions*: characteristics of sites and relations among sites that shape the contention occurring in and across them. *Initial* conditions are those that prevail in affected sites at the start of some process or episode. Example: In Italy of 1966, an array of political organizations and existing connections among them provided the background for the cycle of conflict that occurred over the next seven years.
- *Streams of contention*: sequences of collective claim at or across those sites making singled out for explanation. Example: a series of strikes by workers in a given industry against their firm(s).

(continued)

Box A.2: CONTINUED

- *Outcomes*: changes in conditions at or across the sites that are plausibly related to the contention under study, including transformations of political actors or relations among them. Example: During or after a series of strikes, management fires workers, changes work rules, and/or raises wages.
- *Regimes*: regular relations among governments, established political actors, challengers, and outside political actors including other governments; eighteenth-century England and twenty-first-century Ukraine obviously hosted very different regimes.
- *Political opportunity structure*: features of regimes and institutions (e.g., splits in the ruling class) that facilitate or inhibit a political actor's collective action; in the case of Ukraine 2004–2005, a divided international environment gave dissidents an opportunity to call on foreign backers in the name of democracy.
- *Mechanisms*: events that produce the same immediate effects over a wide range of circumstances. Example: Diffusion of tactics from one site to another often occurs during major mobilizations, thus altering action at origin and destination as well as facilitating coordination among the affected sites.
- *Processes*: combinations and sequences of mechanisms that produce some specified outcome. Example: Major mobilizations usually combine brokerage and diffusion with other mechanisms in sequences and combinations that strongly affect the collective action emerging from the mobilization.
- *Episodes*: bounded sequences of continuous interaction, usually produced by an investigator's chopping up longer streams of contention into segments for purposes of systematic observation, comparison, and explanation. Example: We might compare successive petition drives of antislavery activists in Great Britain (each drive counting as a single episode) over the twenty years after 1785, thus not only seeing how participants in one drive learned from the previous drive but also documenting how the movement as a whole evolved.
- *Cycles of Contention*: episodes combining a variety of actors, their claims, counter-claimants, governments, and institutions.

site has its own peculiarities. Neighborhoods do not behave just like individuals; factories and agricultural communities do not behave like neighborhoods. Yet this book has identified many parallels in the ways that mechanisms, processes, and episodes operate across different kinds of sites. We learn, for example, that repertoires can belong to sets of organizations as well as to sets of informal networks and to sets of individuals.

Conditions are characteristics of sites and relations among sites that shape the contention that occurs in and across them. We might imagine a country, for example, in which one group is a well-established political actor with strong ties to government, while another is an underground opponent of the government currently being harassed by state security forces. The existence of those two groups and of their relations to the government identifies a condition that affects contentious politics within the regime in question.

When looking at mechanisms, processes, and episodes, we have often called attention to *initial* conditions that affect how mechanisms interact, how processes develop, and what outcomes result from those processes. Initial conditions prevail when the stream of contention on which we are concentrating begins. Initial conditions such as the available repertoire of claim-making performances or the organization of the country's government affect how contention actually occurs. Conditions then change during and after contention, as struggle itself alters repertoires, relations among political actors, and other features of the sites.

Streams of contention contain connected moments of collective claim making that observers single out for explanation. We might, for example, treat the entire British antislavery movement from 1785 to 1835 as a single stream on the assumption that throughout the period, earlier mobilizations and their consequences shaped later mobilizations. But we could also focus on antislavery efforts in London alone or on just one intense period of action. A stream may come into view because participants or other analysts already treat it as continuous, as in the mobilization that led to the British parliament's banning of the slave trade in 1807. It may also interest us because of concern with some general process such as democratization. Analysts often line up parallel streams of events that do and don't end up with democratic institutions in order to clarify explanations of democratization in general.

Outcomes consist of changes in conditions at or across the sites under study that are plausibly related to the contention under study, including transformations of political actors or relations among them. In transitions from authoritarian to democratic regimes, previously dominant classes, factions, organizations, or families always lose some of their power. If we ask what happens to former rulers under democratic transitions, we are asking outcome questions. It may turn out that the outcomes we single out did *not* result from the streams of contention we initially observed. In that case, we look for new explanations elsewhere. Part of the adventure comes from determining what actually caused the outcomes in question. For that purpose, we look closely at mechanisms and processes.

Regimes involve regular relations among governments, established political actors, challengers, and outside political actors, including other governments. To identify a regime, we typically begin by locating a *government*: the organization in a given substantial territory that controls the largest concentrated means of coercion—armies, jails, means of shaming people, and so on—within the territory. We then look for political actors outside that government that interact regularly with the government's agents and agencies. We call the actors *members* if they have secure standing in day-to-day politics, *challengers* if they make their presence known collectively but lack secure standing, and *outsiders* if they operate from bases external to the territory under the government's control.

Political opportunity structure figures repeatedly in this book's explanations of contention. Political opportunity structure includes six properties of a regime:

1. The multiplicity of independent centers of power within it
2. Its openness to new actors
3. The instability of current political alignments
4. The availability of influential allies or supporters for challengers
5. The extent to which the regime represses or facilitates collective claim making
6. Changes in any of the above.

From the perspective of a whole regime, the instability of alignments and the availability of allies (items 3 and 4) amount to the same thing. Stable alignments generally mean that many political actors have no potential allies in power. By such a definition, however, political opportunity structure varies somewhat from one actor to another. At the same moment, one actor has many available allies; another, few. For all actors, in any case, threats and opportunities shift with fragmentation or concentration of power, changes in the regime's openness, instability of political alignments, and the availability of allies.

Mechanisms are changes that produce the same immediate effects over a wide range of circumstances. The mechanism we call *brokerage*, for example, operates in essentially the same way in highly varied situations. It connects two previously unconnected social sites and thereby lowers the cost of communication and coordination between them. Social movement organizers often employ brokerage, bringing previously unconnected groups or social networks into the same campaign. Contentious politics also frequently involves the mechanism of *identity shift*, as people who formerly thought of themselves in a variety of distinct social roles come together and realize a unified—if temporary—identity such as worker, victim of environmental pollution, African American, or citizen of the world.

Processes assemble mechanisms into different sequences and combinations, thus producing larger-scale outcomes than any single mechanism. This book deals repeatedly with the process called *mobilization*, in which the resources available to a political actor for collective claim making increase. Relevant resources include energy, ideas, practices, and material objects, to the extent that their application would support the making of claims. Brokerage often plays a part in mobilization, but so does identity shift. In fact, brokerage frequently activates identity shift, as people mobilized around the same issue attribute similarity to themselves and their allies.

Mobilization has an equal and opposite process, *demobilization*, or the decline in the resources available for collective claim making. Beyond open contention, political organizers spend a good deal of their effort on mobilization and on fending off demobilization. Governments, too, direct considerable attention to aiding the mobilization of their supporters and to pursuing the demobilization of their enemies. Government forces' massacre of unarmed peasants of Panzós, Guatemala, only aimed in part at the protesters in the plaza; it also aimed at the demobilization of a swelling peasant movement.

Episodes are bounded sequences of contentious interaction. Mapping streams of contention into episodes aids the detection of mechanisms and processes. This appendix shows how to divide complicated streams of contention into episodes, describe those episodes, decompose them into causes, and then reassemble the causes into causal accounts of episodes, of the larger streams of contention to which those episodes belong, and of processes that recur widely in different sorts of contentious politics. A successful circuit from description to decomposition to reassembly leads back to new circuits; improved explanation of one episode, series of episodes, or class of contention offers a starting point for new explanations concerning similar varieties of contention. We call this the *mechanism-process approach* to explaining contentious politics. Box A.3 sums up the steps we take toward explanation in the mechanism-process approach.

1. Using the major descriptive concepts in table A.1 (political actors, political identities, institutions, etc.), specify the *site(s)* of contention you are studying.
2. Using the same descriptive concepts, describe relevant *conditions* at those sites when the contention you are studying begins.
3. Identify and describe the *stream(s) of contention* at or among those sites you want to explain.
4. Specify the *outcome(s)* whose relation to the contention under study you want to determine.
5. Break the streams of contention into coherent *episodes*.
6. Search the episodes for *mechanisms* producing significant changes and/or differences.
7. Reconstruct the *processes* into which those mechanisms compound.
8. Using analogies or comparisons with similar processes elsewhere, combine conditions, mechanisms, and processes into explanations of specified outcomes.

The eight steps of explanation combine the major descriptive concepts of box A.1 with the major explanatory concepts of box A.2. As we have shown, some investigations call for a different order among the steps. If, for instance, you have a promising account of how a certain process works or how a specific initial condition affects such a process, you will start with a theory about the process and then identify streams of contention that will help to verify or falsify the theory. (We have often used this reverse order of explanation in various chapters.) Sooner or later, however, you will ordinarily go through all eight steps on the way to a new, falsified, modified, or better-verified explanation. Interactions among mechanisms, processes, and initial conditions will constitute your explanations.

When you begin your research, you can adopt a much more systematic procedure than simply browsing web newswires for the day's contentious events. You could, for instance, do any of these projects:

• Single out a particular form or issue of contentious politics (e.g., suicide bombing or attacks on local officials) for description and explanation, starting with a map of where such events occur most frequently, but moving on to see whether similar processes occur at all the locations, and whether distinctive characteristics of the locales affect how and when this variety of contentious politics occurs. In this case, you might be doing a *common process* study identifying similarities across sites, like those in which Berman and Laitin studied suicide bombing.

- Take an established model of some process in contentious politics (e.g., the simple model of diffusion and brokerage presented in chapter 2), find a series of episodes within the same locale in which that process is occurring, and investigate whether it occurs in accordance with the model.
- Even more ambitiously, develop your own model of some contentious process such as mobilization or demobilization, and test it against a variety of relevant episodes.
- Following Kriesi and his collaborators, you could compare a smaller number of countries (in Latin America, e.g., Colombia, Peru, and Chile) to determine whether other features of those countries such as their political institutions, the place of indigenous people, or involvement in the drug trade help to explain similarities and differences in their contentious politics.

For any of these projects, you would need more information on contention's social and political context than you would find in daily newswire reports. For that information, you might turn to standard reference books such as atlases, encyclopedias, U.S. government country reports, political yearbooks, or the countries' own Web sites. You might also want more evidence on individual events. In that case, you might zoom in on national periodicals from the countries that interest you, which are often available online. No matter how and where you assembled your sources, you would be following the steps of box A.3: describing the sites of contention under study, describing conditions at those sites, and so on, through the mechanism-process routine. You would be identifying important streams of contention, dividing them into episodes, looking for recurrent processes within the episodes, and trying to find the crucial mechanisms within those processes: brokerage, diffusion, emulation, and others.

For other analytical purposes, you could also assemble catalogs of episodes at very different scales from Beissinger, Brockett, Kriesi and his collaborators, Rucht, Soule, Tarrow, Tilly, and others. Drawing on North American newspapers, you could close in on a particular issue or form of action—for example, college campus public meetings on freedom of speech or military service. Comparisons among colleges, cities, states, or provinces coupled with background information about the colleges, cities, states, or provinces would then allow you to start an explanation of the character and relative frequency of those meetings. You could also compare much larger events, including revolutions, military coups, civil wars, or strike waves, across multiple regimes and many years. Box A.3 would still give you guidance for organizing your investigation.

One of the book's many applications of box A.3's procedures occurred in chapter 5. There we looked closely at Italian contention between 1965 and the early 1970s. Drawing on Tarrow's and della Porta's work, we went through these steps:

1. Using the major descriptive concepts from chapter 1 (political actors, political identities, contentious performances, etc.), we specified the *sites* of contention we were studying. Tarrow divided his attention among three sites: students, workers, and progressive Catholics, dedicating separate chapters of his book to each of these.
2. Using the same descriptive concepts, we briefly described relevant *conditions* at those sites when the contention we were studying began. Using both Tarrow's and della Porta's accounts, as well as their joint worker, we sketched Italy's contention from the mid-1960s onward to the "years of lead" characterized by widespread clandestine violence.
3. We identified and described the *stream(s) of contention* at or among those sites we wanted to explain. The researchers identified three major streams: *conventional* contention—including the strike wave and marches and demonstrations; *disruptive* contention, mainly during the early part of the cycle; and *violence*.
4. We then focused on the *mechanisms* that brought about the end of the cycle: mainly the *institutionalization* of most forms of contention; the *escalation* of others; and the *selective repression* that helped force a cleavage between the moderate majority and the violent minority of protesters.
5. Those mechanisms concatenated into the overriding process of *demobilization*; it differed from the civil war cycles we saw in El Salvador and Guatemala because, in those countries, *indiscriminate repression* drove the episode into a civil war.
6. Following Tarrow and della Porta, we presented our analysis of Italian contention in the 1960s and 1970s primarily in a *local process* mode: taking established models of processes in contentious politics, finding a series of episodes within the same locale in which those processes are occurring and investigating whether they occur in accordance with the model. We gestured towards *site comparison* and to by alluding to the contemporaneous French cycle of protest, but we did not try to extend our comparisons to *process generalization*, which would have required us to gather enormous amounts of data on the entire protest cycle of the 1960s in Europe and America. Someone else will have to do that work.

REFERENCES

Adida, Claire, David Laitin, and Marie-Anne Valfort. 2015. "Terror in France: Implications for Muslim Integration." In *The Monkey Cage*, Washington Post, January 15. At http://www.washingtonpost.com/blogs/monkey-cage/wp/2015/01/14/terror-in-france-implications-for-muslim-integration/.

Akbar, Anna. 2013. "Policing Radicalization." *University of California, Irvine Law Review* 3: 810–868.

Alexander, Jeffrey C. 2004. "From the Depths of Despair: Performance, Counter-performance, and 'September 11.'" *Sociological Theory* 22: 88–105.

Alimi, Eitan, Chares Demetriou, and Lorenzo Bosi. 2015. *The Dynamics of Radicalization: A Comparative Perspective*. New York: Oxford University Press.

Alimi, Eitan, and Sivan Hirsch-Hoefler. 2012. "The Structure of Political Opportunities and Threats and Movement-Countermovement Interaction in Segmented Composite Regimes." *Comparative Politics* 44: 331–349.

Almeida, Paul. 2003. "Opportunity Organizations and Threat-Induced Contention: Protest Waves in Authoritarian Settings." *American Journal of Sociology* 109: 345–400.

Almeida, Paul. 2007. "Organizational Expansion, Liberalization Reversals, and Radicalized Collective Action." *Research in Political Sociology* 15: 57–99.

Almeida, Paul. 2008. *Waves of Protest: Popular Struggle in El Salvador, 1925–2005*. Minneapolis: University of Minnesota Press.

Almeida, Paul. 2014. *Mobilizing Democracy: Globalization and Citizen Protest*. Baltimore: Johns Hopkins University Press.

Almeida, Paul D., and Marc I. Lichbach. 2003. "To the Internet, From the Internet: Comparative Media Coverage of Transnational Protest." *Mobilization* 8: 249–272.

Amenta, Edwin. 2006. *When Movements Matter: The Townsend Plan and the Rise of Social Security*. Princeton, NJ: Princeton University Press.

Anderson, Benedict. 1991. *Imagined Communities: Reflections on the Origin and Spread of Nationalism*. London: Verso.

Anderson, Benedict. 1998. *The Spectre of Comparisons: Nationalism, Southeast Asia and the World*. London: Verso.

Andrews, Kenneth T. 2004. *Freedom Is a Constant Struggle: The Mississippi Civil Rights Movement and Its Legacy*. Chicago: University of Chicago Press.

Andrews, Kenneth T., and Michael Biggs. 2006. "The Dynamics of Protest Diffusion: Movement Organizations, Social Networks, and News Media in the 1960 Sit-Ins." *American Sociological Review* 71: 752–777.

Aronson, Jacob, Paul Huth, Marc Lichbach, and Chang Kiyoung.2014. "Collective Action, Insurgency, and Sustained Escalation." *IR/CIDCM Workshop*: University of Maryland.

Arrighi, Giovanni. 1990. "Marxist Century, American Century: The Making and Remaking of the World Labour Movement." *New Left Review* 179: 29–63.

Arrighi, Giovanni. 1994. *The Long Twentieth Century: Money, Power, and the Origins of Our Times*. London: Verso.

Auyero, Javier. 2002. "Los cambios en el repertorio de la protesta social en la Argentina." *Desarrollo Economico* 42: 187–210.

Auyero, Javier. 2007. *Routine Politics and Violence in Argentina: The Gray Zone of State Power*. New York: Cambridge University Press.

Avineri, Shlomo. 1971. "Israel and the Palestinians: Reflections on the Clash of Two National Movements." New York: St. Martin's.

Avneri, Uri.2005. "A Miracle of Rare Device." In *Democratic Underground*. http://www.democraticunderground.com/discuss/duboard.php?az=view_all&address=124x98858.

Balme, Richard, and Didier Chabanet. 2008. *European Governance and Democracy: Protest and Power in the EU*. Lanham, MD: Rowman and Littlefield.

Banaszak, Lee Ann. 1996. *Why Movements Succeed or Fail: Opportunity, Culture, and the Struggle for Woman Suffrage*. Princeton, NJ: Princeton University Press.

Banaszak, Lee Ann, Karen Beckwith, and Dieter Rucht, eds. 2003. *Women's Movements Facing the Reconfigured State*. New York: Cambridge University Press.

Beckwith, Karen.2003. "The Gendering Ways of States: Women's Representation and State Reconfiguration in France, Great Britain, and the United States." In *Women's Movements Facing the Reconfigured State*, edited by Lee Ann. Banaszak, Karen Beckwith, and Dieter Rucht, 169–202. New York: Cambridge University Press.

Beissinger, Mark R. 2002. *Nationalist Mobilization and the Collapse of the Soviet Union*. New York: Cambridge University Press.

Beissinger, Mark R. 2011. "Mechanisms of Maidan: The Structure of Contingency in the Making of Colored Revolution." *Mobilization* 16: 25–43.

Bennett, W. Lance. 2005. "Social Movements Beyond Borders: Understanding Two Eras of Transnational Activism." In *Transnational Protest and Global Activism*, edited by Donatella della Porta and Sidney Tarrow, 203–225. Lanham, MD: Rowman and Littlefield.

Bennett, W. Lance, and Alexandra Segerberg. 2013. *The Logic of Connective Action*. New York: Cambridge University Press.

Berda, Yael 2013. "Managing Dangerous Populations: Colonial Legacies of Security and Surveillance." *Sociological Forum* 28:627–630.

Berman, Eli, and David Laitin. 2008. "Religion, Terrorism, and Public Goods: Testing the Club Model." *Journal of Public Economics* 92: 1942–1967.

Bernhard, Michael H. 1993. *The Origins of Democratization in Poland: Workers, Intellectuals, and Oppositional Politics, 1976–1980*. New York: Columbia University Press.

Boli, John, and George Thomas, eds. 1999. *Constructing World Culture: International Nongovernmental Organizations since 1875*. Stanford, CA: Stanford University Press.

Boutwell, Jeffrey, Michael T. Klare, and Laura W. Reed. 1995. *Lethal Commerce: The Global Trade in Small Arms and Light Weapons*. Cambridge, MA: American Academy of Arts and Sciences.

Boykoff, Jules. 2007. *Beyond Bullets: The Suppression of Dissent in the United States*. Oakland: AK Press.

Brockett, Charles D. 2005. *Political Movements and Violence in Central America*. New York and Cambridge, UK: Cambridge University Press.

Bunce, Valerie. 1999. *Subversive Institutions: The Design and the Destruction of Socialism and the State*. New York: Cambridge University Press

Bunce, Valerie, and Sharon Wolchik. 2011. *Defeating Authoritarian Leaders in Mixed Regimes: Electoral Struggles, U.S. Democracy Assistance, and International Diffusion in Post-Communist Europe and Eurasia*. New York: Cambridge University Press.

Burns, Stewart. 1997. *Daybreak of Freedom: The Montgomery Bus Boycott*. Chapel Hill: University of North Carolina Press.

Burstein, Paul, and April Linton. 2002. "The Impact of Political Parties, Interest Groups and Social Movements on Public Policy: Some Recent Evidence and Theoretical Concerns." *Social Forces* 81: 380–408.

Burstein, Paul, and Sarah Sausner. 2005. "The Incidence and Impact of Policy-Oriented Collective Action: Competing Views." *Sociological Forum* 20: 403–419.

Cederman, Lars-Erik, Kristian Skrede Gleditsch, and Halvard Buhaug. 2013. *Inequality, Grievances, and Civil War*. New York: Cambridge University Press.

Collier, Paul, and Anke Hoeffler. 2003. "Greed and Grievance in Civil War." *Oxford Economic Papers* 56: 563–595.

Collins, Randall. 2004. "Rituals of Solidarity and Security in the Wake of Terrorist Attack." *Sociological Theory* 22: 53–87.

Costain, Anne. 1992. *Inviting Women's Rebellion: A Political Process Interpretation of the Women's Movement*. Baltimore: Johns Hopkins University Press.

Dallaire, Roméo. 2003. *J'ai serré la main du diable. La faillite de l'humanité au Rwanda*. Outremont, Québec: Libre Expression.

della Porta, Donatella. 1995. *Social Movements, Political Violence and the State: A Comparative Analysis of Italy and Germany*. New York: Cambridge University Press.

della Porta, Donatella. 2013. *Clandestine Political Violence*. New York and Cambridge: Cambridge University Press.

della Porta, Donatella, and Alice Mattoni. 2014. "Patterns of Diffusion and the Transnational Dimension of Protest in the Movements of the Crisis: An Introduction." In *Spreading Protest: Social Movements in Times of Crisis*, edited by Donatella della Porta and Alice Mattoni, 1–21. Colchester, UK: ECPR Press.

della Porta, Donatella, and Sidney Tarrow. 1986. "Unwanted Children: Political Violence and the Cycle of Protest in Italy." *European Journal of Political Research* 14: 607–632.

della Porta, Donatella, and Sidney Tarrow, eds. 2005. *Transnational Protest and Global Activism*. Lanham, MD: Rowman and Littlefield.

Des Forges, Alison. 1999. *"Leave None to Tell the Story": Genocide in Rwanda*. New York and Paris: Human Rights Watch.

Diani, Mario. 1995. *Green Networks: A Structural Analysis of the Italian Environmental Movement*. Edinburgh: Edinburgh University Press.

Diani, Mario 2015. *The Cement of Civil Society: Studying Networks in Societies*. New York: Cambridge University Press.

Diani, Mario, and Doug McAdam, eds. 2003. *Social Movements and Networks: Relational Approaches to Collective Action*. New York: Oxford University Press.

Dorf, Michael C., and Sidney Tarrow. 2013. "Strange Bedfellows: How an Anticipatory Countermovement Brought Same-Sex Marriage into the Public Arena." *Law and Social Inquiry* 39: 449–473.

Doyle, Michael W., and Nicholas Sambanis. 2000. "International Peacebuilding: A Theoretical and Quantitative Analysis." *American Political Science Review* 94: 779–892.

Drescher, Seymour. 1991. "British Way, French Way: Opinion Building and Revolution in the Second French Slave Emancipation." *American Historical Review* 96: 709–734.

Dunér, Bertil. 1985. *Military Intervention in Civil Wars: the 1970s*. Aldershot, UK: Gower.

Eickelman, Dail F. 1997. "Trans-state Islam and Security." In *Transnational Religion and Fading States*, edited by S. H. Rudolph and J. Piscatori, 27–46. Boulder, CO: Westview.

Eriksson, Mikael, and Peter Wallensteen. 2004. "Armed Conflict, 1989–2003." *Journal of Peace Research* 41: 625–636.

Eskridge, William N. Jr. 2002. *Equality Practice: Civil Unions and the Future of Gay Rights*. London: Routledge.

Evans, Sara M. 1980. *Personal Politics: The Roots of Women's Liberation in the Civil Rights Movement and the New Left*. New York: Vintage.

Evans, Peter. 2005. "Counter-Hegemonic Globalization: Transnational Social Movements in the Contemporary Global Political Economy." In *Handbook of Political Sociology*, edited by T. Janoski, A. Hicks, and M. Schwartz, ch. 32. New York: Cambridge University Press.

Favre, Pierre. 1990. *La Manifestation*. Paris: Presses de la Fondation Nationale des Sciences Politiques.

Fearon, James D., and David Laitin. 2003. "Ethnicity, Insurgency, and Civil War." *American Political Science Review* 97: 75–90.

Fetner, Tina. 2008. *How the Religious Right Shaped Lesbian and Gay Activism*. Minneapolis: University of Minnesota Press.

Fillieule, Olivier. 1997. *Stratégies de la rue. Les manifestations en France*. Paris: Presses de la Fondation Nationale des Sciences Politiques.

Finchelstein, Federico. 2014. *The Ideological Origins of the Dirty War: Fascism, Populism, and Dictatorship in Twentieth Century Argentina*. New York: Oxford University Press.

Franzosi, Roberto. 1995. *The Puzzle of Strikes: Class and State Strategies in Postwar Italy*. Cambridge: Cambridge University Press.

Frickel, Scott, and Neil Gross. 2005. "A General Theory of Scientific/Intellectual Movements." *American Sociological Review* 70: 204–232.

Fu, Diana. 2015. "Disguised Collective Action in China," *Comparitive Political Studies*, in press. University of Toronto Politics Department.

Gabrielson, Ryan, Ryann Grochowski Jones, and Eric Sagara. 2014. "Deadly Force, in Black and White." *ProPublica*. www.propublica.org/article/deadly-force-in-black-and-white.

Gambetta, Diego. 2005. *Making Sense of Suicide Missions*. Oxford: Oxford University Press.

Gamson, William A. 1990. *The Strategy of Social Protest*. Belmont, CA: Wadsworth.

Gillham, Patrick F. 2011. "Securitizing America: Strategic Incapacitation and the Policing of Protest Since the 11 September 2001 Terrorist Attacks." *Sociology Compass* 5: 636–652.

Ginsborg, Paul. 1990. *A History of Contemporary Italy: Society and Politics, 1943–1988*. New York: Penguin.

Ginsburg, Faye D. 1989. *Contested Lives. The Abortion Debate in an American Community*. Berkeley: University of California Press.

Gitlin, Todd. 1980. *The Whole World is Watching: Mass Media in the Making and Unmaking of the New Left*. Berkeley: University of California Press.

Giugni, Marco. 1998. "Was it Worth the Effort? The Outcomes and Consequences of Social Movements." *Annual Review of Sociology* 98: 371–393.

Giugni, Marco. 1999. "Introduction: How Social Movements Matter: Past Research, Present Problems, Future Developments." In *How Social Movements Matter*, edited by Marco Giugni, Doug McAdam, and Charles. Tilly, xiii–xxxiii. Minneapolis and St. Paul: University of Minnesota Press.

Glenny, Misha. 1994. *The Fall of Yugoslavia*. New York: Penguin.

Goldstein, Judith, Miles Kahler, Robert O. Keohane, and Anne-Marie Slaughter. 2001. *Legalization and World Politics*. Cambridge, MA: MIT Press.

Goldstone, Jack A., and Charles Tilly. 2001. "Threat (and Opportunity): Popular Action and State Response in the Dynamics of Contentious Action." In *Silence and Voice in the Study of Contentious Politics*, edited by R. R. Aminzade et al., ch. 7, 179–194. New York: Cambridge University Press.

Goodwin, Jeff. 2001. *No Other Way Out: States and Revolutionary Movements, 1945–1991*. New York: Cambridge University Press.

Gould, Roger. 1995. *Insurgent Identities: Class, Community, and Protest in Paris from 1848 to the Commune*. Chicago: University of Chicago Press.

Graeber, David. 2011. "Occupy Wall Street's Anarchist Roots." *Al Jazeera*, Nov. 30, 2011. <http://www.aljazeera.com/indepth/opinion/2011/11/2011112872835904508.html>.

Guzman Bouvard, Marguerite. 1994. *Revolutionizing Motherhood: The Mothers of the Plaza de Mayo*. Boulder CO: Rowman and Littlefield.

Hadden, Jennifer. 2014. "Explaining Variation in Transnational Climate Change Activism: The Role of Inter-Movement Spillover." *Global Environmental Politics* 14:7–25.

Hadden, Jennifer. 2015. *Networks in Contention: The Divisive Politics of Climate Change*. New York: Cambridge University Press.

Hart, Peter. 1998. *The I.R.A. and its Enemies: Violence and Community in Cork, 1916–1923*. New York: Oxford University Press.

Hassanpour, Navid. 2014. "Media Disruption and Revolutionary Unrest: Evidence from Mubarak's Quasi-Experiment." *Political Communication* 31: 1–24.

Heaney, Michael T., and Fabio Rojas. 2015. *Party in the Street: The Antiwar Movement and the Democratic Party after 9/11*. New York: Cambridge University Press.

Hellman, Judy. 1999. "Real and Virtual Chiapas: Magic Realism and the Left." In *Socialist Register 2000: Necessary and Unnecessary Utopias*, edited by L. Panich and C. Leys, 161–186. London: Merlin.

Hessel, Stephane. 2011. *Time for Outrage!* London: Charles Glass.

Hirsch, Eric. 1990. "Sacrifice for the Cause: Group Processes, Recruitment, and Commitment in a Student Social Movement." *American Sociological Review* 55: 243–254.

Hirsch-Hoefler, Sivan. 2008. "Mobilizing Politics: The Mobilization Strategies of the Israeli Settlement Movement." PhD Thesis, University of Antwerp Department of Political Science.

Hochschild, Adam. 2005. *Bury the Chains: Prophets and Rebels in the Fight to Free an Empire's Slaves*. Boston: Houghton Mifflin.

Hooghe, Liesbet, and Gary Marks. 2002. *Multi-Level Governance in European Politics*. Lanham, MD: Rowman and Littlefield.

Hui, Victoria Tin-bor. 2015. "Hong Kong's Umbrella Revolution: The Protests and Beyond." *Journal of Democracy* 26: 111–121.

Hutter, Sven. 2014. "Protest Event Analysis and its Offspring," In *Methodological Practices in Social Movement Research*, edited by Donatella della Porta, 335–367. Oxford: Oxford University Press.

Imig, Doug, and Sidney Tarrow, eds. 2001. *Contentious Europeans: Protest and Politics in an Emerging Polity*. Lanham, MD: Rowman and Littlefield.

Jenkins, J. Craig. 1985. *The Politics of Insurgency: The Farm Worker Movement in the 1960s*. New York: Columbia University Press.

Jenkins, J. Craig, David Jacobs, and Jon Agnone. 2003. "Political Opportunities and African- American Protest, 1948–1997." *American Journal of Sociology* 109: 277–303.

Johnston, Hank, and Eitan Alimi. 2012. "Primary Frameworks, Keying and the Dynamics of Contenitous Politics: The Islamization of the Chechen and Palestinian National Movements." *Political Studies* 60: 603–620.

Kaldor, Mary. 2006. *New and Old Wars: Organized Violence in a Global Era*. Cambridge, UK: Polity Press.

Kalyvas, Stathis N. 2003. "The Ontology of 'Political Violence': Action and Identity in Civil Wars." *Perspectives on Politics* 1: 275–294.

Kalyvas, Stathis N. 2006. *The Logic of Violence in Civil War*. New York: Cambridge University Press.

Kaplan, Robert D. 1993. *Balkan Ghosts: A Journey through History*. New York: St. Martin's.

Karatnycky, Adrian. 2000. *Freedom in the World: The Annual Survey of Political Rights and Civil Liberties*. New York: Freedom House.

Katzenstein, Mary F. 1998. *Faithful and Fearless: Moving Feminist Protest inside the Church and Military*. Princeton, NJ: Princeton University Press.

Katzenstein, Mary F. 2003. Re-Dividing Citizens - Divided Feminisms: The Reconfigured U.S. State and Women's Citizenship. In *Women's Movements Facing the Reconfigured State*, edited by Lee Ann. Banaszak, Karen Beckwith, and Dieter Rucht, 202–217. New York: Cambridge University Press.Keck, Margaret, and Kathryn Sikkink. 1998. *Activists beyond Borders: Transnational Activist Networks in International Politics*. Ithaca, NY, and London: Cornell University Press.

Keller, William. 1989. *The Liberals and J. Edgar Hoover: The Rise and Fall of a Domestic Intelligence State*. Princeton, NJ: Princeton University Press.

Keogh, Dermot. 2001. "Ireland at the Turn of the Century: 1994–2001." In *The Course of Irish History*, edited by T. W. Moody and F. X. Martin, 321–344. Lanham, MD: Roberts Rinehart.

Keohane, Robert O. 2002. "The Globalization of Informal Violence, Theories of World Politics, and the 'Liberalism of Fear.'" *Dialog-IO* Spring 2002: 29–43.

Kepel, Gilles. 2002. *Jihad: The Trail of Political Islam*. Cambridge, MA: Harvard University Press.

Ketchley, Neil. 2014. "'The Army and the People are One Hand!' Fraternization and the 25th January Egyptian Revolution." *Compative Studies in History and Society* 56: 155–186.

Ketchley, Neil. forthcoming. "Contentious Politics and the 25th January Egyptian Revolution." Unpublished ms., Brasenose College, Oxford University, Oxford, England.

Killian, Lewis M. 1984. "Organization, Rationality and Spontaneity in the Civil Rights Movement." *American Sociological Review* 49: 770–783.

Kitts, James A. 2000. "Mobilizing in Black Boxes: Social Networks and Participation in Social Movement Organizations." *Mobilization* 5: 241–257.

Klandermans, Bert. 1988. "The Formation and Mobilization of Consensus." In *From Structure to Action: Comparing Social Movement Research across Cultures* edited by B. Klandermans, H. Kriesi, and S. Tarrow, 173–196. Greenwich, CT: JAI Press.

Klandermans, Bert. 1997. *The Social Psychology of Protest*. Oxford: Blackwell.

Klarman, Michael J. 2004. *From Jim Crow to Civil Rights: The Supreme Court and the Struggle for Racial Equality*. New York: Oxford University Press.

Klarman, Michael J. 2012. *From the Closet to the Altar: Courts, Backlash, and the Struggle for Same-Sex Marriage*. New York: Oxford University Press.

Koopmans, Ruud. 2004. "Protest in Time and Space: The Evolution of Waves of Contention." In *The Blackwell Companion to Social Movements*, edited by D. A. Snow, S. A. Soule, and H. Kriesi, 19–46. Malden, MA, and Oxford: Blackwell.

Kriesi, Hanspeter, et al. 1995. *The Politics of New Social Movements in Western Europe*. Minneapolis and St. Paul: University of Minnesota Press.

Kriesi, Hanspeter. 1996. "The Organizational Structure of New Social Movements in a Political Context." In *Comparative Perspectives on Social Movements*, edited by D. McAdam, J. McCarthy, and M. N. Zald, 152–184. Cambridge, UK: Cambridge University Press.

Kubik, Jan. 1994. *The Power of Symbols against the Symbols of Power: the Rise of Solidarity and the Fall of State Socialism in Poland*. University Park: Pennsylvania State University Press.

Laba, Roman. 1991. *The Roots of Solidarity: A Political Sociology of Poland's Working-Class Democratization*. Princeton, NJ: Princeton University Press.

Lam, Wai-man. 2014. "Nongovernmental International Human Rights Organizations: The Case of Hong Kong." *PS: Political Science and Politics* 47: 642–654.

Levitsky, Steven, and Lucan Way. 2002. "The Rise of Competitive Authoritarianism." *Journal of Democracy* 13: 51–65.

Levy, Yagil. 2012. *Israel's Death Hierarchy*. New York: NYU Press.

López Maya, Margarita. 2002. "Venezuela after the *Caracoza*: Forms of Protest in a Deinstitutionalized Context." *Bulletin of Latin American Research* 21: 199–218.

López Maya, Margarita, David Smilde, and Keta Stephany. 2002. *Protesta y cultura en Venezuela. Los Marcos de acción colectiva en 1999*. Caracas: FACES-UCV, CENDES, FONACIT.

Lowi, Theodore. 1971. *The Politics of Disorder*. New York: Basic Books.

Lustick, Ian. 1988. *For the Land and the Lord: Jewish Fundamentalism in Israel*. New York, N.Y.: Council on Foreign Relations.

Lutz, Ellen, and Kathryn Sikkink. 2001. "The Justice Crusade: The Evolution and Impact of Foreign Human Rights Trials in Latin America." *Chicago Journal of International Law* 2: 1–34.

Lynch, Marc. 2013. *The Arab Uprising: The Unfinished Revolutions of the New Middle East*. New York: Public Affairs.

Mamdani, Mahmood. 2001. *When Victims Become Killers: Colonialism, Nativism, and the Genocide in Rwanda*. Princeton, NJ: Princeton University Press.

Maney, Gregory M. 2006. "From Civil War to Civil Rights and Back Again: The Interrelation of Rebellion and Protest in Northern Ireland, 1955–1972." *Research in Social Movements, Conflicts, and Change* 27: 3–35.

Mansbridge, Jane. 1986. *Why We Lost the ERA*. Chicago: University of Chicago Press.

Margadant, Ted W. 1979. *French Peasants in Revolt: The Insurrection of 1851*. Princeton, NJ: Princeton University Press.

Margulies, Joseph. 2013. *What Changed When Everything Changed: 9/11 and the Making of National Identity*. New Haven, CT: Yale University Press.

Mathieu, Lilian. 2001. "An Unlikely Mobilization: The Occupation of Saint-Nizier Church by the Prostitutes of Lyon." *Revue française de sociologie* 42: 107–131.

McAdam, Doug. 1983. "Tactical Innovation and the Pace of Insurgency." *American Sociological Review* 48: 735–754.

McAdam, Doug. 1988. *Freedom Summer*. New York: Oxford University Press.

McAdam, Doug. 1999 [1982]. *Political Process and the Development of Black Insurgency, 1930–1970*. Chicago: University of Chicago Press.

McAdam, Doug, and Karina Kloos. 2014. *Deeply Divided: Racial Politics and Social Movements in Post-War America*. New York: Oxford University Press.

McAdam, Doug, and William H. Sewell, Jr. 2001. "It's About Time: Temporality in the Study of Social Movements and Revolutions." In *Silence and Voice in the Study of Contentious Politics*, edited by R. R. Aminzade, J.Goldstone, D. McAdam, E. Perry, W. H. Sewell, Jr., S. Tarrow, and C. Tilly, 89–125. Cambridge: Cambridge University Press.

McAdam, Doug, and Yang Su. 2002. "The War at Home. Antiwar Protests and Congressional Voting, 1965 to 1973." *American Sociological Review* 67: 696–721.

McAdam, Doug, and Sidney Tarrow. 2010. "On the Reciprocal Relationship between Elections and Social Movements." *Perspectives on Politics* 8: 529–542.

McAdam, Doug, and Sidney Tarrow. 2013. *"Social Movements and Elections: Towards a Better Understanding of the Political Context of Contention"* In *The Changing Dynamics of Congtention: The Future of Social Movement Research. University of Minnesota Press*, edited by Jacquelien Van Stekelenburg, Conny M. Roggeband and Bert Klandermans (eds.) 325–346. *Minneapolis and St. Paul: University of Minnesota Press*.

McAdam, Doug, Sidney Tarrow, and Charles Tilly. 2001. *Dynamics of Contention*. New York and Cambridge, UK: Cambridge University Press.

McCann, Michael W. 1994. *Rights at Work: Pay Equity Reform and the Politics of Legal Mobilization*. Chicago: University of Chicago Press.

McCann, Michael W. 2006. "Law and Social Movements: Contemporary Perspectives." *Annual Review of Law and Society* 6: 17–38.

McCarthy, John. 1987. "Pro-Life and Pro-Choice Mobilization: Infrastructure Deficits and New Technologies." In *Social Movements in an Organizations Society*, edited by M. N. Zald and J. McCarthy, 49–66. New Brunswick, NJ: Transaction Books.

McCarthy, John, Clark McPhail, and John Crist. 1999. "The Diffusion and Adoption of Public Order Management Systems." In *Social Movements in a Globalizing World*, edited by D. della Porta, H. Kriesi, and D. Rucht, 71–95. New York: St. Martin's.

McCarthy, John, Clark McPhail, and Jackie Smith. 1996. "Images of Protest: Estimating Selection Bias in Media Coverage of Washington Demonstrations." *American Sociological Review* 61: 478–499.

McCarthy, John, and Mayer N. Zald. 1977. "Resource Mobilization and Social Movements: A Partial Theory." *American Journal of Sociology* 82: 1212–1241.

McCracken, J. L. 2001. "Northern Ireland." In *The Course of Irish History*, edited by T. W. Moody and F. X. Martin, 313–323. Lanham, MD: Roberts Rinehart.

McMichael, Philip. 2005. "Globalization." In *Handbook of Political Sociology*, edited by T. Janoski, R. Alford, A. M. Hicks, and M. Schwartz, 587–606. New York and Cambridge: Cambridge University Press.

Meyer, David S. 1990. *A Winter of Discontent: The Nuclear Freeze and American Politics*. New York: Praeger.

Meyer, David S., Valerie Jenness, and Helen Ingram, eds. 2005. *Routing the Opposition: Social Movements, Public Policy and Democracy*. Minneapolis: University of Minnesota Press.

Meyer, David S., and Suzanne Staggenborg. 1996. "Movements, Countermovements, and the Structure of Political Opportunity." *American Journal of Sociology* 101: 1628–1660.

Meyer, David S., and Sidney Tarrow, eds. 1998. *The Social Movement Society: Contentious Politics for a New Century*. Lanham, MD: Rowman and Littlefield.

Meyer, David S., and Nancy Whittier. 1994. "Social Movement Spillover." *Social Problems* 41: 277–298.

Michels, Robert. 1962. *Political Parties: A Sociological Study of the Oligarchical Tendencies of Modern Democracy*. New York: Collier Books.

Morris, Aldon. 1984. *The Origins of the Civil Rights Movement: Black Communities Organizing for Change*. New York: Free Press.

Mueller, Carol McClurg. 1999. "Claim 'Radicalization?' The 1989 Protest Cycle in the GDR." *Social Problems* 46: 528–547.

Oberschall, Anthony. 1989. "The 1960 Sit-Ins: Protest Diffusion and Movement Take-off." *Research in Social Movements, Conflict and Change* 11: 31–53.

O'Brien, Robert, Anne Marie Goetz, Jan Aart Scholte, and Marc Williams, eds. 2000. *Contesting Global Governance: Multilateral Economic Institutions and Global Social Movements*. Cambridge, UK: Cambridge University Press.

O'Donnell, Guillermo. 1973. *Modernization and Bureaucratic-Authoritarianism: Studies in South American Politics*. Berkeley, CA: Institute for International Studies.

O'Donnell, Guillermo. 2004. "Why the Rule of Law Matters." *Journal of Democracy* 15: 32–46.

Offe, Claus. 1985. "New Social Movements: Challenging the Boundaries of Institutional Politics." *Social Research* 52: 817–868.

Olesen, Thomas. 2005. *International Zapatismo: The Construction of Solidarity in the Age of Globalization*. London: ZED Books.

Olson, Mancur. 1965. *The Logic of Collective Action*. Cambridge, MA: Harvard University Press.

Olzak, Susan. 1992. *Dynamics of Ethnic Competition and Conflict*. Stanford, CA: Stanford University Press.

Osa, Maryjane. 2003a. "Networks in Opposition: Linking Organizations through Activists in the Polish People's Republic." In *Social Movements and Networks*, edited by M. Diani and D. McAdam, 77–104. Oxford: Oxford University Press.

Osa, Maryjane. 2003b. *Solidarity and Contention: Networks of Polish Opposition*. Minneapolis: University of Minnesota Press.

Ost, David. 1990. *Solidarity and the Politics of Anti-Politics: Opposition and Reform in Poland since 1968*. Philadelphia: Temple University Press.

Palmer, Stanley H. 1988. *Police and Protest in England and Ireland, 1780–1850*. New York: Cambridge University Press.

Pape, Robert A. 2003. "The Strategic Logic of Suicide Terrorism." *American Political Science Review* 97: 343–361.

Parthasarathy, Shobita. 2003. "A Global Genome? Comparing the Development of Genetic Testing for Breast Cancer in the United States and Britain." PhD Thesis, Department of Science and Technology Studies, Cornell University, Ithaca, NY.

Pedahzur, Ami, and Arie Perliger. 2006. "The Changing Nature of Suicide Attacks: A Social Network Perspective." *Social Forces* 84: 1983–2004.

Peleg, Samuel. 2002. *Zealotry and Vengeance: Quest of a Religious Identity Group: A Sociopolitical Account of the Rabin Assassination.* Lanham, MD: Lexington Books.

Perrow, Charles. 1979. "The Sixties Observed." In *The Dynamics of Social Movements: Resource Mobilization, Social Control, and Tactics*, edited by M. N. Zald and J. D. McCarthy, 192–211. Cambridge MA: Winthrop.

Perry, Elizabeth J. 1993. *Shanghai on Strike: the Politics of Chinese Labor.* Stanford, CA: Stanford University Press.

Pianta, Mario. 2001. *Globalizzazione del basso.* Rome: Manifestolibri srl.

Pianta, Mario, and Federico Silva. 2003. "Parallel Summits of Global Civil society: An Update." In *Global Civil Society 2003*, edited by M. Kaldor, Anheier, and M. Glasius, 387–394. Oxford: Oxford University Press.

Piketty, Thomas. 2014. *Capital in the Twenty-first Century.* Cambridge, MA: Harvard University Press.

Piven, Frances Fox, and Richard Cloward. 1977. *Poor People's Movements: Why They Succeed, How They Fail.* New York: Vintage.

Piven, Frances Fox, and Richard Cloward. 1992. "Normalizing Collective Protest." In *Frontiers in Social Movement Theory*, edited by A. Morris and C. McClurg Mueller, 301–325. New Haven: Yale University Press.

Pizzorno, Alessandro. 1978. "Political Exchange and Collective Identity in Industrial Conflict." In *The Resurgence of Class Conflict in Western Europe since 1968*, vol. 2, edited by C. Crouch and A. Pizzorno, vol. II, 277–298. London: Macmillan Press.

Polletta, Francesca. 1998. 'It Was Like A Fever . . .' Narrative and Identity in Social Protest." *Social Problems* 45: 137–159.

Raines, Howell. 1977. *My Soul is Rested: Movement Days in the Deep South Remembered.* New York: Putnam.

Rao, Hayagreeva. 1998. "Caveat Emptor: the Construction of Nonprofit Consumer Watchdog Organizations." *American Journal of Sociology* 103: 912–961.

Rocha Menocal, Alina, Verena Fritz, and Lise Rakner. 2008. "Hybrid Regimes and the Challenges of Deepening and Sustaining Democracy in Developing Countries." *South African Journal of International Affairs* 15: 29–40.

Roht-Arriaza, Naomi. 2006. "'The New Landscape of Transitional Justice.'" In *Transitional Justice in the Twenty-first Century*, edited by N. Roht-Arriaza and J. Mariezcurrena, 1–16. Cambridge and New York: Cambridge University Press.

Rosenberg, Gerald. 2008. *The Hollow Hope: Can Courts Bring About Social Change?* Chicago: University of Chicago Press.

Rossi, Federico Matias. 2011. "The Quest for Re-Incorporation in Post-Corporatist Politics: The Path of the Unemployed Workers' Movement in Argentina, 1996–2009." PhD Thesis, European University Institute Department of Sociology and Political Science, Florence.

Roth, Benita. 2004. *Separate Roads to Feminism: Black, Chicana, and White Feminist Movements in America's Second Wave*. Cambridge, UK, and New York: Cambridge University Press.

Rucht, Dieter. 2005. "Political Participation in Europe." In *Contemporary Europe*, edited by R. Sakwa and A. Stephens, 110–137. Houndmills and London: Macmillan.

Rupp, Leila J., and Verta Taylor. 1987. *Survival in the Doldrums: The American Women's Rights Movement, 1945 to the 1960s*. New York: Oxford University Press.

Sageman, Mark. 2004. *Understanding Terror Networks*. Philadelphia: University of Pennsylvania Press.

Samuels, Alexandra Whitney. 2004. "Activism and the Future of Political Participation." PhD thesis, John F. Kennedy School of Government, Harvard University, Cambridge MA.

Sarkees, Meredith R., and Frank W. Wayman. 2010. *Resort to War, 1816–2007*. Washington DC: Congressional Quarterly Press.

Schlozman, Key Lehman, Sidney Verba, and Henry Brady. 2010. "Weapons of the Strong? Participatory Democracy and the Internet." *Perspectives on Politics* 8: 487–509.

Shorter, Edward, and Charles Tilly. 1974. *Strikes in France, 1830–1968*. Cambridge, UK: Cambridge University Press.

Sikkink, Kathryn. 2005. "Patterns of Dynamic Multilevel Governance and the Insider—Outside Coalition." In *Transnational Protest and Global Activism*, edited by D. Della Porta and S. Tarrow, 151–173. New York: Rowman and Littlefield.

Silva, Eduardo. 2013. *Transnational Activism and National Movements in Latin America: Bridging the Divide* New York: Routledge.

Silver, Beverly J. 2003. *Forces of Labor: Workers' Movements and Globalization since 1870*. New York: Cambridge University Press.

Skocpol, Theda, and Vanessa Williamson. 2011. *The Tea Party and the Remaking of Republican Conservatism*. New York and Oxford: Oxford University Press.

Smith, Jackie, and Hank Johnston, eds. 2002. *Globalization and Resistance: Transnational Dimensions of Social Movements*. Lanham MD: Rowman and Littlefield.

Smulovitz, Catalina. 2002. "The Discovery of Law. Political Consequences in the Argentine Case." In *Global Prescriptions: The Production, Exportation, and Importation of a New Legal Orthodoxy*, edited by B. Garth and Y. Dezalay, 27–47. Ann Arbor: University of Michigan Press.

Smulovitz, Catalina. 2012. "'The Past is Never Dead': Accountabily and Justice for Past Human Rights Violations in Argentina." In *After Oppression: Transitional Justice in Eastern Europe and Latin America*, edited by V. Popovski and M. Serrano, 64–85. United Nations University Press.

Snow, David A. and Robert D. Benford. 1992. "Master Frames and Cycles of Protest." In *Frontiers in Social Movement Theory*, edited by A. Morris and C. McClurg Mueller, 133–155. New Haven: Yale University Press.

Soule, Sarah A. 1995. "The Student Anti-Apartheid Movement in the United States: Diffusion of Tactics and Policy Reform." PhD dissertation, Cornell University, Department of Sociology, Ithaca, NY.

Soule, Sarah A. 1997. "The Student Divestment Movement in the United States and Tactical Diffusion: The Shantytown Protest." *Social Forces* 75: 855–882.

Soule, Sarah A. 1999. "The Diffusion of an Unsuccessful Innovation: The Case of the Shantytown Protest Tactic." *The Annals of the American Academy of the Political and Social Sciences* 566: 120–134.

Soule, Sarah A., and Christian Davenport. 2009. "Velvet Glove, Iron Fist, or Even Hand? Protest Policing in the United States, 1960–1990." *Mobilization* 14: 1–22.

Spilerman, Seymour. 1970. "The Causes of Racial Disturbances: A Comparison of Alternative Explanations." *American Sociological Review* 35: 627–649.

Spriano, Paolo. 1975. *The Occupation of the Factories: Italy, 1920*. London: Pluto.

Sprinzak, Ehud. 1999. *Brother against Brother: Violence and Extremism in Israeli Politics from Altalena to the Rabin Assassination*. New York, NY: Free Press.

Stone, Amy. 2012. *Gay Rights at the Ballot Box*. Minneapolis: University of Minnesota Press.

Tarrow, Sidney. 1989. *Democracy and Disorder: Protest and Politics in Italy, 1965–1974*. Oxford: Oxford University Press.

Tarrow, Sidney. 2005. *The New Transnational Activism*. New York: Cambridge University Press.

Tarrow, Sidney. 2006. "Confessions of a Recovering Structuralist." *European Political Science* 5: 7–20.

Tarrow, Sidney. 2011. *Power in Movement: Social Movements and Contentious Politics*, 3d ed. New York: Cambridge University Press.

Tarrow, Sidney. 2012. *Stangers at the Gates: Movements and States in Contentious Politics*. New York: Cambridge University Press.

Tarrow, Sidney. 2013. *The Language of Contention: Revolutions in Words, 1789–2012*. New York: Cambridge University Press.

Tarrow, Sidney. 2015. *War, States, and Contention*. Ithaca, NY: Cornell University Press.

Tarrow, Sidney, and Doug McAdam. 2005. "Scale Shift in Transnational Contention." In *Transnational Protest and Global Activism*, edited by D. della Porta and S. Tarrow, ch. 6, 121–150. Lanham, MD: Rowman and Littlefield.

Tartakowsky, Danielle. 1998. *Le pouvoir est dans la rue: Crises politiques et manifestations en France*. Paris: Aubier.

Tartakowsky, Danielle. 2005. *La part du réve: Histoire du 1er Mai en France*. Paris: Hachette Littératures.

Taylor, Verta, and Nella Van Dyke.2004. "'Get Up, Stand Up': Tactical Repertoires of Social Movements." In *The Blackwell Companion to Social Movements*, edited by D. A. Snow, S. A. Soule, and H. Kriesi, 262–293. Malden, MA and Oxford: Blackwell.

Teles, Steven M. 2008. *Rise of the Conservative Legal Movement*. Princeton, NJ: Princeton University Press.

Teles, Steven M. 2009. "Transformative Bureaucracy: Reagan's Lawyers and the Dynamics of Political Involvement." *Studies in American Political Development* 23: 61–83.

Thompson, Dorothy. 1984. *The Chartists: Popular Politics in the Industrial Revolution*. New York: Pantheon Books.

Tilly, Charles.1986. *The Contentious French*. Cambridge, MA: Harvard University Press.

Tilly, Charles. 1993. *European Revolutions, 1492–1992*. Oxford: Blackwell.

Tilly, Charles. 1995. "Globalization Threatens Labor's Rights." *International Labor and Working Class History* 47: 1–3.

Tilly, Charles. 2000. "Mechanisms in Political Processes." *Annual Review of Political Science* 4: 21–41.

Tilly, Charles. 2003. *The Politics of Collective Violence*. New York: Cambridge University Press.

Tilly, Charles. 2004. *Contention and Democracy in Europe, 1650–2000*. New York: Cambridge University Press.

Tilly, Charles. 2005. *Identities, Boundaries and Social Ties*. Boulder: Paradigm Publishers.

Tilly, Charles. 2006. *Regimes and Repertoires*. New York: Cambridge University Press.

Tilly, Charles. 2007. *Democracy*. New York: Cambridge University Press.

Tilly, Charles, and Lesley Wood. 2009. *Social Movements, 1768–2008*. Boulder, CO: Paradigm Press.

Touraine, Alain. 1971. *The May Movement: Revolt and Reform*. New York: Random House.

Turner, Lowell. 2014. "Organizing Immigrant Workers." In *Mobilizing against Inequality*, edited by L. H. Adler, M. Tapia, and L. Turner, 3–13. Ithaca, NY: ILR Press.

Usher, Graham. 2005. "The New Hamas: Between Residence and Participation." In www.meronline.org.

Vasi, Ion Bogdan, and Chan Suk Suh. 2012. "Predicting the Spread of Protests with Internet and Social Media Activity." Columbia University and Cornell University unpublished paper.

Viterna, Jocelyn. 2013. *Women at War: The Micro-Processes of Mobilization in El Salvador*. New York: Oxford University Press.

Wallerstein, Immanuel. 1974. *The Modern World System: Capitalist Agriculture and the Origins of the European World-Economy in the Sixteenth Century*. New York: Academic Press.

Weinstein, Jeremy. 2006. *Inside Rebellion: The Politics of Insurgent Violence*. New York: Cambridge University Press.

Weyland, Kurt. 2009. "The Diffusion of Revolution." *International Organization* 63: 391–423.

Whittier, Nancy. 1995. *Feminist Generation*. Philadelphia: Temple University Press.

Wiktorowicz, Quentin. 2004. *Islamic Activism: A Social Movement Theory Approach*. Bloomington, IN: Indiana University Press.

Williams, Kim M. 2006. *Mark One or More: Civil Rights in Multiracial America*. Ann Arbor, MI: University of Michigan Press.

Womack, John. 1971. *Zapata and the Mexican Revolution*. New York: Knopf.

Young, Michael P. 2006. *Bearing Witness against Sin: The Evangelical Birth of the American Social Movement*. Chicago: University of Chicago Press.

Zhao, Dingxin. 1998. "Ecologies of Social Movements: Student Mobilization during the 1989 Prodemocracy Movement in Beijing." *American Journal of Sociology* 103: 1493–1529.

Zolberg, Aristide. 1972. "Moments of Madness." *Politics and Society* 2: 183–207.

INDEX

boycotts, 3–4, 21, 37, 92, 114
Boykoff, Jules, 37
Bringing Down a Dictator, 65
Britain: antislavery movements, 3–4, 9, 15, 21, 35, 39, 60–61, 125, 160, 195; France, relations with, 77; Government Communications Headquarters (GCHQ), 170; Hong Kong decolonization, 89–90; Ireland, relations with, 76–80, 93; jihadist groups, 205; political opportunity structures, 77, 80; regime model, 76–80, 86; scale shift, 125
Brockett, Charles, 28–29, 61, 87, 131–32, 173–74
brokerage: Al Qaeda, 195; Arab Spring, 139; Chile, 202; coordinated action, role in, 35, 93; defined, 31; general laws, 172; Georgia, 65–66; Greensboro sit-in, 33; Ireland, 80; lethal conflicts, 172; linking role, 97, 102–3; marriage equality, 226, 229; Nicaragua, 186, 188; Poland, 152, 166; revolutions, 184; scale shift, role in, 125–26; sex workers' protest, 121–22; Soviet Union, 105; transnationalization, 199; Zapatistas, 93
Brown, Michael, 17, 25–26, 38, 109
Brown v. Board of Education, 31–32, 50, 54, 158
building occupations, 51, 53, 87, 120–23, 128, 131–32, 154
Bulgaria, 178, 219
Bunce, Valerie, 177, 179
Burma, 67, 113, 180
Burstein, Paul, 162
Burundi, 180, 182
Bush, George W., 54, 56, 157

Cambodia, 185
Canada, 56–57, 67, 78, 219
Cape Verde, 67
capitalism, 4, 61, 90–91, 132, 196, 222
Carter, Jimmy, 186
Catholicism, 3, 54, 76–77, 79–80, 93, 122–23, 147, 150, 152–55, 177
Cavallo, Miguel, 203

Central African Republic, 183
certification, 14, 36–37, 103, 113, 139, 149, 152–54, 166, 172, 184, 188, 226
Chad, 183
Chamorro, Pedro, 186
Charlie Hebdo attacks, 98, 108
Chavez, Hugo, 86, 88
Chechnya, 177, 180–82
Chiapas (Mexico), 9, 100–104, 109–10, 196
Chile, 67, 201–3, 219
China, 57, 59, 63, 66–67, 89–91, 146, 185
Christianity, 10, 63, 80, 109, 123, 128, 140, 154, 177, 183, 205
civil rights movements, 11, 17, 19, 31–33, 39, 50–55, 113–14, 131, 229
civil wars, 21–22, 36, 39, 58, 76, 119–20, 131–37, 140, 172–73, 180–84
Clarkson, Thomas, 3–4, 15, 20, 125, 149, 200, 215
climate change, 151, 197–98, 201, 210–11; *See also* environmental movements
Clinton, Hillary Rodham, 137, 163
Cloward, Richard, 161–62
Cold War, 17, 50, 147, 181, 199, 201, 210
Coleridge, Samuel Taylor, 4
collective action, 7–13, 27, 39, 50–51, 62–63, 97, 121, 125, 141, 148, 154, 158, 162–63, 208, 216, 226
Colombia, 180–81, 219
Columbia University, 41, 43, 124
commercialization, 164–65
communism, 5–6, 17, 50, 62–63, 109, 123, 145–47, 151–52, 177–78
contention: composite forms, 79–80, 82–84, 120; conditions, 28, 45, 115; confrontational performances, 17–19, 40, 50, 55, 87–88, 91, 128–29; contained forms, 60, 62–63, 76, 86, 112, 122, 198; conventional performances, 16–18, 50–52, 55, 87–88, 91, 128; cycles, 119–20, 123–24, 126–31, 140–41;

ABOUT THE AUTHORS

Charles Tilly was Joseph L. Buttenweiser Professor of Social Science at Columbia University, and before his death in 2008 was the author of *Identities and Social Ties* (Paradigm 2005), *Trust and Rule* (Cambridge 2005), *Democracy* (Cambridge 2007), and *Contentious Performances* (Cambridge 2008). He was the first winner of the Albert Hirschman Prize for distinguished contributions to the social sciences from the Social Science Research Council.

Sidney Tarrow is Maxwell M. Upson Emeritus Professor of Government and Visiting Professor of Law at Cornell University. His latest books are *Strangers at the Gates: Movements and States in Contentious Politics* (Cambridge 2012), *The Language of Contention: Revolutions in Words, 1789-2012* (Cambridge 2013) and *War, Rights, and Contention* (Cornell 2013). He is a fellow of the American Academy of Arts and Science and a holder of the John McCarthy Prize for Social Movement Scholarship.